TRIUMPH

A Journey of Healing from Incest

TRIUMPH

A Journey of Healing from Incest

TRYSH ASHBY-ROLLS

McGRAW-HILL RYERSON
TORONTO   MONTREAL

9927

AUG 31 1993

TRIUMPH: A JOURNEY OF HEALING FROM INCEST

First published in 1991 by
McGraw-Hill Ryerson Limited
300 Water Street
Whitby, Ontario, Canada
L1N 9B6

Care has been taken to trace the ownership of any copyright material contained in this text. The publishers welcome any information that will enable them to rectify, in subsequent editions, any incorrect or omitted reference or credit.

1 2 3 4 5 6 7 8 9 0 D 0 9 8 7 6 5 4 3 2 1

Canadian Cataloguing in Publication Data

Ashby-Rolls, Trysh
   Triumph : a journey of healing from incest

Includes bibliographical references.
ISBN 0-07-551315-3

1. Incest. I. Title.

HQ71.A83 1991   306.877   C91-094778-3

Cover Photo: "Child in the Meadow." Mary Patricia age eleven, summer 1954, the only photograph in which I felt pretty as a child. By now the sexual abuse has ended.

BOOK DESIGN: CAROLE GIGUERE

Printed and bound in Canada by John Deyell Company

To honour Mary Patricia, the child who
endured and survived

With special love to Rob

In loving memory of Jerzy Milisiewicz

And with thanks to all who have been — and still
are — part of my journey.

CREDITS

CONTENTS

FOREWORD

Trysh Ashby-Rolls was still recovering appalling memories of incest when I met her, but her story wasn't the first one I had ever heard. My friend of some twenty years, the gifted novelist Sylvia Fraser, had just published *My Father's House*, an account of her gradual awareness that her father had subjected her to incest from her infancy until she was in her teens. Over many dinners in candlelit restaurants I listened as Sylvia struggled to piece together what had happened to her, one fragment of horror at a time, and I knew how painful it had been for her to decide that she had a responsibility to write about it.

Soon after Sylvia's book was published in three countries, a letter came to me at the *Globe & Mail* where I was writing a column. The person, Trysh Ashby-Rolls, said she was dealing with incest memories and she was finding it both an exhilarating and awful experience. She had invented ways to cope and she thought some of them might be helpful to others. Was I interested in writing about her?

I certainly was. Her letter, for one thing, was uncommonly sprightly and intelligent. She sounded like a woman I would enjoy meeting in any context. The subject of incest, however, was one that had become a media phenomenon and I was intrigued on that count alone. Almost overnight, it seemed, sexual abuse was revealed to be almost as fixed an experience in childhood as bandaged knees. Experts were saying that some form of sexual abuse happens to one in three girls and one in six boys. Reports documented the crippling consequences. Close to ninety percent of women in Kingston's appalling Prison for Women had been sexually abused in childhood; it was said that more than eighty percent of prostitutes, men and women, were sexually dysfunctional because of incest.

I first learned the extent of childhood sexual abuse in October 1984, when I moderated a panel at the Clarke Institute of Psychiatry that was advertised to be about Violence in the Family. I expected it would concentrate on wife-battering and I prepared for that topic. To my surprise the panellists were more preoccupied with incest. Lorna Grant, who coordinated the Metropolitan Toronto Special Committee on Child Abuse, devoted her presentation to exploding myths about sexual abuse of children.

It was not true, she said, that most sexual abuse of children is caused by villainous strangers who lurk around schoolyards to waylay youngsters. Instead, almost all sexual abuse—ninety percent—occurs in the child's own home and the perpetrator, a word new to me to describe offenders, is someone known and trusted by the child. Also, she said, the degree of abuse is not an indicator of the lifelong damage the child will suffer. Fondling can be as traumatic as penetration, depending on the child and the situation. Neither is it true that an affectionate perpetrator does little lasting harm; the truth is that a child fondly seduced with gifts and attention is profoundly confused because misery and shame have come packaged as love.

And so it went during that evening's discussion of family violence. The participants spoke in sensible, brisk tones as they described the emerging social problem, but something very different happened when they finished. People in the audience went to microphones, their faces streaming tears, and told a hushed auditorium about the incest in their lives. We all went home shaken.

That same year the Fifth International Congress on Child Abuse and Neglect in Montreal was stunned as paper after paper, speaker after speaker, all described the havoc and extent of childhood sexual abuse. That winter the topic of incest simply exploded out of the closet and took over the national agenda.

Incest *survivors*, as they bravely called themselves, began to meet and share their stories. The similarities astonished and heartened them, but to proceed with their healing they had to teach therapists how to help them. Few therapists had the insight or training to meet their needs. Counsellors were running to one another saying, *"What is this?"* Women survivors of incest who consulted male psychiatrists for help sometimes were told that they were imagining things. Men survivors went to incest workshops and were turned away by women who wanted to comfort one another, but not them.

I met a psychologist in a small community in the Maritimes who told me she was burned out. She was the only person in town working with incest survivors and she had a waiting list.

Like many other journalists writing about social issues, I tried to report on what was happening. Whenever I did, dozens of men and women contacted me to tell their personal stories of abuse. What they had in common was the intense emotional pain they were suffering and, in every case, a history of disrupted relationships that was blighting their hopes of adult happiness.

They also shared a compulsion to be heard—and always for the same reason. They wanted others with similar backgrounds to know that they weren't alone, that they weren't crazy, and that there was hope.

The letter from Trysh Ashby-Rolls in January 1989 sounded what had become a familiar theme but it had a distinct quality, a thread of elation. She was healing, she told me joyously, and she wanted to talk about it. We arranged to meet in her small, exquisitely furnished downtown house. She served me tea elegantly and told me, often with a brilliant smile I found disconcerting and incongruous, about her horrible childhood.

It was a relief when she began to speak of the ways she was managing her anger and her grief. Her ingenuity was simply splendid. She had begun by trashing her bedroom, she told me sunnily, but then she discovered something that left no mess and was just as gratifying. "I whack the bed with a tennis racket, as hard as I can." She was full of such strategies, some as basic as warm milk for sleeplessness and others, like a symbolic burial in her backyard of the abused child within her, deeply complex and powerful.

Mindful of the thousands of adults in the same pain, I said, "Of course, you'll do a book."

When I wrote about Trysh Ashby-Rolls the next week in the *Globe* I devoted most of the space to her techniques for healing herself.

"She is parenting herself," I wrote, "and she is the good, loving parent she didn't have. She buys herself roses. She bakes herself cookies. During a particularly bleak period, she went to bed and drank warm milk out of a baby bottle and nipple. She has a teddy bear, a piano, plants in a sunny window, and beside her bed is a silver teapot and white china cup. . . . " That day telephone calls poured into the *Globe*, overwhelming the staff. People were hungry to know more about the phenomenal woman who was fighting back with such wit and bone-wisdom. Trysh called. I was apprehensive that inadvertently I had written something to embarrass her or add to her anguish but, to my relief, she was jubilant. She was besieged with calls from radio and television people across the country, she said. They wanted her to talk about her strategies for dealing with incest memories and she was delighted to accept.

A few days later, with media attention still building, she told me that she was giving serious consideration to my suggestion about writing a book. Maybe she owed it to others, she thought; maybe she owed it to herself.

"Do it," I insisted.

We didn't see one another again for almost two years but we kept in touch. She wrote me that she was moving to the West Coast to find the space and privacy to finish her own growth and start on the book. Every few months she wrote that both projects were going well. Then I happened to be in Vancouver one evening late in 1990 and someone gave me a note. It was from Trysh, saying that she would see me after the speeches.

When we met I almost didn't recognize her. The woman I saw in Toronto in January, 1989, had a quality of muffled tension and anxiety that made me fear that she might break. The Trysh Ashby-Rolls who hugged me in Vancouver was bubbling with the joy of living. She was out-going, beautiful, and at peace with herself.

Her book is about a very long journey through hell. In places the pain she experienced is almost unbearable to read, but it is almost about a miracle—the triumph of an unquenchable spirit.

Susan Swan, a brilliant novelist, once wrote that "healing, rebirth and the evolution of self are the central goals of experience." Here's to Trysh, healed and reborn; whole. She's good news.

—JUNE CALLWOOD

ACKNOWLEDGEMENTS

This book could not have come into being without the love, support, and encouragement of many friends, acquaintances, colleagues, teachers, and even strangers, to whom I am profoundly grateful. Your contributions have been invaluable.

My deep appreciation and thanks to June Callwood, John Ridge, and Robert McConnell, who suggested, in the same week, that I write my story. How could I ignore the message?
— June, you not only got me started, but your marvellous letters inspired me to continue.
— John, you have never doubted my ability to write.
— Rob, you are my dearest friend, from whom I never stop learning. May all your fish be golden — you deserve the best.

A heartfelt thank-you to:
— Richard Perrin for getting me on my feet.
— Lori Haskell, without your gentle compassion and understanding, I could not have started down the tunnel.
— Pamela Sleeth, your caring and honesty have helped me reach the light without blinding myself.
— Sandra Butler, Leona Gallant, Sharon Hanley, Marcia Jacobs, and the authors of innumerable books, for being my teachers and guides.
— Heather Brooks-Hill for your financial generosity until the advance came through, for being an outstanding role model, and for being part of my women's support group with Karen Cowitz, M. J. Matthews, Clarice Ondrack, Penny Patterson, and Ruth Wagner. The unconditional, loving support of each one of you moved me toward unconditionally loving myself.
— Jean Sharp for being Mary Patricia's friend, and continuing to be mine.

—Jane Davidson, for being my second mother.
—Emma, Molly, and Cameron, for being playmates to my Child Within.
—Tim, Hélène, Eric, Rick, Deb, Janice, Bill, Ghislaine, Leigh, Bill D., Annele, Marlee, Nancy, Michel, Pam, Deborah, Dan, Sabrina, Steve, George, Michael, Michael F., Jess, Rosemary, Michael, and my Saturday lunch buddies at Café Pierrot for welcoming me so warmly into my new community, and being wonderful friends.
—The Writers' Forge, ACOA group, and Transition House for making me feel at home.
—Tristram, for teaching me that it's never too late to be a good parent. I love you.
—Adrienne, for your guts, courage, and cooking.
—Isa Milman, for your generosity of spirit.
—Bev Shaw and your staff at Talewind Books; Joanne Bacon at the Metro Toronto Special Committee on Child Abuse; and the staff at both Toronto and Vancouver Public Libraries for your help with research.
—Anna Weyburg, my assistant, for providing an oasis of calm, and being there when I needed you.

I honour the support of:
—Helena Aalto, Tamara Alferoff, Krys Angel, Harvey and Mary Armstrong, Robin Barber, Jeremy Carver, François and Nicki Chamberland, Nicki and Robin Clarke, Josh Burman, Susan Crean, John Delmage, Joyce Frazee, David Hanley, Geraldine Hawke, Kiku Hawkes, Hollyhock Farm, Cortes Island, Kristina Jensen, Jann Johnson, Betty Kaser, Letha MacLachlan, Morgan McConnell, Chris McGoey, Cindy Merkley, Janina Milisiewicz, Terry Mitchell, Jochen Mueller, Beverley Pace, Susan Penfold, Michael Playfair, Janet and Don Priston, Tracé Porteous, Colette Pyselman, Sylvia Senensky, Anne Simmonds, Alma Skae, Chris Staples and Photo Works, Mary Sutherland and Lovecraft, Carolin Taron, Shirley Turcotte, Caroline Durston Vereker and Rio Caliente, Karen Walker, Jean Weaver, Mary Williams of Oakland, Ca., Suzanne Rice Young, Adrienne MacLennan of Metro Toronto Police, Constable Terry Bell of the RCMP, Detective Inspector Peter White and the staff at the Sussex Police Station who made a gruelling day a lot easier. The Wellesley Hospital, Toronto, for taking good care of me during some of my worst times. The staff at Jimmie Simpson Recreation Centre, Toronto, for arranging a protected exercise time for me.
—Julia Day, Margo Gilmore, Penny Joy, Megan McConnell, for your constructive criticism, feedback, and suggestions on the manuscript.
—Peter L. Austin for opening the door to book publishing.

— Don Loney for believing in my project from Day One, having the courage to publish my story, and supporting me all the way.
— Marian Dingman Hebb for negotiating me a splendid contract.
— Charis Wahl for trimming my flowery phrases and asking some provocative questions.
— Lenore Gray for your attention to detail; Heather Somerville for your expertise; and everyone at McGraw-Hill Ryerson who helped bring *Triumph* to fruition. Long may we all work together.
— To all the survivors of incest and childhood sexual abuse who have shared your stories with me, thank you for that privilege, and for letting me know I'm on the right track. Especially Kimberly, Denise, Joanne Barrie Lynn, Erin, Mary L., and Anastasia. Remembering your resilience and courage in our healing circle gets me through the difficult times.
— Imo for putting up with short walks, or no walks at all.
— The Goddess, Her Consort, and The Four Directions for blessings and balance in my life.

INTRODUCTION

Telling the truth is dangerous. Very few people want to hear it. Statistics do not agree on exactly how many women and men are the survivors of childhood sexual abuse in North America. Whatever those figures are, they are shockingly high and, ultimately, meaningless. For they don't touch hearts; they say nothing about the pain endured by the casualties. Individual stories do.

My story, my healing journey, is not unique. I have written it, not for retaliation or revenge but to reach out to other survivors, to those who support us — our partners, friends, counsellors, teachers, families, colleagues — and to those who want to gain greater insight into healing the devastation of incest and child sexual abuse.

Not everyone can listen. Those whose pain is very great and who are protecting themselves will deny, trivialize, and try to invalidate my experience. Some will turn their backs — some already have. Others may work to silence me, for those who must keep secrets, even from themselves, attempt to stifle those who would speak their truth. Nonetheless, I have endeavoured to show the real state of things, but it is my view only. Truth has many sides.

I want to share what has happened to me to inspire you, the survivors, on your own journeys of healing; to offer encouragement when your instinct tells you to give up; to let you know you are not alone. It helps me, too, to know there are many of us travelling in the same direction. It *is* possible to heal, to live a life of dignity and serenity. My way is not the only way; we each find our own path. The more of us who walk it, the more likely we will save our own lives and break the broader pattern that has destroyed so many.

PART ONE

VICTIM

Recovery from sexual abuse is a continuing process. The first stage of that process is recognizing that we were victimized.

T. Thomas, Surviving with Serenity: Daily Meditations for Incest Survivors

Remembering our vulnerability as children makes it possible to understand the effects of the violation and exploitation that is child sexual abuse. We can see how the abuser's invasion of childhood and his manipulation of a child's vulnerability wreaks havoc that takes years to undo.

Women's Research Centre, Recollecting Our Lives: Women's Experience of Childhood Sexual Abuse

CHAPTER ONE

A BIRD'S EYE VIEW

We treat ourselves for the rest of our lives the way we were treated as children.

Alice Miller, For Your Own Good

Spring came early to southern England in 1943. Almond trees bloomed on February 2, pale petals against a cloudless sky. From that same sky, the night before, German bombers had dropped their arsenal on the capital city. As dawn approached and the all-clear sounded, I slid into the world, to my mother's consternation and the midwife's surprise. She remarked, "If the child can survive this, she can survive anything." This inspired me often in later life.

My mother wanted to call me Mary (a name I grew to hate); my father, Heather. The compromise was Mary Patricia. Had I been a boy I would have been called Spenser, my great-grandmother's family name. It is easy to see how my parents attracted each other. Both came from shame-bound, dysfunctional families with overwhelming needs for love. They clung to each other like orphans. It was a marriage doomed to fail.

My father was related to the Rolls family of Rolls-Royce. He was born in Wales in 1913 into a life of privilege: wealth, elitist private schools, Cambridge—all the fine things of life and the traditional cruel discipline that accompanied them. His father was a violent-tempered, dictatorial British army colonel; his mother a socialite more interested in being an international bridge champion than a mother. Clearly exasperated and frustrated in the latter role, she dumped my father, age three, on her mother's doorstep, which he never forgot. His grandmother packed him home immediately.

My father had physical problems—spasms caused his head to nod and his eyes darted back and forth. His mother's infidelity with his father's regimental chief, and the inevitable scandal of divorce that followed, led him to retreat into his intellect and imagination, both of which were considerable. My father's brilliance walked a fine line between genius and madness.

At university he developed a love of acting and announced that he wanted a career in the theatre. Shocked, his mother ordered him to take up a more suitable profession. As always, he obeyed and became a chartered accountant.

My mother, a year younger than my father, was born out of wedlock to a domestic housekeeper in 1914. She was abandoned by her father into the hands of the well-meaning relatives—among them his sister, Ada—who bailed him out of his "little scrapes." He was a naval commander who had distinguished himself at the Battle of Jutland during the First World War. (Eventually, he was transferred to Vancouver, Canada, where he died an alcoholic in 1959.) The family regarded their tiny charge as a bad seed and set about reforming her wilful character through religion and strict discipline. She was certainly beaten and probably sexually abused, although the evidence for the latter is circumstantial. Women who marry child sexual offenders almost always have their own history of childhood sexual abuse.

Being responsible, fitting in, and selflessly looking out for others were her daily lessons. Laughter was discouraged, fun unheard of. Never allowed to have more than one toy at a time, the appearance of each new toy meant the departure of its predecessor to "the poor." She learned to make fine lace, to sew exquisitely, and to play the piano well enough that she hoped, not unreasonably, to turn professional. A bout of diphtheria in childhood left her physically weak and prone to infection. Nevertheless, she was sent to boarding school at age five, no doubt to "build character."

When my mother was thirteen, her beloved adoptive mother died of a chronic illness that had dogged her throughout my mother's childhood. At the will-reading my mother learned that she had been adopted; the news deeply shocked her. The family refused to discuss the matter, and it was years before my mother learned the full story of her origins. Less than two years later she ran away from home for good, rather than stay alone with Aunt Ada.

A mutual friend, who had dated my father and found him "rather sinister," introduced my parents. Obsessed by my mother's innocent beauty and willingness to please, my father worshipped her. Feeling cared for and special for the first time in her life, she loved her Prince Charming unconditionally and idealistically. He wrote her romantic letters and sonnets, showered her with flowers and champagne, took her dining and dancing throughout fashionable London, and proposed with a diamond-and-sapphire engagement ring. They were married in London in 1939.

The expectation of living happily ever after soon was shattered: their Paris honeymoon was cancelled by the outbreak of the Second World War.

The bones rattling in their family closets—alcoholism, sexual and physical abuse, sexual escapades and their consequences, violence, compulsive gambling, and abandonment—went unheard and unacknowledged. According to my father the marriage went unconsummated for two years, and my mother became desperate to have a baby. When she did become pregnant in 1942, both my parents eagerly anticipated my birth. They called me their "love-child."

Becoming parents strains even the strongest bonds. Long-buried pain resurfaces. If it is not repaired, it is acted out, often in damaging or self-destructive ways, spilling over from one generation to the next. A partnership of two insecure and wounded children masquerading as grown-ups, struggling with both a flesh-and-blood infant demanding constant attention and a war-torn environment, was an emotional time bomb. It exploded after we moved to a new home on the outskirts of London. I was fifteen months old.

At first, my parents adored me, especially my father. Filled with confidence and loving trust, I would run to him, chortling with delight, for him to hold close in his strong, safe arms. Then, without warning, he changed. My mother and I fell subject to his violent fits of rage: he battered her and pushed, hit, hurled, and sexually molested me. The old white house, its windows draped with blackout curtains, became a battle zone so threatening that getting outside to "play bears" was a relief. Rather than risk our rat-infested air-raid shelter, we lay flat on our bellies under the fruit bushes making a game of hiding from the V-2 missiles of the Blitz. Even after the terrifying, earth-shattering roar of a direct hit on neighbourhood homes, the garden felt safer than the house.

My little sister was born in July 1945, and Aunt Ada moved in to help. Then in her seventies, she had become a religious fanatic so rigidly opposed to alcohol that she would not even touch the sherry-laced Christmas trifle. Almost crippled from an old hip injury and very deaf, with an irritating habit of humming tunelessly while she worked, Ada took us over. It was she who called the police when my father beat my mother, she who took it upon herself to discipline me in my parents' absence. And when my mother exhibited signs of emotional stress, Ada issued an edict: "We'll have no nervous breakdowns in this house."

Family life escalated into chaos. My father started disappearing for weeks on end. There were allegations of affairs with younger women who "needed his help" and evidence that he was binge drinking. He may also have been involved in more sinister activities involving children. At about this time he saw a psychiatrist who diagnosed him as being either schizophrenic or having a personality disorder. Since my father functioned more than adequately in the workplace, rising in time to a top executive position, the former diagnosis is unlikely. Alcohol can sometimes create personality changes dramatic enough to resemble mental illness. Whatever the cause of his erratic behaviour and extreme mood swings, he tolerated therapy for only a short time, pronouncing himself "cured." My mother turned in desperation to her mother-in-law's second husband. It was her duty, he snapped, to stand by her husband. She found a sympathetic ally in her new family doctor, a paternal man thirty years her senior whom we would dub "Papa." He would play a major role in our lives and he and my mother eventually retired together. He suggested a lawyer. The lawyer advised, quite correctly, that if she left the marital home she would lose her children and forfeit all her rights to property. The law clearly stated that women and children were the property of men. My mother bravely accepted her predicament.

My father left when I was nearly four. After he had gone my mother realized I had witnessed the fight, my father putting on his brown trilby, picking up his suitcases, and screaming that he wanted freedom. For many years afterwards the scene was blocked from my conscious memory, except for the slam of the front door and the ensuing silence. I knew only that it was all my fault. I had been abandoned because I was bad, unlovable.

After that night, I never trusted anyone to touch me. The only time I let my mother hug me was when I was half asleep. I retreated into a world of my own.*

My father's desertion brought some measure of relief, but he closed the joint bank account he held with my mother and left us literally penniless. Living on credit and discreet charity my mother maintained the appearance of a middle-class widow. The courts granted her a divorce in 1950 on the contested grounds of my father's "unreasonable behaviour." She got custody of us children. My father was not granted any visitation rights. My mother said he was ordered to stay away from us because of his violence.

In 1952 our home reverted to its lessor, the local council. My mother had no alternative but to suffer the "disgrace" of public housing and paying rent. Insisting that her daughters attend private schools and take piano and ballet lessons like other girls of "our" class, she took in boarders. I bitterly resented the lodgers, especially if I had to change bedrooms to accommodate them. When nobody was around I made a thorough search of each new roomer's belongings, helping myself occasionally to a small item. (Surprisingly, there were never any complaints of missing property.) Only my favourite, Jean, escaped having her room rifled. She made friends with me, listened to my concerns, and answered my questions. We had a lot of fun together.

"Uncle" Jim made me feel uneasy, although I liked playing with his typewriter. "Granny" Daly terrified me. It was like having two Aunt Adas. Willie was a nice enough woman, but her guinea pig shared a cage—and terminal disease—with my much-adored pet rabbit. Old Major F. took his meals with us. While he waited for my mother to serve him, he would rock back and forth in his chair, wiping his nose slowly with his forefinger and thumb. As she put his plate in front of him he would say, "Aah!" and smooth back his hair with his wet fingers. No comments were tolerated about the lodgers or their idiosyncrasies, except from my mother.

We had some strange rules at our house. No wearing sneakers or chewing gum—only common children and Americans did such things. No singing at the table. No strumming on the piano. No

---

*Had anyone known the behavioural and physical indicators of children who have been sexually abused, it would have been easy to pick me out as an incest victim. But these traits have only been defined recently. See Appendix A. Most of the signs listed by the Metropolitan Toronto Special Committee on Child Abuse (July 1990) as possible indicators of sexual abuse were apparent in me from the time I was very young until I entered my twenties.

shouting in the garden—what would the neighbours think! Shouting at Aunt Ada in the house was all right; that was "talking loudly" because she was "hard of hearing." No getting angry, or grumpy, or too enthusiastic. No peeing in the bath water. No touching "down there." No showing off. "It's not the done thing" was my mother's catch-phrase. Talking unemotionally about neutral subjects was always best, but I never quite knew what those subjects were, and being without emotion was impossible. If I didn't talk, my mother would ask: "What's the matter? You're so quiet." For a long time I thought we were just another stiff-upper-lipped British family. Now I understand the unwritten rules of all dysfunctional families: Don't Talk. Don't Trust. Don't Feel.

After the divorce my mother lived from one day to the next, depressed, physically ill, and taking various prescription pills. A buddy of my grandfather "taught her to drink." She felt so deeply ashamed that her ideal marriage had ended in divorce that it was kept a secret—as was my father's violence, the fact that we lived in public housing, and that we had to scrape to get by. When my father was mentioned she referred to him as "Poordaddy"—all one word.

My mother lived only for her children, and filled her overwhelming need for love through us. She wanted us to have the normal upbringing that she had missed out on, emotionally and materially—an impossible task demanding enormous self-sacrifice. We became an extension of her, the little girl she had been and, in many ways, still was. I got the same message that she grew up with: I was lovable as long as I was good, in other words obedient, sweet-natured, quiet, and industrious—impossible, unrealistic expectations. The resentment and frustration my mother carried often caused her to lash out at me or to smother me with overprotective devotion. As a caregiver when I was ill she became kindness itself: uncritical, non-judgemental, unconditionally loving. Although I have no doubt that she loved me in the best way she could, the only time I ever felt loved, relaxed, and comforted was when I was sick. With no reliable role models, she had no idea how to raise a child consistently. She knew only that everything had to be perfect.

At four and a half I started school: smacks for a misread word, a tongue-lashing for not making it to the bathroom in time. Still, I liked school: for several hours a day I could escape from home. One day I returned home for lunch to find my mother's apron hanging over the front gate. Aunt Ada, whom I hated and feared, ordered me to eat my lunch. It was a boiled egg, and it was rotten. Sickened by its sulphurous stench and certain that the old woman was trying to kill me I fled, hysterical, back to school. Aunt Ada had said nothing about my sister being knocked down by a car or my mother taking her to the doctor.

Under normal circumstances I loved the walk to and from my classes. I made friends easily with passers-by, did my share of doorbell ringing and running away, and stole flowers from immaculate gardens. I always had a store of anecdotes to tell my mother. Because I knew I was inherently bad it didn't matter that I exaggerated some of the details—indeed sometimes made them up. My mother often believed my lies while dismissing the truth with one of her favourite expressions: "What a tale our cat has!"

With other children I felt either inferior or superior. I hated being in their houses when their fathers came home from work. I wanted so much to have a family with a father, yet they scared me. There was one family in particular whom I admired—Elizabeth's. It didn't seem fair that such a disagreeable child should have so much. When I tried to explain to my mother that I wanted a daddy like Elizabeth's she entirely missed the point by retorting, "Why on earth would you want her father? He's only in trade." He was a greengrocer.

One day Elizabeth's mother turned up at our front door to "clear the air." I had been biting her daughter. I was immediately put to bed in a darkened room, without supper. I was told I was ill; evidently being angry meant that I was sick. "Papa" the doctor was sent for. He talked to me very gently. I don't know what he said, but I never bit another child again.

Once a week Miss Warner came to the house, and I was duly ensconced with her for an hour at the drawing-room piano. She always wore a hat. I was convinced a brown one meant she was in a bad mood. More smacked fingers—for playing wrong notes. I thought that if my father was at home things would be better. I hadn't seen him since he'd left. At the piano, it all became too much. "I want my Daddy, I want my Daddy," I sobbed over the keyboard.

And so in my sixth year, unwittingly and with the best of intentions, my mother made the arrangements that began years of Saturday outings. He took us to lunch, to the cinema, to his London apartment, to the zoo, to the fairground, and to the countryside for picnics. On most of these occasions, sexual activity took place between him and me: fondling became oral sex and, eventually, penetration. When I was nine he raped me in a clearing in the woods near Box Hill, Surrey.

For weeks after, I hid the symptoms of a vaginal infection. "Papa" considered it improper for him to examine me and sent me to a gynaecological clinic. There, the doctors were sufficiently alarmed at their preliminary findings to order an examination under general anaesthetic, so as not to traumatize me. My mother told me that "sometimes little girls stuff things inside themselves." Jean, the lodger who was my friend, remembers my mother's distress and the sound of her sobbing during the night.

At about this time other disturbing medical problems were noted. I developed acute pain in my heels, making it impossible to walk normally. An orthopaedic surgeon diagnosed a rare bone disease and strapped my legs in plaster casts. He also suggested a series of back operations. These were turned down by "Papa" who thought the surgery too dangerous and unpredictable.

When I started junior high school in the fall of 1952, my legs still in casts, I wore eye glasses for the first time to correct astigmatism and had new braces on my teeth. I was also struggling with the embarrassment of sanitary napkins to protect my underwear from the gentian violet being used to treat my vaginal infection. I felt ugly, ashamed, and terribly lonely. I had no friends and my academic performance was dismally disappointing. I believed I was stupid.

My mother began working full-time for "Papa" despite her constant illness, surgery, and exhaustion. My father's request to take his daughters away for Easter 1954 meant a rest for her and a seaside holiday for us. I was eleven, my sister nine. He took us to a hotel in a village on the Isle of Wight. There I was forced to strip naked for a group of paedophiles, photographed, and forced to perform obscene acts. I was gang-raped twice. I didn't see my father again until I was seventeen.

Two years later I went back to the Isle of Wight on a day trip organized by the counsellors of my summer camp. We spent the afternoon at Alum Bay, collecting multicoloured sand at the top of the cliffs overlooking the Needles. Suddenly I missed my footing, deliberately ignored a sturdy plant that could have broken my fall, and hurtled toward the sea below.

I was hospitalized for six weeks; my legs remained lifeless. I had neither bladder nor bowel function. X-rays revealed no broken bones, and tests ruled out polio. When sensation suddenly returned it was thought I had multiple sclerosis. It didn't occur to anyone—then or later—that the accident had been a suicide attempt or that the injuries had exacerbated pre-existing damage within my spinal column.

For a child who has been sexually traumatized, has lost her sense of power, feels isolated and stigmatized—the hallmarks of child sexual abuse—puberty is the beginning of years of turbulence. When I turned twelve, I became terrified of my burgeoning female shape. Menstruation was a shameful and painful secret— "the curse," my mother called it. I exercised slavishly and meticulously monitored everything I ate. Occasionally I would feel compelled to stuff and purge. Anorexia and bulimia nervosa were the only ways I could feel in control.

During a three-month stay in hospital when I was seventeen, I was again diagnosed with multiple sclerosis: I would spend my life in a wheelchair. My bladder function was diminished and I suffered intermittent severe back pain and acute abdominal pain. A second opinion produced a diagnosis of spinal cord cancer, with a life expectancy of three years. A surgeon suggested that I had a hysterical personality. "It's all in your head," he said. I implored him, literally on my knees, to do exploratory abdominal surgery, promising to see a psychiatrist if nothing abnormal was discovered. After deliberating for three weeks, the surgeon operated and removed a grapefruit-sized cyst he found on my left ovary.

I mounted a full-scale rebellion against all the values I'd had drummed into me. I ran with a crowd who abused drugs and alcohol, and indulged in wild parties and sexual promiscuity. Danger fascinated me, made me feel alive. Sex got me all the attention and affection I craved. I would go off with any male who promised love and devotion. Relatives warned that I'd end up in a mental hospital or in jail.

I first fell in love at nineteen with a twenty-three-year-old musician from a rich American family—a drifter, a heroin addict, and an alcoholic. I met him in Paris in 1962. I expected him to marry me and make me happy for the rest of my life. After a brief affair, in which I became pregnant and miscarried, he returned to the United States. (In 1983, he came to visit me and proposed. I turned him down. Three years later he was murdered by a prostitute he lived with in Mexico.)

I first saw a psychiatrist when I was twenty, after a holiday in Spain. I had spent the summer of 1963 hitch-hiking with a girlfriend before starting my second year at drama school, to which I had won a scholarship. During the vacation, on a dare, I picked up an aristocratic French Algerian in a nightclub in Benidorm, on the Costa del Sol. He invited me to a party at his villa, in the remote countryside thirty miles from town. He was on leave from the army, where he was in an intelligence unit involved in the torture of captured Arabs. He was a sexual deviant and psychopath who idolized Hitler. I was mesmerized by him. For two weeks he raped me repeatedly, forced me into degrading acts confined under lock and key; he tortured me with burning cigarettes, beat me, and threatened me with a gun. When I attempted suicide he threw me, bodily, out of his house. Humiliated, injured, and carrying a genital infection, I made my way home to England.

I badly wanted to tell my mother what had happened but she refused to listen. "Papa" prescribed Valium and sleeping pills. Unable to function at drama school, I was asked to leave. The thought that I'd gone crazy terrified me. "Papa" sent me to a psychiatrist. I was overwhelmed by fear, positive that I was mad—like my Jekyll-and-Hyde father. When I found it hard to continue paying for private therapy sessions, the doctor insisted that I come free, every day if I wished. He seemed the only friend whom I could confide in and trust not to relay any information to my mother. I was always his last appointment, before he returned to his pregnant wife in the suburbs. I would unpin my long hair and, at his request, bare my breasts to let him kiss and feel me. He betrayed his position of trust just as my father had.

During this time I got a few bit parts in television between secretarial jobs. Through one of those, in 1964, I met my husband-to-be. The man I proposed marriage to was several years older than me; I was sure he would take care of me forever. I was heavily addicted to tranquillizers, taking them with alcohol to induce blackouts and using sleeping pills to combat insomnia. I had frequent nightmares and lengthening depressive episodes between periods of frenetic activity. Sometimes agoraphobia would paralyse me: I would hide in my house, or develop physical symptoms and childishly implore my husband to stay with me. When we were first married in 1965, I would cling to him hysterically as he prepared to leave for his office, terrified that he would never return. Yet when I felt on top I would audition successfully for parts on television and in the theatre.

My daily intake of Valium was up to a gram by the second year of the marriage; my husband took the pills away, forcing a dangerous cold-turkey withdrawal. He refused to let me see a psychiatrist, insisting that we could handle the problem ourselves. He did not "believe" in psychiatrists, and persuaded me that he could help me more than any shrink could.

In July 1967, my husband wanted to move to Canada. We settled in Toronto; but by 1970, deeply dissatisfied and convinced that the "quality of life" lay in Britain, he insisted on returning home with our infant son, Tristram. The upheaval was too much for me. Leaving Britain had been a chance to start a fresh life, to escape. On our return, I took up tranquillizers and drinking again, often soon after I woke up.

When Tristram was fifteen months old, in January 1971, I plunged into a severe psychotic depression and was sent to the locked back ward of a mental hospital. I was prescribed large doses of powerful mood-altering drugs that I would take for the next twenty years. I regressed to infant behaviour, refusing to leave my bed even to go to the bathroom; force-feeding was ordered. I was expected to stay in hospital for two years and be in and out of mental wards for the rest of my life.

During the first few weeks my father appeared and announced to an astonished psychiatrist that "none of this is my fault," before abruptly leaving. (He had remarried by this time and fathered three more children—two daughters and a son, brain-damaged under mysterious circumstances.) I regained normalcy surprisingly fast and went home three months after admittance. Several months later my husband decided that we should go back to Canada permanently.

The return to Toronto did little to improve our marriage. I was still excessively dependent and clinging, constantly ill or depressed, drinking heavily and using both prescription and illicit drugs. For several years, I regularly saw a psychiatrist who did little more for me than the one in London. On one occasion he simultaneously fondled me and another female patient at a party where marijuana was being used. He also asked me to arrange a sex triangle with a woman friend with whom I had admitted being intimate, and suggested we all "use poppers and acid together." After revealing details of my sado-masochistic sexual fantasies to him I made a nearly successful suicide attempt.

He refused to let me delve into my childhood memories, which I longed to explore, saying it was too dangerous. (My mother had told me a few details about the early battering and abandonment in a dismissive way, so the events seemed trivial.) Instead, the psychiatrist urged me to make peace with my father, and in 1976 I returned to England for six weeks to visit childhood haunts. I stayed with my father for three days. To my bafflement, he made odd comments about my "dear little panties" and volunteered that the "seat of his troubles was because he was a transvestite." I didn't see him again.

In 1976, the psychiatrist convinced me to get involved in an esoteric mystical school. I participated in a six-week training in the Colorado mountains the following year, and returned to Toronto only reluctantly and at the insistence of my husband, who said Tristram needed me. The thought of my little boy overcame the temptation of heady freedom.

If there were faults on my part there were also faults in my husband. He was an old-fashioned, rigidly controlling, emotionally withdrawn man, unable to express his feelings. He had never regarded me as special, and he considered me and our child to be his property. He believed my duty was to fulfil his needs. He seemed jealous if Tristram took up too much of my attention; sometimes he physically prevented me from attending to the baby when he cried or needed feeding during the night. Later, he lashed out at him in anger, and although he protested his love for Tristram, he was generally cold and punitive.

Although I trained as a prenatal counsellor and worked part-time, I was discouraged from pursuing a career, further education, or outside interests. My husband frequently criticized my few friends. Then he rejoined a cult he had been active in during his late teens. The cult advocates wife and child abuse; when he told his tutor that I refused to obey his wishes, he was advised to "beat her, lock her up, and rape her if she declines sexual intercourse."

Sex with my husband had never been satisfying and always left me angry and frustrated. Underlying our lovemaking was a disgust on my part that became total revulsion when he took to dressing up in a red cloak and adorning himself with leather dog collars, chains around his genitals, and a knife in his belt. Fearing the consequences if I refused, I accepted his fantasy. Stoned on a joint or two, I'd dress up as a stereotypical prostitute and pass into oblivion as soon as I was finished with.

Finally, I could stand it no longer. After a brief but fulfilling love affair and the launch of my own small business (started despite my husband's protests), I took my son and moved into a run-down flat. For all its drawbacks it seemed like freedom, until disaster struck.

One day, while I was renovating the kitchen, a small cabinet fell off the wall, striking me on the temple. The concussion brought on hallucinations and a severe depression. I was admitted to a psychiatric ward. The hallucinations were pleasant enough— the garden of my childhood home rather than the blood, worms, and men yelling obscenities at me that were the images of my previous breakdowns.

By the time I left the hospital, I'd lost all my business contracts and all my money. My husband refused to help, telling me to "reap what I had sowed." Then, on the orders of his cult tutor he courted me, sent me armloads of flowers, and asked me to remarry him, "on his terms." I refused. He agreed to contribute a very small weekly sum, with the instruction that it be used solely for food for our son—and his hamster.

I had few marketable skills, and those I had never seemed to match the jobs available. I ran out of food and subsisted on oatmeal for three weeks until I collapsed. In desperation I applied for emergency welfare while my lawyer forced a court case. When the court-ordered support payments began I used part of the money to retrain for a career in the media. Life looked up. The matrimonial house was sold and I bought one of my own.

As my confidence grew I made new friends and acquaintances and began dating. I was much in demand by men, yet the involvements never lasted long, and were usually one-night stands. Still, I was sure that one day the right man would come along. Sometimes I thought I'd met him and would pin my dreams on him, trying to catch and tame him. It never worked.

I found work as a television writer, producer, and host of a local current-affairs show after a stint as Canada's first news director and anchor on cable television. This brought some fame if not fortune. I wrote for magazines and worked for a while at the CBC; but my potential success was spoiled by mysterious pain in my lower back and right leg, and loss of bladder function. On my fortieth birthday a rehabilitation nurse taught me how to expel my urine artificially. Tests showed nothing abnormal, and I was told it was "all in my head."

Depression continued to interrupt my life. My worst episodes occurred each April and I admitted myself to hospital whenever I felt suicidal. In 1984, I was diagnosed manic-depressive and put on lithium, a mood stabilizer that ultimately destroyed my thyroid gland.

My misdiagnosis was not unusual. Incest survivors are often thought to be manic-depressive or suffering from personality disorders. Nobody told me I carried most of the distinguishing features of an adult who has been sexually abused as a child: depression, suicide attempts, self-mutilation, addictions, eating problems, extreme mood swings, high tolerance for pain, phobias, difficulties with and a need to sexualize all relationships, and isolation. And, like me, an extraordinarily high percentage of women molested as children are raped as adults.

Only one doctor—a child psychiatrist I once consulted about my son—had ever asked me if I had been sexually abused as a child. My answer was no; yet it was an honest answer. All memory of the sexual horrors of my childhood had been erased from my conscious mind during the trauma, and buried behind the protective mechanisms of denial and repression.

PART TWO

SURVIVOR

The focus on coping, resistance and survival . . . draws attention to the strength women display despite their experiences of victimization through shifting the emphasis from viewing women as passive victims of sexual violence to seeing them as active survivors.

Liz Kelly, Surviving Sexual Violence

But we must always be aware that survival is a TEMPORARY state, one that will be replaced by something better.

Mike Lew, Victims No Longer: Men Recovering From Incest

CHAPTER TWO

CATALYST

I have never met anyone in the whole of my life so well equipped for happiness as I was, or who laboured so stubbornly to achieve it. . . . It was not merely this effervescent sensation in my heart, but also the belief that here lay the truth about my existence, indeed about the world.

Simone de Beauvoir, The Prime of Life

I was attracted to Rob as soon as I met him but I didn't know that this handsome, elegant man would become one of the most important people in my life. The magic of New Year's Eve, 1986, was the prelude to an extraordinary adventure that was to change my life.

In itself the meeting was fairly ordinary boy meets girl stuff: passionate glances, the accidental brush of flesh, the inevitable "What do you do?" Auld Lang Syne, the pop of champagne corks, and the jubilant screams welcoming 1987 were our cover. His kiss was long, ardent, and surprisingly tender.

I had dressed for dinner as if I'd achieved my goals of independence and emotional stability. The shrinks had added large doses of thyroid medication to the lithium in an effort to control the mood swings; but it had left me with shaking hands.

A short, intense affair with a dancer, which had ended the previous August, had left me with the feeling that I shouldn't get involved with men. I simply didn't have what it takes. "Never trust a man," Mummy used to say. I had a deep, if denied, longing

to be in a relationship that I covered with the sassy air of a free
spirit. I wanted a life without constraint or responsibility—if only
I could find happiness. Love equalled pain.

Although I was intelligent, perceptive, and intuitive, I had little
faith in such gifts. I saw myself as sunny, funny, sexy, and street
smart—with talent that needed only "discovering" for me to
achieve all I wanted. For years I carried a stage in my head, with
an imaginary audience to applaud.

Underneath the image lay another side that I fought desperately
to conceal: bizarre sexual images that haunted my dreams and
disturbed my waking thoughts and fantasies, and a fragile little
girl craving unconditional love, security, attention, and approval
who longed to be rescued by one special man. I imagined a New
Age knight in shining biodegradable armour.

Rob was in town negotiating his legal separation agreement.
For a year he'd been living on a houseboat in Sausalito that belonged to a Californian woman with whom he'd fallen in love.
For her he'd willingly sacrificed his twenty-two-year marriage,
close ties with his children, and corporate success. He paid a high
price for what he called freedom (and others less kindly described
as "midlife crisis"): he'd allowed his lover to run through most
of his money, and the relationship was on the rocks.

A mutual friend introduced us that night. She'd just broken
up with her man and confided that she'd started an affair with
Rob the previous day. They couldn't be an item already, I told
myself. He was fair game. Her disclosure added spice to the drama
unfolding in my imagination: trips to California, romantic inter-
ludes when he came through Toronto en route to Montreal where
the Californian Woman had business interests. I knew he found
me attractive. There was no way I would pass him up.

"Here we go again," said a voice inside my head. Another
smaller voice counselled, "You've waited all your life for this man.
Don't play games. Show him who you really are." I was puzzled.
Rob was familiar somehow with a sincerity that I'd never before
encountered. He seemed to offer all that I craved. But reveal the
real me? I didn't even know who I was.

I waited, but his invitation didn't come until ten days later when
I had about given up hope. Would I have dinner?

I had never eaten Japanese robata before. It was an orgy of
sensuous delight. I felt part child on a special treat, part story-
book princess. Rob seemed genuinely to care about me. I confided
that I was manic-depressive—to test him. It made no difference.

The illness had been in his family, too. I was bewitched. He made me feel beautiful. Smart.

We had more drinks—and kisses—curled up on my uncomfortable Sally Ann couch. I plunged right in. "Wanna go upstairs and play?"

My euphoria died as soon as we reached my bedroom. Rather than seducing me, he was lying in my bed while I struggled to undress. Suppose I failed to deliver. I wanted so much to please him. The hook snagged on my skirt. Panic set in. Flaccid genitals repulsed me. Erections threatened. If I went down on him would he think me a whore? (Sometimes I felt compelled to perform fellatio. It made me feel powerful to hold a man between my teeth.) What if he smelled? What if I did? He was so nice. I didn't deserve him. I knew he'd go away.

Slipping in beside him I blurted out, "I can't have orgasms."

"Now," he murmured. "We're going to do this very very slowly." I melted.

Performance anxiety, guilt, and too much alcohol put paid to any thoughts of supercharged sex that first time. It was an intercourse of affectionate intimacy—touching, looking, exploring, and getting-to-know-you talking. We wove fantasies that crumbled our defences, bringing us intensely close. It would be the same whenever we made love.

Once he ran his hand over the flat surface of my tummy. I felt inexplicably sad, very small, very vulnerable. I thought it ugly, fat, and conspicuous. I kept it well covered with large blouses and voluminous skirts.

I wept and told him how my father had battered and abandoned me, how terrified I was still of being abandoned. For the first time in my life I let another human being come truly close. I could let him touch my emotional raw spots and feel safe. I knew he would never intentionally harm me.

He came to see me whenever he could during the next six weeks. Our meetings were unplanned, unpredictable, and secret. Rob continued his other affair. He also maintained his liaison with the Californian Woman, flying to Montreal, Dom Perignon in hand, for a celebratory weekend when his separation agreement came through. But when he appeared on my doorstep he looked more like a lost little boy than Don Juan. His needy, hungry look, like that of a destitute orphan, was irresistible. He seemed so vulnerable; to have turned him away would have been to turn from myself.

He left Toronto on my forty-fourth birthday, after taking me to lunch and promising to arrange a ticket for me to visit him. His last words were, "Whenever you feel unhappy, think of San Francisco." I could think of nothing else.

Rob had advised me, taken care of me, offered solutions to my every problem. At last a man I could trust. I waited by the telephone. He called a week later to get my address. To send my ticket? Sorry, he didn't have time to chat. He was late for a dinner engagement. People were waiting. He'd call again. Yes, he still cared. He hung up. I burst into tears.

Two weeks passed. My back hurt and I was limping. The doctor diagnosed sciatica and sent me to bed on pain-killers. How was I going to get to California? "I miss you so much, Rob," I bawled into my pillow. "I'm lonely. I hurt. I want you." I hadn't meant to chase him but surely I had excuse enough to call. "Please leave a message," a woman's voice exhorted me on his answering machine. I did.

I dreamed of searching for him aboard his houseboat. I walk up a long flight of red-carpeted stairs looking . . . looking. "Rob!" I call. Silence. He is out with her. I am not forgotten, just overlooked.

Rob's return call restored my spirits. He'd seen a cheap flight via New York. He spoke quietly, as if not wanting to be overheard. "I'm sending you a package."

Rob called again the day Federal Express delivered his gift: several thoughtful items including a tape to ease insomnia. I was disappointed it was not an airline ticket, but I thanked him anyway. I kept on about visiting him, whined about my back, about whether he cared. I talked incessantly, clinging to him. I hated myself. Why was I always so self-centred? I knew it would be a long time before he'd call again.

My obsession for Rob grew—fed by his silence—until I couldn't concentrate. I was fired from my job, I started smoking again, I couldn't eat. My hands shook so much that I could barely write my name. I shut myself in the house and stared into space.

The Voice of Conscience derided me. "You shouldn't have been messing with your friend's lover. Besides, he's gone back to the Californian Woman. Forget him. He isn't honest. He drinks too much. He uses dope. Sooner or later he'd leave you without a word. He's the kind that needs a woman. He's just another in your bad apple collection."

I refused to listen. Depression enveloped me. April already, almost Easter. I always got depressed in April. Men always hurt me, abandoned me. I had to be flawed—why else would they leave me?

I counted my stash of pills. There were enough. I'd swallow them with wine, push them down with bread. Take, eat. This is my body. This is my blood. Do this in remembrance of Rob.

Suppose I proved a failure at death as I was at life? Just another pathetic specimen drowning in self-pity. Suppose they got me, half-dead. Again. Nothing had really changed. With Rob happiness had not lasted. It never did. I wore suffering like an old familiar coat. "You could take it off," said the Small Voice. I admitted myself to hospital.

The nurses welcomed me back. I'd been a regular customer at Seven North for years. It was a refuge; one of the few places where I felt I belonged. A psychiatrist said he was sorry to see me again and immediately reduced the dose of thyroid medication, afraid I might have either a heart attack or a manic episode. When neither occurred he said I should go off the lithium.

I left more messages for Rob. How could he fail to respond in my hour of need? When he called it was to reassure me. Yes, he cared. He was sorry he hadn't called before—he'd been very busy. He'd try to come and see me.

"All the way from San Francisco?" asked my psychiatrist. I stared at him, then rushed out of the room. I knew I wasn't worth it. I went home for the weekend.

My girlfriend invited me to dinner and talked about the big business deals Rob put together with the Californian Woman. My alarm mounted. The woman sounded powerful, a jet-setting rich Vogue-model type with wardrobes of clothes and apartments all over the world. My friend spoke of Rob's recent stay, of her disappointment that he hadn't called.

I slunk back to hospital burdened with guilt. I'd betrayed her. I would have to confess. Rob had sworn me to secrecy: it was up to him to tell her, he'd said. I was about to betray him. I waited three days, then dialled her number.

"I had a dream about you and Rob last night," she said brightly. "You were having a fling."

"It's true," I confessed. I felt like a child caught out by her mother. I denied nothing. She'd half-guessed all along: my distinctive perfume on his clothes, my telephone number in his jacket pocket. I wanted her to reprimand me, chastise me. She hung up.

I refused to leave my bed. I couldn't stop crying. I shouted at the nurses to leave me alone. The psychiatric resident looked in.

He was leaving for his Easter break. Would I please try and tell him what was happening? I described the garden at my childhood home. It made no sense to either of us.

I left more messages for Rob. Anything to get him to call. I couldn't understand why he'd gone away, apparently loving me, yet barely keeping in touch. Suddenly his unpredictability, once so appealing, was a curse. I felt dead. To make matters worse I picked up an intestinal infection and was put into isolation on Good Friday. Visitors were prohibited: I was the bad little girl of my childhood, banished to my room in disgrace.

On Easter Sunday my girlfriend called. She'd told Rob. Twenty-four hours later he and I talked. He seemed relieved that the truth was out. Angry that I'd done his dirty work for him, but unable to express such a dangerous emotion, I asked if he was upset with me for telling.

"No, I'm not angry with you."

"Do you still care about me?" (My constant question.)

"My feelings for you are as strong as they were in January," he replied. "But I don't want to encourage you to need me even though I know you need me and my support."

"If you don't care," I threatened, "I'll say goodbye and go away and forget you."

"I do care," he insisted. "I care very much."

He said he still wanted me to come to San Francisco and promised to call the following day. "I might have a different phone number," I said. "I'm being moved back into the ward."

"I'll find you," he said. "I'll always find you."

The Small Voice whispered, almost inaudibly, "He won't call, but he will be back. Be patient."

Telling the truth cleared one hurdle: it salved my conscience, but it did not expiate my need to be punished. After leaving the hospital I spent more and more time with my girlfriend. She seemed to like having me around and I wanted to please her, make things up to her. As long as she was in control our relationship worked. I, the perpetual child, welcomed her Big Mummy stance. She took charge of me, mopped up my tears, told me what to do, and listened endlessly to my problems. She provided solutions, scolded, and encouraged me. I became more and more the three-year-old Mary Patricia. I yearned so for affection that I allowed my friend power over me, chained myself to her, yet always feared that at any moment she might strike me or lash out verbally and banish me.

As I gradually realized the implications of our relationship—that I was re-enacting my father's abandonment and my deliverance into the hands of a mother unable to fill my emotional needs—I grew increasingly disturbed. Fighting painful memories became a full-time occupation. My weapons were compulsive behaviours: workaholism, chain-smoking, binging and purging, abusing alcohol and drugs (both prescribed and illicit). Then I hit upon the addictive qualities of sexual activity. I needed more and more to keep me numb.

It started with a one-night stand in May, when I ran into my former lover. The experience restored my confidence in my attractiveness. As I slowly accepted that Rob was gone—at least for the time being—I allowed myself sadness, but I kept a tight lid on the anger bubbling beneath. Its energy manifested itself in sex.

My libido geared into overdrive. Masturbatory fantasies whirled in my imagination, spurred by alcohol and drugs, pornography, and the companions columns. I entered into an erotic correspondence through the ads and talking dirty to strange men late at night helped.

Meanwhile I wrote Rob—letters I did not send, filled with blame and recrimination. In June I mailed two decent paragraphs from New York, hoping he'd think I'd gone away to forget him. I did not fool myself. I still thought of him constantly but I'd made a stand. I could move ahead in my life.

I met John mid-July at a barbecue. He was an older man who reminded me of my father. He told me I excited him, that he'd been married a year but had started divorce proceedings, that getting mixed up with me would be a bad idea.

The Small Voice warned, "Leave him alone." I couldn't. I felt driven to conquer him sexually. I invited him to dinner, at which I provided magic mushrooms. It was the only time he ever stayed overnight, and even then he left at dawn.

I described my sexual fantasies in detail and, for the first time, acted them out. I'd play a little girl, and he took delight in spanking me, strapping me, and tying me up while I pleaded for more. The more he demeaned me, the more I begged. The more I begged, the more turned on I got. "Daddy, Daddy, Daddy," I moaned. It was an invocation from the depths of my unconscious uttered at the height of passion. My breathing indicated orgasm, but I was cut off from all bodily sensation.

I was also capable of cruelty: once I gave John a thrashing worthy of a professional dominatrix.

I masturbated several times daily, while reading the responses from my erotic correspondents: a female nurse, who enclosed explicit photographs, and two men in their sixties, one of whom I dubbed "Uncle Tony." All three were into sado-masochism. I signed my letters Mary Patricia. With John's consent I arranged a threesome with Uncle Tony, in which I was to play the part of a naughty schoolgirl. I cancelled when Uncle Tony refused to use a condom.

No amount of sex could satisfy my compulsion; the acts brought neither relief nor pleasure. I recounted my exploitations as titillating stories that belied the agony of my guilt and shame.

My escapades came to an abrupt halt in November. Within one week the nurse sent me a handmade wooden paddle with explicit instructions on its use while administering enemas, Uncle Tony showed me his whip, my third correspondent sent word that he was coming over to discipline me, and I narrowly escaped being raped by an advertising executive I picked up in a bar. He was too buzzed on cocaine and booze to do more than fumble, but I was terrified.

I had a dream: Rob waits for me in a greasy spoon. When I meet him I'm shocked at his seedy appearance. He wears ostentatious jewellery in memory of the Californian Woman who has deserted him. His self-absorption hurts and alienates me.

Over the summer I'd begun to see how I had contributed to Rob's treatment of me. Had he really behaved so shabbily? Had I built what had been between us into more than it really was? I'd sent him a present for his birthday in September—an articulated brass fish that "Papa" had put in my Christmas stocking when I was eight years old. It was my most treasured possession. Rob's daughter Megan had taken it to him with a note saying the "Golden Fish" was magical and would bring him luck, happiness, love, and success. She told me he'd been thrilled with it.

Then I had two odd dreams: Rob asks after me. He thinks of me often. He wants to see me. He says he'll be in Toronto soon. In the second, he and I make a treacherous journey high in the mountains away from civilization. I carry his little boy in my arms and hold my own three-year-old girl by her hand.

I could not understand the latter dream.

He called me in October during a brief visit to Toronto. "This is your incredible disappearing man."

"Who?"

"Thank you for the fish. It came at the right time. It was the only present I got."

"It was because I loved you, I still love you, and I'll always love you." The intensity of my reply took me aback. Rob was silent.

"I don't think we're right for each other," I rattled on. I was so afraid of rejection.

"You may be right. But there's an undeniable attraction," he answered softly.

"Oh well," I said too brightly. "Who knows what's going to happen." He told me he had moved back to Canada. I heard later that he was living in the Californian Woman's apartment.

The conversation ended. I was angered that he didn't have time to see me. He'd ruffled my false sense of peace, opened old wounds.

In early December I called Rob and lied to him that I would be in Montreal the next day on business. Could we have lunch? He regretted that he'd be in Chicago.

Damn.

Christmas approached. John made vacation plans that didn't include me. I was sick with bronchitis and cystitis when he called. "Take me with you," I pleaded. He refused.

"What are you doing right now?" he asked.

"Writing to my father," I answered. "And as usual can't think what to say."

"Ask him all the questions you've ever wanted to," John growled.

"Good idea," I said. I had a lot of questions.

Just before his departure for the Caribbean, I called John's house. A woman answered. His wife.

I dreamed: I am searching for John and find Rob instead—seriously ill with lung disease in a hospital. He looks grotesque. He's willing to have a fling with me although he's gone back to his wife and family.

The following night I dreamed again: Rob comes to Toronto with his wife and family. He wants to see me. I'm afraid to see him again and run into the crowded city streets.

Christmas Eve dawned optimistically clear and crisp, the sort of day it's good to be alive. Rob called. He told me that his relationship with the Californian Woman was over. He'd moved his stuff out of her place and was living alone. I tried to be absolutely honest. I told him how much I'd like to see him again but that I was afraid of being hurt. "It could happen," he said. "There are no guarantees. I'd like to see you again, too."

Would I like to spend a few days with him in the Laurentian Mountains? He'd arrange the ticket and confirm times and meeting place next day.

He was as good as his word. The plane took off into a perfect sunset sky on Boxing Day. I made a fervent wish on the first twilight star: let this be my liberation, and not my execution.

CHAPTER THREE

A PROMISE IN THE SNOW

Human beings, especially at an early age, are amazingly resilient. . . .
Errors can be made and errors can be corrected; and tenderness, care,
and understanding can help bring about new beginnings at any age.

June Singer, Love's Energies

I meant to act the cool glossy-lipped sophisticate, hat jauntily askew, ready with a witty greeting. My fantasy evaporated into the chill Montreal night as soon as I saw Rob waiting at the airport. I hurled myself into his arms.

We drove to the cottage, catching up on our news like two old friends, for whom there had been no real separation. I stole sidelong glances at him, appraising the man I'd last seen eleven months before. Memory had exaggerated his looks to film-star proportion, but the real man appeared more vulnerable than I remembered.

The first night I vacillated about sleeping in his bed. I'd told him on Christmas Eve that our vacation might be platonic. I didn't tell him that I was sexually burned out and had been ill. Indeed, I still felt below par. Fear of rejection if I said no, several glasses of wine, and the freezing night made up my mind. With his body curled around mine, I relaxed. The warmth of his touch made it impossible to hold back my feelings. Our lovemaking was a sublime mix of tough and tender.

We spent our days talking, laughing, hugging, playing, cooking, shopping, and fetching water from a hole through the ice. Despite Rob's objections I lugged heavy pails up the hill for bathing, cooking, and flushing the toilet. "You're stubborn," he observed, when I refused to quit.

"Damn right," I yelled back. "And obstinate. They're the marks of a survivor." Eventually, however, I chose other tasks. I wanted to be Rob's peer and sensed his silent approval of the assertiveness I had developed in his absence.

The weather was crisp and perfect. Rob cross-country skied; I walked. "Next time I'll bring my skis," I laughed, realizing that I'd dare try the bumpy slopes with him.

We experimented with drugs; under the influence Rob encouraged me to tell him the details of the time he'd been away; to shout my anger and yield up my pain; but he categorically denied that he had abandoned me. "I always intended coming back," he said. "When I was free and clear."

"How can I believe you?" I asked. "How do I know you won't do the same thing again?"

He explained the importance of being open and honest with each other to avoid misunderstandings and made it clear that he was unwilling to get deeply involved again just yet. He'd felt as trapped with the Californian Woman as he had in his marriage. "Relationships with women are like a drug," he said, "I get addicted."

I promised not to put all my eggs in one basket, agreeing that monogamy wasn't for me, either. But I hoped that, perhaps, if I loved him enough, he'd change in time. We agreed that neither of us wanted to marry again nor did either of us want more children.

On other occasions, however, he painted me a different picture: in two or three years we'd live together. He wanted to accumulate enough financial security so he'd have plenty of time to do the things he enjoyed and nurture his relationship. Well, maybe it'd be one or two years, "but first I need to learn to live on my own."

The idea of living with Rob scared me, but I was thrilled. I imagined our apartment in Chicago or Montreal, retirement co-ops we'd build in Northern California and on the Gulf island property he owned. While he made his millions I'd write novels, become another Danielle Steel. I even dreamed that my dreams were reality.

The Small Voice piped up, "Whoa! Too soon. Too fast. Slow down."

We resonated together. I was in love. Rob told me he could not feel love, and its geography had brought him only heartache. I, too, asked the age-old question: what is it? I knew I had found it. Rob's aura of affection could only be love. I felt loved. Yet, how could I guard against abandonment? We decided to make a personal contract.

There could be no guarantees; nor were there proposals or vows. But the commitment we signed in the snow and on paper was cemented with an exchange of gifts. I told Rob he could keep "Papa's" Golden Fish unless he fell in love with someone else. Rob gave me his grandfather's silver spoons, set with nuggets from the former family gold-mine, on the same understanding. As we slid across Green Lake to Deer Island he took my hand. We smiled at each other. I'd never felt happier.

Two days later, en route to Toronto, I ripped the back page from my notebook and tore it into tiny pieces. It was a list of all my lovers, male and female. An era had ended.

A letter from my father was awaiting me at home, announcing his intention to visit me in May. That, he wrote, was the only way he could answer my questions. Suddenly I had everything. "My Daddy's coming back," I yelled like an excited kid. "My Daddy's coming back!" "And Rob's come back, too," the Small Voice said, very quietly.

Rob and I celebrated New Year's Eve, 1987, with the mutual friend who'd introduced us. We discussed the past openly: 1988 would be the year of new beginnings. Little did I know it would bring a major test of our new-found bond: serious illness and its aftermath.

In January I was diagnosed with severe pelvic inflammatory disease and confined to bed. I was in and out of hospital. Narcotics kept the abdominal pain under control, but when the virulent infection failed to respond to intravenous antibiotics I faced a total hysterectomy. Friends questioned whether Rob would stay by me despite his obvious attentiveness.

I had other concerns. I dreamed of being chased by Nazis. I journey down the canals of my Fallopian tubes in a punt steered by an elderly, white-haired, familiar man; I am accompanied by a young child. I go into hiding, wanting to sunbathe and swim naked. After a long long time I come out at the other side of a tunnel safe, peaceful, whole.

Convinced that I was moving into the last stage of my life I made out my will. I wasn't afraid of dying, only that it would happen before I was ready.

February swept towards March. I retreated inside myself to a treasure chest of vivid, long-forgotten childhood memories. Sometimes I questioned reality. Once, at home for a few days, I went for a short walk—against doctor's orders—steadying myself on the icy sidewalk with a black, floppy umbrella. The sky was blue and the air smelled sharp and clean. A neighbour hollered at his children, a crow squawked as another chased it from a tree, and pigeons cooed, mating happily in the eves of a house. Yes, the world functioned normally outside the immediate experience of my bedroom. I pinched myself. Yes, I was real. Yes, I was alive. I returned home and fell into a profound sleep.

I dreamed of Uncle Tony. He takes me to a bar on a train. We travel through a long, dark tunnel. We come upon a small child sucking a baby bottle. Uncle Tony enjoys caning the child viciously. The child sustains cuts and bruises. I stand by helplessly, then get angry and tell Uncle Tony to get out.

The removal of my reproductive organs on March 4 brought release. Their usefulness was over, but mine was not. I suddenly felt capable, intelligent, warm, and loving. I began to look beyond the next six weeks of convalescence toward the rest of my life. Rob promised me a long weekend in the Laurentians.

I was released from hospital just before Easter, at the beginning of April. Rob came to Toronto to celebrate. He introduced me to his son and we went out for special dinners. We painted faces on eggs and made them paper hats. In bed I fed him strawberries dipped in chocolate and slathered him with Drambuie-flavoured honey, which I licked off, giggling. Sex might have been off limits; sensuous play was not.

"Don't leave me again," I whispered. "Don't go away again—please."

"No," he replied softly. "I mistreated you so last year and caused you so much pain . . . "

"I don't want to possess you," I tried to explain, "but I want to be with you. You make me feel like a whole person."

"I worry sometimes that you love me too much," he replied, sadly.

Rob flew back to Montreal. I settled down to try to prepare a novel for publication and get back to normal health. I thought of the hysterectomy as my resurrection. Little did I know that I had yet to endure my crucifixion.

The first hint that something was terribly wrong had come in the hospital. I dragged my right leg when I walked and I felt numb through my buttocks and thighs. I told no one. But when an excruciating attack of sciatica hit in mid-April, I spoke up. I was ordered back to bed. In a few days, sensation was gone in my right leg and I could not wiggle my toes. Rob drove down from Montreal and took me to Emergency.

A harried young doctor, his hospital I. D. card marked "Temporary," examined me thoroughly and proficiently, but seemed to forget that there was a human being behind my symptoms. "S-One nerve compression," he diagnosed, pleased with his cleverness. "Go home. I want you flat on your back for two weeks. No moving. Then we'll see."

"What's the prognosis?" I asked, scared out of my wits.

"Probably surgery," he replied, beating a hasty retreat towards the door. "But you've just had one operation. You wouldn't survive another yet."

Spinal cord damage? Why, God? What have I done? Tell me what crime have I committed? Death would be sweeter. Back surgery? "Papa" said it was dangerous. Hadn't I had these same symptoms at nine years old? The pain was the same. And at thirteen, after hurtling fifty feet towards the sea? Life in a wheelchair? The doctors promised me that when I was seventeen.

I shut my eyes and imagined how I would live. I could still be happy, productive, and self-sufficient. I could even have a social life. I pictured a ballroom. I sit, elegant and self-assured in my wheelchair: loving and loved. Rob dances with a woman in our party. I regret deeply that I have never danced with him. He comes toward me. We are completely familiar, totally trusting, comfortable together.

BANG! The fear comes. He might not choose to spend his life with me. Not because he doesn't love me but because it might be too painful for him to see me incapacitated. He might be ashamed of me and my useless legs. My genitals felt fuzzy now, as though I wore thick diapers. My sexuality was already restricted to my breasts, mouth, and left hand. I had not told the doctor that I had diminished sensation in my right arm. Getting to Green Lake would be a chore. I'd have to be pulled in on a toboggan. I would be a burden, a duty, a liability, a source of resentment. I refused to be any of those things. The unthinkable snapped into consciousness: I'd have to spend life without Rob because of a disability. I thought of him impaired and elderly. My sharp-witted beloved friend? I would stand by him as best I could.

The Small Voice whispered, "And he will you." I had to trust, that was all there was to it.

My father was due to arrive in three weeks. I wrote telling him about my illness, that he was still welcome to come but he'd have to pitch in and help my friends and the home-nursing service that Rob had organized to caretake me.

The pain increased. I charted how often and how many pills I took. If death was approaching it would happen naturally, not by accident. Sometimes I felt overwhelmed with fear and grief. Rob seemed always to be there. He'd read to me, bring food and soothing comfort. He arranged practical matters and provided financial support. I ceased to question him, surrendering myself to whatever was to be.

I thought back to the only time I had ever really felt loved: when I was sick. Then my Mummy read to me and paid me kind, gentle, loving attention as Rob was doing. I remembered that when I was well I felt unloved, controlled, and guilty as though she were constantly disappointed in me, angry with me, punishing me, sending me to my cold green room, with its jail-like safety bars on the windows and its coin-gobbling gas meter.

My father went away because I was bad, because I didn't love him enough. My mother emotionally abandoned me for the same reason. All the secrets, all the shame were my fault. It was like having an elephant in our house, covered over with a sheet that we tiptoed around as though it didn't exist. We all knew it was there, but we never discussed it or dared show emotion about it. I began to realize that I had been considered crazy from an early age. "Just like your father," Mummy had said so often. So I acted out, got hospitalized and labelled. Yet the therapy I'd had along the way had mostly been useless. Somewhere I'd been sold a false bill of goods. I stood now at the gateway of some dark inner journey whose tortuous path I would travel alone.

I turned inwards to focus on the shadowy recesses of my past. The Small Voice said Rob would be there "until the light comes." Rob guided me when I floundered in the mire; he caught me when I fell over the twisted roots of my existence; he led me toward the sunlit clearings where suddenly everything made sense. Because his loving support was unconditional and because he constructed an emotional framework of safety, I was able, eventually, to remember all that had happened to me.

My father called from England on the day I could no longer stand the pain. "I didn't lose any money on my ticket," were his first words. He told me briskly that the exchange rate was the same as when he purchased his traveller's cheques. He did not ask how I was doing. "I'll come in the autumn when you're better," was his only allusion to my illness.

With a sickening thud I realized "My Daddy" was never coming back. I had no "Daddy." He was a figment of my imagination. The reality was that he cared only about himself and money. I said goodbye, knowing that the dream was over.

An ambulance took me back to the emergency department. This time two separate teams of doctors poked and prodded—one lot from Neurosurgery, the other from Orthopaedics. Neurosurgery won. A faceless orderly trundled me away on a stretcher to Four North. A nurse gave me a shot of Demerol.

I called Rob. The Californian Woman identified herself. There was nothing going on between them. I knew it as soon as he walked into my room. He looked haggard. Tests were to be started the next day. "You don't have to be brave," he said.

It was a howl of anguish, pain, agony. It surged up from deep inside me yet did not seem part of me. It seared the length of my sciatic nerve. There were no coherent thoughts, only sobbing. There was no sense of control, only that I had to give myself over totally to the howling scream of terror.

Strange men stand around the table. Each nerve into which they place the needle causes me to tremble. Spasms of movement like orgasm grip me. I groan and gasp as in the throes of sexual passion—making love with Rob at Green Lake. No, must not think of that now. Inappropriate. "Get her on her side," someone shouts. There is panic. Silence. More spasms. I am trembling, shaking badly. I have a headache as they touch another nerve. "Where's the pain?" "In my hip." "Is it radiating?" "No." "Down your leg?" "No." "Try 12 . . . Try 7 . . . Try . . . ?"

I cannot hear. I cannot see. There is only blackness, suffering, coming closer, closer. I cling to the pillow. The needle pierces, an intolerable blinding mind-blowing shattering knife-sharp pain. HOWL . . .

"I want to go home. I want my Mummy." I weep silently, uncontrollably. I want to suck. A nurse gives me an ice cube. She is a motherly sort with an ample bosom. I want to nestle close, be protected.

I'm not crying any more. They've put Xylocaine down the nerve. I feel nothing. I'm in a room full of monitors and hi-tech equipment.

Next night Rob brings a gourmet picnic dinner and non-alcoholic champagne. He hands each patient in my room a glass. I put up my hair and adorn it with a carnation—no mean feat for one lying in a crib, sides up, almost helpless. The muscles have wasted in my leg, I am spastic, have migraine headaches, and trouble getting my breath.

Later I reach back to the battered, screaming child lying in the corner of the drawing-room, discarded like a broken doll. The pattern on the ceiling-rose and the bottle-green light fixture mesmerize me. My father's face is blank, white, frozen with a rage locked deep inside him. There is no cuddly all-embracing loving Daddy. There never was. I ache for touch, for love, to be told I am worthwhile and good.

Dr. Perrin says I am a completely sane and normal woman. There is good reason to operate but it will be exploratory. What if, I want to say, there is no bone to remove; no twisted, knotted, nerve cord; no cancer—no reason for this constant pain, these muscle spasms? Will you sever the nerve so the pain will cease forever? Will I have no real legs to stand on?

I am in hell. Its gates are stainless steel; bedpans clanging. Ghouls and ghosts dwell here, multifaced demons past and future. The spasms in my back are excruciating. Please God, let it end.

In one corner of the ceiling two dead friends laugh together, drinking coffee in the Heavenly Canteen. They chat of social inequity, universal daycare, repealed abortion laws, the legalization of marijuana, and Amnesty International.

"Please Paula, Susie, let me come to you. I want death with no more pain."

They reach down from the ceiling tender, loving, strong. "Come," they beckon. I feel tremendous pulling in my solar plexus. Then I pull back. I cannot go just yet and leave Rob behind.

The elderly patient in the next bed is trying to teach the woman with the inoperable brain tumour not to babble. The lady with Huntington's disease screeches in her sleep. The quad down the hall is screaming, "Get away nurse. Help." The old boy who's had a stroke bangs his spoon against the bedrail. He cannot speak. He is incontinent. Splosh. Bang. Whack. He's thrown his dinner on the floor.

They stuff me full of pills. "Rob, stay with me," I beg. I know I'm in the Wellesley Hospital and who I am. But, "Please Rob. Don't let them hit me. Don't let them hit me." I rock myself to and fro, my fingers in my mouth. My father looms over the side of my crib in the nursery at home. I must be going mad. I ask to see a shrink.

The shrink orders the Valium stopped. I am not mad, he tells me. "The tranquillizers are opening memory spaces in your brain." I am abreacting.

I throw up and accidently wet the bed. The nurse patiently changes my bedclothes and my nightdress. There is no hand across my bottom, no sense that I am bad. Nurse tucks in the sheets and pulls up the safety sides. Lightning illuminates the room. Furtively I put my thumb in my mouth. I am comfortable and comforted. Pieces of an invisible jigsaw puzzle are falling into place.

Pills. Shots. The doctor has ordered heat but it has yet to come. I am disoriented. My head throbs. I am vomiting and peeing at once. I drift away again to Susie and Paula, guardian angels. Death sits on my bed, its bony skeletal hand outstretched. Rob says I have a wonderful life ahead. The other patients say he'll marry me.

There are pins and needles in my plum-purple five-toed foot. "This little piggy went to market," my mother used to sing. I can't wiggle my piggies, Mummy. The nurse rearranges my leg across a pillow. "Don't hurt me. Please don't hurt me," I beg her. My hairy legs are shrunk to the bone. Rob insists I'm still beautiful. My mirror reflects a woman I do not know—pale, thin, grey-haired. I'm barely holding. I must not fall down the chasm: don't want to reject you, Rob, must not abandon you. I promised in the snow. He tells me proudly that I'm changing in ways I know nothing about.

On May 17, 1988, chock full of morphine, I am wheeled into the operating room. The Great Magician Perrin incises my lower back with his ritual knife and lets out the demons. The location is at the first chakra, site of life-affirming energy. Survival.

Slap, slap. "Wake up." The operation is over. "What did they find?" I ask. No one will answer me. No one speaks to me at all. Everyone is as cold as the life-support equipment in the recovery room.

The cold, starched nurse has gone. I drift upwards, gently disappearing into myself. I feel no pain, only that some part of me is being pulled—the shining, beautiful part five fingers below the navel that is invisible: my soul. I see a long, dark shaft. Tiny light particles spill from an infinite, brilliant, white-lit place. Higher up more stars twinkle: the bright lights of rebirth.

I am dying. I cannot breathe. I'm being pulled, but I made a promise in the snow. I promised not to abandon him. No, I am not coming. I am not coming.

"Six breaths . . . eight. She seems very anxious and frightened." A man speaks loudly. An oxygen mask is strapped to my face. I am hooked up to a heart monitor; two extra intravenous drips are in my right arm, one in my thumb. "We had to shunt in lots

of medication to counteract the previous medication," the anaes-
thetist is telling me. "It was having a bad effect."

I want to laugh. Did he know that I was staring Death in the
face and chose to live? I chose. Glad I saved you from having
to explain, doc. His report would probably have read, "She died
of complications."

Next day I tell the hospital chaplain. Yes, she said, she knew.
She'd arrived as I stopped breathing and witnessed the life-saving
dramatics. She'd gone to conduct funeral services for a woman
about my age not knowing if she'd find me alive or dead when
she returned. When I tell Rob the terror in his face reminds me
of a hunted animal.

The neurosurgeon got me out of bed the day after the surgery.
Extending the same strong skilful hands that had removed the
scar tissue strangling my spinal cord and two root nerves, he
gently but firmly showed me how to sit up, dangle my feet over
the edge of the bed until I stood with one leg on the floor. His
eyes are piercing blue.

"Tell me about your work," Perrin insists.

I talk animatedly about writing, about producing, about my last
stint at the CBC. Slowly I realize that my right hip is dropping
and my right foot rests flat on the floor. I smile broadly. I am
standing on my own two feet. I wince with pain.

"Breathe! Breathe!" shouts the Head Nurse. "Remember your
Lamaze breathing." What is this? A birth? Gradually the doctor
lets go of my hands. We maintain eye contact. He's so much
shorter than I thought; perhaps I've grown. I feel ten feet tall.

"Nurse," he says, "pull up a chair for Dad."

A chair is moved in front of me. For Rob? The room seems
huge; the people very tiny. I tower over them, strong and powerful.
Suddenly I realize what Dr. Perrin has said. "What did you call
him?" I roar from my gut, from my very soul. "My father was
evil. And some of what you have just cleaned up was caused by
him."

When I'm in bed Rob asks me how I feel. "Important," I murmur.
"I'm somebody. Not just a disc case at the bottom of the operating
list." How outraged I'd been!

"You look," said Rob, "as though the burden of a lifetime has
lifted."

CHAPTER FOUR

FLASHBACKS AND MEMORIES

Unpleasant experiences gain power over us by being denied or hidden, but they can be made to relinquish that power when they are brought out in the open.

Dr. Susan Forward and Joan Torres, Men Who Hate Women and the Women Who Love Them

I had been believed. Scar tissue. Spinal cord damage. I'd thought a cancer grew so deep inside me that the doctors couldn't find it or left it unacknowledged. I had never accepted that it was "all in my head." For two years I'd known my body was deteriorating, but it seemed useless trying to convince anyone. The labels "neurotic" and "psychotic" are hard to eradicate. Not only had I been injured plummeting down a cliff, I had also been battered. My body remembered the pain of my father's blows. The seed of my troubles lay in early childhood—the place the shrinks had said was dangerous to look at.

Fires stormed through me as I projected my family onto my caregivers. Great Aunt Ada merged with the diminutive Scottish nurse, her white hair pulled back into an immaculate bun. I trembled with terror when she jabbed my tender skin to check my neurological responses or when she yelled, "Don't pee in the bed."

Dr. Perrin's arrogant young sidekick also frightened me: his real crime was that his eyes were dark brown like my father's. I resented, and felt responsible for, the little old girl in the next bed. She blended with my mother, whose love was conditional upon my meeting her needs.

"Breathe in." Rob's hand rests lightly on my abdomen. "Imagine white light filling you with healing energy." His calm manner returns me to the present. "Breathe out. Let go all the pain."

I gaze at him adoringly. He is a gift. "Shut your eyes." His tone is gently firm. "Very few people can sleep with their eyes open." I am afraid that he will leave. I close my eyes. He waits outside my room, protecting me from too many visitors.

The weather turns hot. My new room-mates are all dying; they want the ceiling fan shut off. I must get out.

"Walk, keep moving," Dr. Perrin had said. "Breathe. Keep breathing," Rob had said. It's Sunday. "Please," I implore an overworked young nurse, "I want to go to church."

Bzzz. Boing. Babble. Noise. "No, Mr. Mackenzie, you can't get up." Two buzzers sound simultaneously. Nurse is under stress.

"Please, I want to go to church."

"Ask the porter."

"Porter? Will you take me?"

"Sorry," he replies, "have to bathe a patient." I'm going to suffocate.

"Nurse, please, tell me how to get to church."

Another nurse smiles. "You take the elevator to the main floor, turn left and the chapel is across the hall."

The service is almost over by the time I get there, each step a major effort. Step. Step. Step. Step. The Gestapo physiotherapists have put me through my paces to perfection. Left. Right. I'm thirsty. I feel faint. The congregation is singing a hymn about passion and pleasure. In my head, Rob and I make love. A sunbeam casts a blue shadow through a stained glass window. It's a beautiful day. Dr. Perrin told me last night that I can make love whenever I like. Then I most certainly can go outside. To hell with asking permission. I'm a grown-up.

Brilliant sunshine pours through the great glass windows in the main hall. I ask the receptionist to open the doors. They're too heavy for me. "Yes," I nod in answer to her question. "I'm allowed to go out. Doctor said." The lie washes over her. She's a stranger I'll never see again. I burst out, "I was a cripple when I came in here. I thought I'd spend the rest of my life in a wheelchair. I had spinal cord surgery five days ago. I can walk again." She gapes.

As I walk on the grass, looking up at the trees pregnant with buds, I thank God for my wholeness, for the rest of my life, for all the people who love me, especially Rob, and pray that I don't become obnoxious. Today is Pentecostal Sunday, birthday of the Christian Church. Am I being born again? It feels like my birthday, but this is no religious experience. I have taken charge of my own life.

Back in my room a profound relaxation floods my body. I fall into the first natural sleep I've had in months. I've been taking narcotics for so long, I've become addicted. I realized it three days ago when I looked in the mirror, and I've refused painkillers ever since. The staff don't like the word "addicted," but I recognize the signs. The diarrhoea is getting worse, my head throbs, and I'm hallucinating.

I virtually ordered Dr. Perrin to release me, threatening to sign myself out otherwise. He said I could go if I promised to "send him a copy of the book." I could barely dress myself. The staples still in my back, Rob took me home: it had been a week since the operation.

As I stood with Rob by the elevator I realized that he had become my elemental father—in spite of me. I was almost completely dependent on him. He was the one who'd offered warm wet washcloths through crib bars for me to suck on after the surgery. It was with him that I had taken my first steps alone. "Look Ma, no hands," he'd said gleefully as I let go of the walker.

Home in my living-room I staggered, toddler-like, towards him. As he reached out his arms something fearful triggered. I started to cry. Claustrophobia closed in. "Outside," I muttered through my tears. "Gotta get outside."

Rob helped me onto a canvas chaise longue in my sunny garden. Birds sang in a neighbour's tree, ablaze with magenta blossoms. Instinctively I pulled off my dress, opened the buttons of my chemise and pulled off the straps. Rob began to stroke my breasts as I reached for his zipper. I hitched up the skirt of my petticoat, then drew up my knees and protectively put my hands between my legs. I'd been unable to bend down to put on panties and my nakedness felt dangerous. Oddly, I felt too small, too tender and young for sex. Rob changed the subject to lunch, discouraging my ardor. Perhaps he sensed my ambivalence and need for extreme gentleness. Even the soup was manageable only when lukewarm. I was new born into a transformed world.

Nightmares, from which a white-coated Sir Knight Perrin emerged triumphant, terrorized our nights. I woke screaming and sweating so profusely Rob brought towels to dry my trembling, emaciated body. I was still withdrawing from the drugs but I knew that something else was happening, too, something psychological.

On Rob's last night, some monster in my unconscious made the garden seem the only safe place. Painfully, I crept downstairs, sweating with the effort. Rob saw me go but didn't interfere. I was deeply grateful. It was time to reclaim some adult independence.

Outside I looked up at the stars and told the whispering trees that I was an old wise sexually experienced virgin; child-woman, madonna-whore. I went back to bed and watched Rob get up for the bathroom. On his return he stood at the end of my bed and waved. I knew it was him, but his towering dark shadow triggered terror in me. I became hysterical.

He lay down beside me, comforting me. "Please, please stay," I begged him. I can be good, I thought, I can be still if only you'll protect and guard me.

It is dawn. Rob's arms are around me from behind where I cannot see him. I want to make love. I must make love. We are touching, stroking each other.

"Am I safe?" I ask, puzzled by my own question.

"Yes," he replies, "You are perfectly safe."

He guides my hand between my legs. I want to give myself to him. "I am traditional and old fashioned about some things." I tell him about giving him my virginity. Why am I so hung up on virginity?

The pins in my back force me into utter passivity. Rob is infinitely tender and affectionate. My fingers are over my clitoris. "I like to do it through material," I say, pulling down my long T-shirt. Why do I hate touching naked genitals, even my own?

There is no hurry, no agitation. Like ripples in a stream bubbling happily over stones, eddying about wild watercress and lilies, comes the quivering spasm of release. Warm waves spread outwards from a central vibration, surrounding us.

My first fully felt orgasm with a man. It had neither engulfed nor overwhelmed me. I did not feel swallowed up, hurt, abused, or coerced. I had given and received love. Out poured a mass of questions.

Why have I always been sexually so passive? Why, in order to get off, have I always needed bizarre fantasies about being beaten or spanked for wetting my bed or my panties? Why have I always been so terrified and fascinated by bodily functions? Why did I cry myself to sleep every night when I was little, comforting myself by masturbating? Was I really such a sexy little girl? *Are* little girls sexy?

Rob stayed for a few days, pampering me and stocking up the refrigerator with gourmet foods fit for a princess. I thought he was cruel leaving me before the staples had been removed: it meant taking care of myself all alone. I very badly wanted him to stay with me; but he wanted to get back to the cottage he'd rented outside Montreal to hook up his computers. Perhaps he would take me home with him to convalesce.

But as I watched Rob walk slowly to his car I realized that my illness had been a harrowing experience for him too. He looked exhausted and overburdened. The Small Voice whispered, "It'll be a while before you see him again." Sadly, I knew it to be true. I was beginning to trust that inner voice. It had told me he'd come back. He always would.

I dreamed about blackness and chaos. Rob goes away and comes back, is ever-present. Loving Daddy goes away and is lost to me forever. Rob, my ex-husband, and my father are all one. They go away. I am helpless and bereft.

Spinal cord surgery is not the entire answer; there is a hidden, deeper trauma. I am infinitely curious to uncover it.

The first clues about the secrets I hid from myself came in a series of vivid dreams. I described their images in my notebook, but what really disturbed me was that I woke from them rocking myself in a frenzy of compulsive sexual agitation, shame, guilt, sadness, and incredible loneliness.

I dreamed of an innocent baby with a powerful, cold grandmother. In a subsequent dream the same child grows into a beautiful little princess with long, golden hair. She's trapped in a tower, suffocating, terrorized in darkness.

Night after night shadows haunt my room. My father standing at the end of my bed? Only after dawn is it safe for me to stop prowling the house and return to bed. I fall into an exhausting, nightmare-riddled slumber.

A house: claustrophobic and unsafe. Underpants. Get outside. Terrifying bathrooms. Being private. Locking the door.

Dreams. Images. Flashbacks: hairs in the bathtub. They've always disgusted me. A key. The lock on the bathroom door. Why am I remembering such odd details so vividly? Why are they accompanied by fear?

In July the memories started: snakes in the toilet bowl. No toilet paper. Of course, they are not snakes at all. I see the colour, shape, and size of the stools. My father is there. It's a memory

I've had before, but not thought of for years. There is something scary about it. Darkness surrounds it. What does that mean? Why do I want to push the memory away?

Why was I in the bathroom with my father? In my family, in our class, privacy in the bathroom was mandatory. What went on behind closed doors in the very best of families? What things were never spoken of, that even other family members knew nothing about?

I first remembered what was safe to remember. The memories were never coherent but small, apparently insignificant details repeated over and over in the exact same way. By probing the darkness surrounding these flashbacks, I was gradually able to open myself up to whole sequences; gradually I could piece together the jigsaw puzzle of my childhood. But it was not mere recollection; I relived what had happened, re-experienced my feelings, deep-frozen at the time the trauma occurred. After four decades in what doctors call "post-traumatic shock syndrome," I was defrosting.

The record goes round and round on the turntable. The needle sticks in the groove. "Someday My Prince Will Come." There are six songs on three black 78 rpm records with yellow centres: Walt Disney's "Snow White." I am in Daddy's study. Does he sleep on this single bed? Is this before he will leave Mummy and never return? Then I must be about three years old. He plays me records in his room; he pays attention to me; he is kind. The pattern on the curtains is smallish, reds, greens. Animals of some kind.

I seem to be watching from across the room. He sits on his bed, my Daddy. I stand in front of him, close to him. I've twisted my dress up to my waist. I wear little-girl white panties. I am afraid. I am angry. I want to cry. I feel ashamed. What is he doing? My Daddy has my panties down. He touches my tummy. He does something between my legs. The feeling makes me excited, makes me want to pee. I mustn't. Mummy would be angry.

A raw physically burning rage bursts into the here and now. I want to kill my father. I clutch my pillow, the comforting fat fluffy pillows Rob gave me. They are my father's face, my father's flesh. I have been betrayed.

Somewhere in my house are childhood photographs, which might offer further clues. I track down the albums in the back of a closet; I have not looked at them for years.

Through a magnifying glass I gaze at myself from babyhood to thirteen, Mary Patricia, the ugly little girl I had been. But it isn't an ugly child who looks at me from the black-and-white snaps. I am beautiful, innocent.

Bits and pieces, higgledy-piggledy memories that made no sense: my father wears evening clothes; he refuses to take me dancing. The Bridham Hotel, Bembridge, Isle of Wight. 1954. A clearing in the woods. Box Hill. Blood. Worms. 1952. An enormous switch-back. Festival of Britain. 1951. Slides. It's raining. I'm afraid. It's not safe. No other children are around. Chessington Zoo where, he wrote me in 1981, "I have taken 'all' my children."

Some Saturdays Daddy takes us to the cinema. We're crossing George Street in the rain. He looks like a huge giant in his beige raincoat and brown trilby. I'm five. "Fucking Jesus Christ!" he yells. Will he get violent, beat me up right here in the street? A car hasn't stopped for his charming smile and haughty wave. The world should stop for the British Ruling Class. (I laugh at the memory. How I am my father's child!)

I always choose the movie. And make my little sister sit between me and Him. Lunch first at Wright's. The cream makes me sick. The cream was fresh, they assured "Papa" and Mummy, who make enquiries. It wasn't the cream! Daddy took me to the toilet . . .

A kettle at his apartment. A single hotplate. A lavatory under the stairs. My father took me there as well.

A finger in my vagina. I told Daddy I needed to pee. He pulls down my knickers and lifts me. In public. In the grounds at Wind-sor Castle. I am humiliated.

I was confirmed at age eleven. I did not know why but I felt undeserving, ashamed, unclean. What happened at the Isle of Wight? The holiday is mostly a blank.

The floodgate opened. I began to understand my questions. They made sense of so much of my life: why I was always so passive sexually, why I always felt compelled to be sexual, es-pecially with controlling, dominating men. And with certain women. I began to understand the degrading sexual fantasies and the exciting revulsion of certain sexual activities. And why, during early teenage sexual experiences, I felt guilty, ashamed, and ter-rified when boyfriends, pants bulging, rubbed up against me. I understood why I froze, why I had to do what they told me. I was my father's whore, his slave child doing what I was told. I was raised obedient, polite, pretty, and good. No wonder I was such easy prey to every Peeping Tom and flasher: the man in the bus with his fingers under me, the dentist who lifted young girls' skirts, Uncle Jim fondling my nipples while I typed, the artist in the farmhouse, the nurse when I was seventeen. Helping me to urinate. How many more were there?

Carolin massages the knots of tension in my body, especially in my back; the same places Rob scarcely touched yet I cried out in psychic pain. My massage therapist's expert hands release the burning physical nerve pain this steamy August afternoon.

A terrible dreadful scream constricts my throat. I am in the nursery. I see the white painted crib; my baby sister in it. I'm in a big-girl bed. I must be two or three. I feel anxious, sick to my stomach.

A door knob, white china, turns on the nursery door. A little Vyella nightie, sprigs of tiny flowers on it. Being pushed up. I see my little tummy, tiny belly button, the hairless pubic mound and tiny clitoris.

Something unspeakably horrible is happening to me in the midst of an exhaustion so profound I crave oblivion. Even Ward Seven North beckons invitingly.

There's a grey fog behind me. It's dangerous to move. A leather belt. I am being beaten. I watch from a long way off. I want to run but I'm too afraid. I breathe hard—panicking. He is there and I am blocking something. I cannot go on. I cannot feel. All I know is that I am an innocent, vulnerable girl, angry that this is happening. A pillow comes towards me, dark and suffocating. To stop the scream? So Mummy, asleep in her bedroom, will not hear? The scream stays strangled in my throat.

The panic and the darkness recede. He leaves. I feel bewilderment and a sense that I hurt. The danger is past. I need comforting. What has happened is a blank. Babies don't know the difference between breast and penis: why do I think that?

Then I remembered the vaginal infection. I was nine, questioned all night in the hospital. It was after Box Hill, place of terror. How did I get a vaginal infection? The implications are abominable.

Slowly I peeled the layers of denial to expose the malignancy that had infected my whole life, every cell of my body, my mind, and my soul: Incest.

CHAPTER FIVE

CHOOSING TO HEAL

And Yellow decided to risk for a butterfly.

For courage she hung right beside the other cocoon and began to spin her own.

"Imagine, I didn't even know I could do this . . . If I have inside me the stuff to make cocoons—maybe the stuff of butterflies is there, too."

Trina Paulus, Hope For The Flowers

No wonder life had been one long, chaotic struggle. I'd funnelled all my energy into an intricate web of survival skills, until my body screamed, "Enough!" What an opportunity to disentangle from the past and recover completely. Opportunity, yes; but was there any alternative?

My first task during that introspective summer of 1988 was to maintain the tranquillity that followed each discovery about my past. To do so, I had to create order and balance. Exhaustion from the double surgery made it difficult, but the physical healing complemented the internal healing and provided a means to devote myself to it full-time.

The pain in my back was constant. Deep breathing got me by most of the time; I used analgesics only when it became unbearable. I could still hardly sit; walking, shopping, getting into the shower, even cleaning my teeth, were Herculean events. I could lift only the equivalent of two small cans of soup—one in each hand—and my leg sometimes crumpled limply. It would likely take two or three years to get back to normal, but I was determined to do it as fast as possible.

Two days after the staples were removed I started exercising at the local swimming pool. I travelled the two blocks by taxi until I could manage the walk. At my one month post-operative check-up Dr. Perrin congratulated me: I'd worked so hard that I'd surpassed all expectations. Basking in his admiration I proudly showed off the developing muscles in my once shrunken legs.

"I want you in that pool every day for the rest of your life," Perrin said firmly.

I had to ask the question. "What's the prognosis?"

"The scar tissue will grow back." He spoke quietly, used to telling people awful things.

"How long before I'm . . . ?" I could not admit the word "crippled."

"Maybe months. Maybe years. Go on with your life. It's all you can do."

Armed with a long list of spine-jarring activities I must never, ever do, I left. I'd use visualizations to beat the odds.

I thought it would take a few months to get over the incest. All I had to do was grieve my lost childhood. Hadn't I read somewhere that working through denial, anger, and sadness to acceptance takes about six weeks? Surely it was a matter of guts and hard work. I was strong. "Tough as an old leather boot," Rob had told me.

I just needed to forgive "Poordaddy" and forget. Perhaps it was only curiosity that made him look at a female child's genitals. Hadn't I once wanted to do the same thing? Maybe his "fondling" (which the dictionary still defines as "to touch or handle lovingly") just got out of hand, that's all.

"Weak pun," muttered the Small Voice. "He did a lot more than 'fondle.' Curiosity! Don't give me that. You wanted to explore a little girl's private places after you'd been raped in Spain. Remember how excited and terrified you were? You kept your impulses under control; your father didn't. Don't make excuses."

I made plenty. Perhaps Mummy didn't give him enough sex. She always said he was sick. He was a victim himself once. She must have known. She should have left him. She should never have married him. It was her fault. She was an adult. She should have protected me. Perhaps I'd led him on. She should have stopped him. Crazy circles of Blame Mummy.

Deep breaths. As long as I breathed In and Out I stayed in touch with reality. I wasn't mad. I focused on externals: the changing shapes and colours of leaves against the hazy Toronto sky. I'd never felt saner, but I was using rationalization and minimization to keep the childhood horrors at bay. Shameful secrets thrive under the protection of denial.

I was learning that mother-blame is as commonplace and counterproductive as self-blame. I did not have to protect Poordaddy. What he had done was criminal. I did not have to love an unloving parent.

It was time to stand on my own two feet. I'd been a victim long enough, always able to find someone or something to lean on, to fill the huge yearning space inside. I felt as if I'd woken up from a lifelong nightmare. I was alive, grown-up; no longer alone. I had rights: to be here, to be heard, to get better. I would face the hollow ache of unmet childhood needs.

Rob had shown me the meaning of love by supporting my changes, great and small. He was the first person with whom I'd had real intimacy, by whom I'd felt accepted and loved for being who I really was. He had never used, manipulated, or violated me. He was the only man I had never been afraid of.

It was a natural mistake to turn him into a god, to focus all my attention on him and love him obsessively. Until I could tear down the fantasy I had created, until he could understand that he didn't have to caretake me in order to feel lovable and valuable, we would never develop a healthy relationship. Yet, paradoxically, it was my projected fantasy that started my internal healing. I did everything at the beginning "as if" Rob was with me.

I started by turning out every drawer, every cupboard, sorting years of accumulated junk. (Rob would say I needed to clean out the old to make room for the new.) Then I had the bathroom renovated. Rob would approve. The shower had needed to be fixed for ages. New wallpaper and tiles lifted my spirits. Without knowing it, I was learning to affirm my worthiness. I polished an ornate silver coffee pot until it gleamed. I was worth the work. I pretended to serve Rob as I poured myself Earl Grey tea into a beautiful bone-china cup. Tea from a coffee pot? What would Mummy say! (Rob would laugh, "Here's to Mummy!") I laughed.

I set the dinner table with lace placemats, pretty napkins, and a rose from the garden. A fat bumble bee searched among its fragrant petals and I thought of Rob making love to me. I touched myself tenderly. My fingers became his.

I'd heard nothing from him for three weeks. Was he in hiding? Was the tax man after him? Was the Californian Woman in trouble? Had he gone running to help?

Why couldn't he trust me? I'd help you darling. I would understand, be there. Was Bell on strike? I'd heard the lines were cut between Ontario and Quebec. Some services had been out five days. But I'd called his office twice. And his landlord once. I was told "Robert's car has gone." Gone? Gone where? For how long? Since when?

Instead, I got on with my life. I was so much stronger since the surgery. Yet, I felt ashamed not knowing Rob's whereabouts. Was there another woman? I stuck pins in a drawing of a voodoo doll, listened to Leonard Cohen sing "I'm Your Man," and despised my own suspicious accusation. I felt neglected, hurt, and worried. I turned up the volume on my Walkman until the music blared loud enough to blot out the pain. Then I was stunned and amused to realize I felt angry—not long ago I would have been depressed. I was beginning to change. There was hope.

I devised a plan. I'd noticed that when I was fighting to take care of my physical needs, I became so immersed in what I was doing it was impossible to think of anything else. If I applied the same focus to my emotional needs perhaps Rob would become less of an obsession.

My goal, initially, had been to change myself to please Rob. I wanted him to be happy and knew that happiness, for him, meant being free. So I could let him come and go as he wished by developing the strong, independent woman inside me. What I had not yet learned was that Rob's happiness was entirely his responsibility and nothing to do with me at all. Only I could change *me*. I made a commitment to devote the summer to healing. What did I have to lose? If Rob never came back, working on *me* would still be a good investment.

I broke my days into segments, paying attention to developing as many aspects of myself as possible. I didn't think I could do much about my past—it was gone!—but I could nurture my present self by taking care of my body, mind, emotions, and soul. I made a list of tasks and goals I wanted to achieve.

I followed my list assiduously, devoured library books, and wrote copiously in my journal recollecting the pieces of my childhood. As changes in my body became increasingly apparent, with friends telling me how marvellous I looked, my optimism increased. By fall I would be "cured"!

I wanted to comfort the terrified child, but my father has her in his arms. I leap on his back, swing him around. Clutching him by the throat, I push him up against the wall. "You are accountable to me now," I shout. He lets the child go—me. I feel strong and powerful. I visualize my father as if through a telescope the wrong way, and he dwindles to the size of a pin. He can't do me any harm.

I'd learned the visualizations from NLP (NeuroLinguistic Programming). They helped me feel less helpless, but did little to stop the sea of confusing feelings that new flashbacks and memories unleashed.

I lie awake in the night, not knowing the time, refusing to look at the clock. If I am to cure myself of insomnia it's imperative that I don't worry about the time or the number of hours I sleep or don't sleep. I need to pee but if I get up I'll wake completely. I must learn to sleep through the night. I must stop worrying about it. I always wake before dawn feeling so unsafe, thinking of my father's stealthy footsteps across the nursery carpet. I sneak a look at the time: 4:45 a.m. I'm doing much better! Last night I woke at 3:00. I praise my progress. No drugs. No panacea.

The anger comes again. Clean, cold anger. Feeling feels dangerous. Why such anger? At Rob? Maybe some. I dig deeper. It's at my father. He can't hurt me now, yet my feelings overwhelm me.

I feel constricted in my chest. I am splitting and fragmenting; but I am not dissolving into depression. That's something to be thankful for. Part of being alive is intolerable. It's the burning feeling. I'd give anything to deaden it, but holding feelings down is worse. Is the burning in my back and leg? Is it burning shame?

It was all my fault. My clitoris betrayed me; let me down. Mummy said it stuck out like a boy's. She told me that once when I was in the bath. Daddy must have been sexually abused. He split off his little boy part and became his persecutor. I egged him on. I am guilty. I can't forgive myself. I couldn't speak to Rob, even if he does call. He wouldn't want me now. If he saw me trying to comfort myself with the baby bottle . . . If he knew I feel so alone, so frightened—like a tiny child—he'd come. No, that's the very thing that puts him off me. It's my father's fault. But they say if only you forgive . . . I'm so muddled.

I tracked Rob down in mid-July. He told me he needed to be on his own for a while to discover who he was and what he wanted. I tried to understand that his decision was not about me but about his own pain as the adult child of an alcoholic; that he had his own legacy of physical and emotional damage. His heal-or-die struggle was about to begin. "Do you want to continue building on what we have?" I asked.

"Yes," he answered decisively.

I sent him letters and anything pertaining to healing that I could find. I wanted to help him in his trouble, although I felt useless. I'd never been the supportive one before; but I wanted to make the most of this opportunity. Two whole individuals growing and sharing—it could work. I wrote our names side by side in my notebook. They looked good together. The Small Voice said, "You need at least two years, alone, to function fully." "If you don't come back, Rob," I whispered aloud, "it'll be because I'm not who you want. My love will go on and I shall go on." I was planting the seeds of unconditional love.

I dashed off a letter to my father telling him I forgave him. (I asked Rob to mail it from Quebec, feeling safer if my father were to think I'd left Toronto.) The act was meaningless. I felt no forgiveness, no relief, and try as I might, I could not forget. Indeed, I was feeling worse.

Everything was rising to the surface in dreams and nightmares, flashbacks and memories, triggered by everyday events. Sometimes I felt as if I wore a headband marked "Incest Victim." The hook was in my back and I did not know how to get it out. How could the incest have been my fault? My father was bigger and more powerful than me. I had no say as a little girl. At three I had no power, no choice.

But now, I do have power and I make my choices. I am an incest survivor. I choose to break the family code of silence. I do not have to love my father. I do not have to hate him. I do not have to feel anything for him. I just want to let him—and my childhood trauma—go.

But what if I am not believed? Rob believed me. I told him haltingly in such a strangled whisper I had to repeat myself for him to hear. My revelation did not surprise him. I asked him not to come back until summer was over. I was scared that if he came close I'd back off and he'd feel rejected. That would hurt us both. I needed time. But I couldn't do it by myself—I needed professional counselling.

My friend Jochen believed me. He'd guessed ten years earlier. He suggested a New Age doctor he knew who'd dreamed not to sit his final psychiatric exams, who believed himself to be psychically connected to R. D. Laing.

My friend Penny believed me. She suggested I see Lori, a feminist counsellor whose practice was dedicated to child sexual-abuse survivors.

In late July I called them both.

CHAPTER SIX

CRISIS AND CHAOS

Incestuous assault is any manual, oral or genital sexual contact or other explicitly sexual behaviour that an adult family member imposes on a child by exploiting the child's vulnerability and powerlessness. The vulnerability of the child stems from a specific lack of information about the unacceptability of the behaviour because of her early state of psychological and psychosexual development. Her powerlessness stems from the inability to say "no" to an adult member of her family.

Sandra Butler, Incest: Whose Reality, Whose Theory

Telling R. D. Laing's reincarnation about my father's abuse was liberating. The doctor said my understanding and connectedness to my inner journey was very advanced. I was flattered and made another appointment, but it didn't feel right. He'd suddenly stretch into yoga postures, as if I wasn't there; he left the number of his Florida retreat on my answering machine. The last thing I needed was a co-dependent guru.

Lori's manner was almost grave and, at first, disconcertingly direct. She listened attentively to my every word, as if she might otherwise miss something vital. When I got to know her better I discovered her to be highly compassionate, articulate, intellectually brilliant and with a great sense of humour.

I dreamed about islands, needing to reach Lori by a certain date. I have to hurry—she keeps moving. I am being stopped by a crowd of men forcing me to be silent every time I get close to her.

Lori had immense respect for the healing process. It had taken me forty-five years to get to this point, she said; I wouldn't heal overnight—or in six weeks. I would not wake up one day magically "cured." Lori would act as my guide, pacing me carefully. Step by step we would examine what happened to me in the context of my family's dynamics, the abuse itself, the ways I'd survived it, and its effects on my life. Also we'd look at my present relationships, work, and daily life.

Lori expected me to honour boundaries that would keep our work consistent, predictable, safe, and protected. She would encourage my self-reliance and healthy dependence. She would be honest with me: if I was standing in the rain telling her it was not raining, she'd point out the discrepancy. She would never, ever touch me. I was not to use her telephone as a hotline; I must gather a support network of friends. There would be crises but I was a *survivor*, not a victim. I had lived through the worst, the abuse. With courage I could endure remembering, re-experiencing my buried feelings, and grieving for the child I'd been.

At our third meeting Lori confronted me: she would not allow me to continue seeing her and the New Age doctor, too. I was playing them off against each other. I had to make a choice.

I left her office feeling a mixture of betrayal, guilt, rejection, abandonment, humiliation, and rage. When I got home I sobbed and howled and rocked from side to side on my bed, a wounded little girl again.

If I disobey your rules, Lori, what will you do? Will you punish me? Will you send me to my room, threaten me with your beating stick? You say you care about me. Mummy said she loved me and, making to kiss me, bit me on the face. She struck me about my head until I saw stars. Well, at least you won't touch me. I think Mummy really hated me; she was angry that I ruined her relationship with Poordaddy. It was after I came along that "he changed," wasn't it? Then he unleashed his fury on us both. Did I betray Mummy? Take away her man?

Why am I so disturbed by you, Lori? Why are all women so judgemental, critical, untrustworthy? Rob says *all* women can't be like this.

Rules, Lori, rules? Mummy had rules! About not singing at the table or making a noise in the garden. About not getting water on the bathroom floor. Once, a man in a bus put his hand inside my knickers. Mummy said I ought—her favourite word—to have stood up and shouted. My voice strangled with embarrassment, I couldn't cry out. I still can't. If I wasn't allowed to shout in the garden, how could I shout in a crowded bus?

Mummy didn't hear my distress or humiliation and terror. She implied that I hadn't done the right thing.

What use are rules?

Lori, of course, wasn't talking about rules, she was talking about boundaries. There had never been any of those invisible, safe, flexible perimeters of self-protection in my dysfunctional, shame-bound family: I had been invaded sexually, physically, and emotionally.

I didn't want Lori to see behind my facade. All I did was talk, terrified to give up the tiniest bit of control, terrified of hearing something I didn't want to hear, terrified of silence. Mild pre-cancerous cells had shown up in a recent Pap smear, but I wouldn't let her see me cry. I hated Mummy seeing me cry. I wanted Lori to think me as strong as a horse.

Inside it was a different story. I wanted to cling to Lori, be comforted, sit on her knee, be a little child: respected, loved, treated well, cared for, listened to. I was reaching far beyond Lori, back to a parent who never was. I wasn't sure I could continue my sad journey. Yet there was no going back.

I stopped seeing the New Age doctor. In exchange I tested Lori's patience to the limit, until I was sure I could trust her. She was safe, protective, predictable—the vital frame in which I could reveal my terrible secrets. With her support, and the support of close friends, especially Rob and his daughter Megan, I was able to let my worst memories surface. There were so many in the fall of 1988 that I felt caught right in the eye of Hurricane Gilbert, then lashing the Yucatan Peninsula.

Aunt Ada. I keep thinking about Aunt Ada. She lived with us from the time I was two until I was seventeen, when she died. I hated her. Yet there's blackness around her, no memories. Did she do something to me too? Wasn't it she who beat Mummy when she was a child? Strapped her for running away, wetting her pants, not practising the piano. Six of the best bent over the piano stool.

The dog leash. Brown leather hanging by its strap on the hook on the wall to the left of the front door. The dark, claustrophobic broom closet. The downstairs washroom. We called it the cloak-room. I hated it, its smell. Aunty used it.

I hated Aunty's room. Except for the encyclopaedias: an old gold-covered set and a red-covered set. There was a perfume bottle on her tallboy; sometimes it held lavender water. On the mantelpiece were two ornaments that fascinated me, one a farm woman scattering seeds from her apron. Mummy said they were hideous. Aunty had big paper-cutting shears on her desk and a paperweight she'd brought back from Niagara Falls. Travel meant freedom. Did she write about her journeys in her journal? What else did she write about? I wonder if she wrote about the day my little sister was born?

Ada gave me beetroot for high tea that day. I hated my baby sister. That's a memory I've long remembered. While Mummy says I greeted her with delight, I remember my suspicion. Another interloper to watch out for. Daddy was nowhere around, though not yet left for good.

If I have blackness around Aunt Ada who abused Mummy as a child . . . if I remember the intrusive way Mummy spoke of my clitoris and washed my genitals in the bathtub—"doing my tail-end" she called it—I want to retch with these sickening thoughts . . . if Daddy battered and sexually abused me . . . battered and God knows what else he did to Mummy . . . what an evil house I lived in. No wonder Mummy never took me to a psychiatrist. What atrocities might have been uncovered. "Papa" said psychologists and psychiatrists were quacks and charlatans.

I feel despair. Mummy always said she loved me. Rob says he does everything "as if" he loves me. Am I lovable? I think not. Daddy did things to me that grown-ups do or wish that they could do. It's in all the pornography. I had no idea why pornography fascinated me, why I wanted to produce documentaries on the subject as an objective TV journalist. Children being forced to . . . I went completely numb, speechless with shock, guilty that I felt nothing about what was so familiar. Less than a month later I cracked up.

What did I do? What did I do? I only wanted to be loved. I ran to you, Daddy, for love. And you betrayed me with your probing fingers, your beatings, and your penis. No one saw. No one heard. No one rescued me.

Carolin gently massages me. The scented oil revolts and sickens me. My body is numb. Yet I'm turned on. I remember Aunt Ada's gnarled old fingers.

The memory is vague. Being locked in the broom closet underneath the stairs. It's dark, airless. Every detail of every item stored in that closet is clear. The feather duster brushes my nostrils. I hate feather dusters. My friend Ruth has one in her bathroom. I have to shut my eyes when I go there or I can't pee.

I always had trouble peeing; I hated anyone to know I performed the shameful act. After my baby was born my urethra, constricted during the birth, had to be stretched to normal with steel dilators. Just before they took me away to the lunatic asylum in north London in 1971 the same problem returned. A doctor told me it was "all nonsense. But if I would enjoy the dilators . . . " He stabbed at me so hard my urethra bled. Gin and Valium helped afterwards.

There's a special brush hanging in the broom closet for doing the banister rails. I hate it too. Although I do love dusting with it. Hit them hard. Punish them. Hurt them. The rail between the two soft edges of the brush. Bang. Bang. Penis in vagina?

What is that scent? It's not mentholatum, rubbed on my chest for bronchitis. It's not the linseed in the poultice Mummy put on my shoulder. "Papa" gave me penicillin for pneumonia when I was six. Spoonfuls of thick, white medicine, but it had no smell.

"It's lavender," said Carolin. Aunt Ada's lavender bottle, antique with a pewter top.

I open the oven door to see if my dinner's ready. I feel like such a bad girl. The flashbacks can't be real. Perhaps I don't exist. I put my arm against the element and feel nothing. The oven is set to 400 degrees. Dispassionately, I watch my skin sear to crimson red. I am dead. I take a cloth and pick up my dinner. My hand goes limp, the dinner smashes to the floor. I scream and hit my hand. Bad hand. Naughty hand. Naughty girl.

Ada let me out of the broom closet because I couldn't hold it any longer. And when I wet my knickers on the cloakroom floor she pulled them down and strapped me with the dog leash. I had to clean the floor. I tried to be good, but my body let me down. Would not stay controlled. Must be controlled. For my own good.

Ada stands by the old gas stove in the kitchen. I am two and a half. My baby sister is being born in the master bedroom at the front of the house upstairs. I am tied to the table. She holds something shiny in the blue flames. A knitting needle or a crochet hook. I don't want to know any more.

Penny came and made tea. Rob listened on the phone. Both supported me, comforted me, helped me hang on. I'm not supposed to call Lori but I do.

"How could anyone do such a thing to a little child?" I screamed in Lori's office.

"She tortured you."

"I must have made it up." I wanted to retract what I had told her. I was overwhelmed, appalled. I knew what I remembered was real, but I didn't want it to be real.

"It happened. You could not possibly have made it up." She applauded my courage and strength. I went home exhausted to soothing music and a bath, my baby bottle.

For several days after each major memory I felt so much better, freer, more peaceful. The slow process of my internal healing was as visible as my external healing.

The bathtub and my bed were "safe" places in which to allow the memories to surface. The pain of remembering was indescribable. I wished to get seriously ill again, an excuse to avoid what was coming. A second Pap smear came back negative.

I was having recurring dreams, which I'd had for years, of worms and blood and shit. They were coming more often now. And about pushing out my father's penis. I remembered the picnic at Box Hill. I remembered about the vaginal infection and called Jean, my lodger friend. She remembered Mummy crying in the night. Nobody explained. Nobody said anything.

The doctors exchanged worried glances. Mummy's "sometimes little girls stuff toys inside themselves" shamed and humiliated me. I was admitted to an adult gynaecological ward, given a private room, and a general anaesthetic. Someone stayed beside my bed all night asking questions. I repeated over and over again, "I have a mummy and a daddy and a sister and a doggy and a cat." Had I already buried the truth? Or was I so terrified of what had taken place that I tuned it out with a protective chant?

The clearing. Woods. Tops of trees. Slim trees, silver birch, I think. Rough short grass. I need to poop. There's no toilet paper. Are there leaves to wipe myself? We look at the poop, Daddy and I. There's a winding path going up, up, up Box Hill. Box Mountain.

Mummy laughed when I told her about my mountain. In memory her laugh is derisive. She'd forgotten that I was small. I was supposed to be a Big Girl. I was nine.

There are worms in my poop. White writhing skinny worms. I'm scared and disgusted. Daddy says, "You *must* tell your mother about the worms." I'm confused. I have to tell about being with

Daddy. I *have* to tell. "You *must* tell her about the worms." *Only* tell about the worms. I must obey.

There is no toilet paper. There are no leaves big enough to use to clean myself. I'm bad because I have worms. I'm bad because I'm dirty. My pants will get all stained. Mummy will punish me. Bad girl.

I can see the trunks of the trees all the way down to near the ground where they touch the grass and the grass around the trunks. Spikes of green, stubby, coarse grass. Not soft grass. It is summer, or nearly summer, and there are clouds, puffy white in azure blue. I see them all lopsided somehow as though I'm falling. It's like being dizzy or being turned upside down. Or being pushed. My eyes concentrate on the distance, on sky and leaves, on trees and trunks, on bark and grass. Are the birds singing? Are children shouting happily in the distance beyond this nightmare in the clearing?

Like a huge shadow he is over me. Above me. Around me. I concentrate on the trunks, on the bark, on the grass, to blot out what is really happening, to make it go away.

"Please Daddy. No, Daddy. Please no, Daddy, no." I'm crying. Sobbing. Do I ask aloud or in my head? I lie still, small and passive, a frozen, unfeeling little body in the grass. Far away there's a hurt feeling between my legs but not happening to me, like something seen at the movies, yet knowing exactly how it feels.

A thundering in my ears, my heart beating in terror, pounding in my ears. My clitoris is swollen. Excited. I want to pee. I'm filled with shame and fear. Pain pushes deeper, deeper. No! I'm full up. Stuffed full.

"A fishbone's got stuck . . . here," I tried to tell Mummy. At last I summoned the courage to explain about the peculiar hurting. I could only equate the sensation with what I knew—a fishbone stuck in my throat. I pointed, scared, between my legs. She laughed, ignored me, dismissed me.

No one ever taught me the real words. Tail. Tail-end, that's all I knew. Nothing of clitoris or vagina. Boys had "willies." I still feel uncomfortable saying "penis." When I taught pelvic floor exercises during prenatal classes they thought me the most liberated of women. "Pull up the muscles between your legs. Com'n, you guys, too. Pulling up your testicles a bit is very useful for jumping fences." Roars of laughter, naturally. Little did they know I was on auto-pilot.

I understand the lifelong recurring nightmare: shit, worms crawling, and blood. And screaming all my life for Mummy. She did not hear. I might have been invisible. Sometimes I wished I was. Often I go to the mirror just to check I'm really here.

Shortly after the Box Hill memory vague flashbacks started. Then memories of door knobs and a strange room. "Isle of Wight. Isle of Wight," the Small Voice sang.

I wanted to avoid it. I reverted to taking Percodan and staying in bed all day. It didn't work. I realized that the more I tried to stall, the more pain and rage and fear I felt. I wanted 1988 and all the memories to end. But they continued, still lifes of my life.

The Isle of Wight collided with Spain in my internal meanderings; I will never return to either place. Other children laugh in the distance. My reality was locked rooms with a tortured, dark brown-eyed man. I did not understand that being beaten with a leather belt, being forced to suck him off or submit to his tongue were violations. It all seemed familiar, comforting; there was no pain, even when he burned me with cigarettes. It was what I deserved and expected ever since I'd started being sexual with men. I was the aristocrat's little slave girl whore.

I'd been well trained, seduced by my own flesh and blood. I'd been turned into a doll, a plaything. My own father betrayed me, destroyed my trust. I was used and abused behind locked doors in a hotel in the Isle of Wight.

Those windows wore net curtains to keep out prying eyes; I remember no view. I remember only being lonely and ugly. That was why Daddy wouldn't let me go dancing with him.

No. I am not and never was ugly. It was YOU, Daddy, who made me feel that way. You, in that room with the blue velvet drapes that came to the window ledge. You in that room with the wash-basin and drinking glass. You, in that room with a dark-coloured dressing table and twin beds. You, Daddy, who raped me. Repeatedly.

You brought a man up there, a pimple-faced youth wearing something white, his hair dirty blond. Was he a waiter? My genitals were whipped with something sharp, a switch, or cane or stick, while I cowered on my bed, my backside bared. I got another licking before being made to suck. It was the first time, I think, I ever saw an erection close up. It looked swollen and violent as if it would do me irreparable harm. It measured at least one foot sticking out from unbuttoned trousers. I was smaller then. Everything seemed bigger. I am sickened writing this.

It's in my mouth. Suffocating, repulsive, choking me. I'm rolled on my tummy. It's rammed in between my buttocks, stabbing me. My clitoris is pulled and my cunt probed by sweaty fingers. I'm messy with ejaculate and perspiration. The little slave girl performed for you, Daddy. I left my body and watched from the ceiling. I watched the corners of the curtain and your white dishevelled shirt. I smelled your breath.

I see your face close up, Daddy. You take your glasses off. They have tortoiseshell frames, I think. You leer, call me "dear" and "darling." The hairy mole on your lip leers too. In your excitement your head bobs back and forth uncontrollably, shaking and twitching from the nervous tremor; your eyes dart to and fro. You sweat. I stand naked while you kneel, prying open my legs to look, to feel, to slobber. I make no sound. My terror stays strangled in my throat.

The waiter's black bow tie holds my attention while he and another and another and another . . . four hardnesses come inside. Did the waiter alternate with Daddy or were there several of them?

I hear the rustle of taffeta or shot silk. A woman lifts her red dress over me, so I cannot see. I catch a glimpse of black garter belt and stocking top. Garter belts and stocking tops revolt me, as does taffeta and shot silk.

My Daddy wore a dress, a curly platinum-blonde wig, pale make-up, and a slash of livid lipstick across his cruel mouth. He raped me. He and his pimply faced friend and the others whose faces I cannot yet recall. I feel their pricks inside my eleven-year-old body.

Another room with smoke and bright lights. I am naked. I look down from the ceiling at a little girl. Photographs are taken of me. Flashbulbs pop. The door is locked: a Yale lock on a brown door at the foot of some stairs. The drapes are burgundy red. I don't know where I am. But you are there, Daddy, smiling and dressed impeccably in evening clothes.

I suppose you told Mummy you were taking us for a nice Easter holiday by the sea. And she, thinking we'd have fun, persuaded us to go. I was anxious and afraid. I never trusted you, Daddy, but I'd been taught to say "Yes, please." I was reared to be silent and submissive and good.

It was useless fighting the memories; but in the safety of my bathtub I could allow the horrors to seep from my pores, then cleanse and rinse myself.

A wooden toilet seat. A man's cap. The tall legs of a bar stool, glasses, bottles. An outhouse, flagstones on a path, weeds, a fence. A man with ice-blue bloodshot eyes, wearing a hat.

There were chairs in a semi-circle, a small stage, a bar, an unlocked door at the back that led to an outside toilet at the end of a yard. A man took me there. He was short, stocky like John, like a man I recoiled from who stared at me in the bank recently. He had pudgy hands with stubby fingers and wore a flat cap. He grabbed my arm and I, defiant, tried to resist. He struck me across the face. As I leave my body I watch the man's hand smacking across the memory-picture. I feel it on my face. My left cheek stings.

He drags me, kicking and screaming, to the outhouse, forces me to sit on the wooden toilet seat, legs apart, to pee. I smell tobacco and beer, his stale sweat, his genitals. He breathes hard and fingers me.

I am flung against the wall. Everything goes dark. Is he above me, blinding me? I feel nothing. I am dead. I leave my body and watch dispassionately as I am raped by the toilet.

Months later I'd remember being handed from man to man. Being made to masturbate and suck them. Being masturbated, forced to urinate on a newspaper while they jerk off. I am slow to do what I am told. A man swats me on my left buttock with his belt. Accidently, I fart. They laugh. The crossword puzzle is in the right-hand corner of the newspaper. I hear urine splash on newsprint. I am ashamed. I remember only the first man in detail. Then oblivion. One day, when it's safer, I'll remember the rest.

I don't know where Daddy was during this, but afterwards he was there. In the bathroom. "I hate you, Daddy. I hate you." I tried to beat him with my fists. He beat me, then ordered me to bathe. He watched unemotionally from the door as I scrubbed and cleaned my pre-pubescent body in the old deep white tub. To wash away pain, dirt, blood and semen and urine. Tears trickled down my face.

When I got home I said nothing. Crawling between spotless cool white sheets in my own grown-up bed, I never wanted to leave the safety of my bed, my house, my street. I never wanted to go out again. Not for years would the world feel safe.

It's close to Christmas, 1988. I feel safe enough to feel the memory of my suicide attempt two years after the Easter horror. Hurtling, bumping, shaking, jarring my spine sliding toward the sea.

I don't know why I was saved any more than I remember being rescued. I probably lost consciousness. I remember pins and needles in my legs, then numbness and being carried. I remember a train and having to change at a place called Brockenhurst, where our luggage was stolen while I was being carried to another platform. Mummy was waiting at Waterloo Station, looking worried. I was scared she'd punish me. I was ashamed. They took me away in an ambulance to an isolation hospital. "Papa" was away. His locum thought I had polio.

So many misunderstandings, so little love. As I entered my teens, sexuality raged between my legs. I searched for answers in pornography, sex shows, fantasies, promiscuity, drugs, and booze. I looked for answers in psychology books, reading them secretly so Mummy wouldn't know that what I found confirmed my craziness. Satisfied, I settled for being unsettled. The depressions rolled in, their regularity contributing a sombre order between bouts of manic energy.

Glass shards, knives, and razors dance in my waking nightmare. Cut, stab, puncture my skin, slash my arms, bite through my flesh. I want to feel the agony of the wounded child, tear her from me and run. The viaduct. Blood spatters, bones shatter. My broken body lies on the highway. I want relief from this longing to be loved, from this torment and pain.

"Don't kill yourself," Rob said. "Or your father wins."

CHAPTER SEVEN

CHILD IN THE MEADOW

The Child Within refers to that part of each of us which is ultimately alive, energetic, creative and fulfilled; it is our Real Self—who we really are.

Charles L. Whitfield, Healing the Child Within

"Close your eyes. Take a deep breath. And another one. Let your whole body relax. You're quite safe. Count from one to ten. Slowly. One. Two. Three. Keep breathing. Four. Five. Six. Seven. Eight. Nine. Ten."

Rob is calling from Montreal. It's February 1988. He speaks quietly, his mouth close to the telephone.

"You're in a lush meadow. Look down at your feet. You're standing in long green grass dotted about with bright yellow buttercups—the kind you put under your chin when you were a kid.

"At the edge of the meadow is a forest. The trees reach way up into the sky. All kinds of animals and birds live there. Deer. Raccoons. Crows. Mice . . . "

"I don't like mice," I interrupted.

"You'd like this kind," Rob continued, unperturbed.

"Look beyond the forest and you'll see snowcapped mountains. Eagles fly up there."

I visualized a beautiful magical place.

"On the east side of your meadow, to your right, is a stream. It has gently sloping banks with lots of good places to sit and dream. A little girl sits there right now. She's eleven years old. Her name is Mary Patricia. Can you see her?"

"Yes," I whispered, tears pricking my eyes.

She's wearing a plaid shirt and shorts and brown leather Start-Rite sandals. To save money her mother has cut the scuffed front ends off and her toes stick out. She'll get new ones before school starts. Her arms and legs are long, skinny, and brown from the sun. Freckles dot her oval face. The sun highlights flecks of blonde and auburn in her brown hair. She wishes she was blonde like a princess. Her eyes are brown. She usually doesn't think of herself as pretty, but she is.

Her back is to me. She's very far away. She seems very sad or angry. She doesn't want to speak to me. She doesn't want to know me. I sense she's terribly lonely.

"Ask her to help you with the memories. Ask her to be your friend and ally. You'll have to earn her trust. Be trustworthy and predictable. Teach her, take care of her, and meet her needs and you'll never be alone again. Because neither will she. Ask her for her energy, for her playfulness. Be open to her and you'll find who you really are."

I'd always felt like a needy child, but this was different. I would be separate from her and responsible for her. The trouble was I'd been out of control and abusive to my son. I'd neglected his needs half the time. When I wasn't palming him off on friends and babysitters, I was absent emotionally behind marijuana or cigarette smoke, alcohol or pills. Working compulsively. Hardly giving him a thought. I knew so little about him and his life. I didn't even know where he was most of the time, although sometimes I worried about whether he was safe and keeping out of trouble. If I couldn't parent my own child, would I be any different with this Child Within?

I slipped a tape into the Walkman Rob had given me. I'd have been ashamed to admit even to him that a part of me loved the songs from *The Sound of Music*. Now I knew it was my Mary Patricia part. I closed my eyes and went back into the meadow. Back to the stream. I wanted to ask the child for strength and courage, but she still would not turn toward me. I wanted this child to come to me, to hold her in my arms and love her unconditionally. If I could.

I allowed myself to *be* Mary Patricia—not the performer who wanted an audience, nor the little scapegoat who got punished for acting out, who manipulated or complied—but the little child who lay somewhere inside the body of a grown-up woman quietly hugging her teddy bears. For this night she was safe and secure, bathed in unexpected love.

As I lay there in the dark I visualized my ideal parents, protective caregivers with whom it was safe to feel vulnerable and very small. "Elizabeth," the woman I longed one day to be, stood to my left. To my right stood that selfless part of Rob who so caringly tended me after the hysterectomy and helped me walk again after the spinal cord surgery. Dimly, I understood that I was meeting three parts of myself: the Child, Mary Patricia; the Good Mother, "Elizabeth"; and the Good Father, who for now I called "Rob."

My "Good Parents" and Mary Patricia talked about loneliness, about being alone, about being loved. I felt peaceful, sleepy. "Elizabeth" and "Rob" whispered goodnight and, merging with Mary Patricia, I drifted into a deep refreshing sleep knowing that I had discovered distinct vital resources: archetypes I could call upon and develop to help me grow and heal.

I found it very difficult staying in touch with Mary Patricia at first. She appeared very demanding and needy. How dare she continue to interrupt my life? Hadn't she been told often enough that Daddy changed after she was born? Everything must have been her fault. She'd caused enough trouble!

I'd tried to turn friends into substitute parents, especially Rob with his compulsion to caretake. Now, if I could keep my newly discovered internalized parents to nurture my Child Within, I'd break that old pattern. But the loving mother was elusive.

Later, with Lori, I realized that I didn't know what it meant to be truly loved. My mother and father had used me to fill their own unmet childhood needs; my husband had considered me a keeper of home and hearth. And, although Rob offered respect, admiration, and affectionate caring that I'd never known with any other human being, I felt loved by him sometimes, abandoned at others. He wasn't even certain of his own feelings. If I could love my self, if I could love Mary Patricia, I would not have to fasten, leech-like, on Rob or anyone else. "How, Lori? How do I do that?"

Lori suggested I write the Child Within a letter, but the results were disappointing.

Dear Mary Patricia:

Today I hate you, little girl. Today I don't recognize you, can't empathize with you, and am quite unable to protect you. I feel only empty and numb. I burned my arm on Saturday and it felt like it happened to someone else, not me. I suppose that's what it was like for you when your Daddy raped you and your Mummy punished you and Aunt Ada did stuff to you. Well, it was your own fault. You must have been in the way, a nuisance. I know about that because I told my son he was a nuisance once and I remember hearing your mother telling you that, too.

I know your Daddy said you had to tell about the worms. Why didn't you have the guts to tell about what else he did? Ah well, I suppose she would not have believed you, said to you, so haughtily and skeptically, "Where d'you get an idea like that?" I'm not sure if I can believe you either.

Blood you tell me. Blood from your anus. So now you're suggesting you were sodomized? You think that was done to him when he was a kid? How on earth do you know that? That's a terrible thing to say. You were probably constipated. You often had constipation when you were a child. I remember your mother insisted you take Syrup of Figs, Milk of Magnesia. "Eat your vegetables," she said. "Eat more fruit." You've probably made everything up to get attention.

As for screaming that you want to kill your father—well, it's a good thing you quieted down so fast. The neighbours might have heard you. Thought you crazy. Then you thought you were invisible. Ha! Everyone can tell you are an incest victim. They all know it was your own fault. You asked for it. Saucy minx. Your mother always said, "It'll only end in tears. I'm warning you." And if you carried on—and you stupid little brat you always did—she said, "Go to your room. You're in disgrace. You'll have to be dealt with." She threatened you with her beating stick, didn't she? She should have given you a damn good hiding.

You're getting turned on now, aren't you, you dirty little thieving bitch. I expect you enjoyed what he did to you, didn't you? That's why you never told. You stole when you were little. I know, I watched you. I should have slapped your fingers and stopped you. You should have known better. You did get your fingers slapped—playing wrong notes on the piano, reading the wrong words in kindergarten. Served you right. You're so stupid. You always screw up. Why do you even bother to try?

Go back to bed. Get in a crib. Stay there. Warm milk in a baby bottle! My patience is running out. You slept really well but you sure wasted a lot of milk. You mustn't waste good food. We can't afford it. Think of the starving millions. Sure I gave you the same leftover milk last night. Because you complained you hurt. I hate it when you cry.

Blood in your underpants. What was wrong with your mother examining your underpants? It was her job. He raped you in the woods when you had worms, did he? The nurse shoved an enema tube up you—another violation, you tell me. Yes, I know. You had a vaginal infection and your mother cried. None of it proves anything. Your mother always said you exaggerated, so why should I believe you?

Now listen to me, Mary Patricia. No more talk of suicide, please. Shape up or I can't ever be nice to you. You're fucking up my life. Stop telling me how lost you are; how small and vulnerable you feel. Don't get angry like that. It scares me that you'll get violent or explode or something. And, really dear, Rob doesn't need to hear all this garbage. He wants you smiling sweetly, being good. So do we all. Stop thinking all these nasty thoughts. They're dirty and abusive and we just don't talk about these things. You had as good a childhood as anyone if only you'll think of the happy times.

Now, no bawling or you'll go to your room. No, you won't have to wash me in your bath. That *is* a disgusting thing to make a child do to a grown-up. But you must certainly be made to keep silent. Aunt Ada once said that to you, didn't she? I wonder what she did to you. No, don't tell me. I don't want to hear.

Go to your room and stop this nonsense. I can't be doing with you right now. I'll be nicer to you later, if you're good. Right now I feel dislike for you rather than hatred. I just need a break from you and your rotten memories or I'll have to pack my bags.

from
Big Trysh

"Who wrote that letter?" asked Rob.

"I did," I replied, ashamed of myself.

"I think it was written by a cruel controlling mother who lives inside you," he replied in his usual gentle way. "What happened when you were a little girl wasn't your fault."

I read the letter to Lori. "The incest happened," she said matter-of-factly. It *had* happened. Part of me knew she was speaking the truth. The other part didn't want to believe.

"It wasn't your fault," Lori said distinctly. "It wasn't your fault," she repeated. Her words rang like Sunday church bells. "It wasn't your fault." I had been an innocent child, not a seductive siren. *It was not my fault*. It is *never* the child's fault.

I went home and hugged the child who'd become this confused, unhappy, controlling, needy grown-up trying to keep out all possible hurt while desperately hurting inside.

"What would you like for supper?" Elizabeth asked. "Rice pudding," Mary Patricia replied. She didn't mention how nasty

I'd been to her, but seemed happy to be taken notice of. When I put a favourite childhood dinner on the table she clapped her hands with glee. For the first time in weeks I laughed and cried at the same time. We were okay.

I dreamed about being pregnant, about giving birth to Mary Patricia, about her being in danger. I reassure her, "I'm here for you."

At the beginning of my healing journey it was especially important to take care of my Child Within. I was physically weak and all my childhood pain was rising to the surface. Lori told me that each injury—from the violence, the molestation, the rapes, the torture—was stored inside my body in my senses and my cells. It must come out. I'd been numb for so long. It would be a year before I'd have intervals without pain.

Sometimes the only way I could reach Mary Patricia, and her me, was to imagine stepping into her skin, trying to feel her from the inside. Other times I alternated between her and the adult me.

"Why did my Daddy hurt me?" Mary Patricia asked one day in the bathtub. More bad memories had come. "Why didn't my Mummy protect me?"

"I don't know," I replied. "But I'll take care of you. We'll get through this together." Out of nowhere came a soothing lullaby Mummy used to sing me. I sounded like her as I sang. My hatred for her vanished for a moment. I remembered being cradled in her arms, gazing into her beautiful green eyes. Remembered her young soft face. Of being comforted and held. Something released in me. I'd forgotten my mother's lovely side.

Slowly, day by day, I approached Mary Patricia, so young, a mere baby. I had to kneel beside her, win her trust. Her pain was great, her wounds deep. She ached to know that she was wanted, was loved no matter what. I had to encourage her to know that she was precious and unique. I wanted to cradle her in my arms and slowly bring her closer and closer to me. I poured all my strength and love into her. "You are safe now, Mary Patricia. Safe for always."

I took long warm baths. I lay in the sun. I went to Carolin for massages. I curled up on my sheepskin rug or nestled among rugs and pillows. Like a baby, I wanted tactile sensation. "A baby's come to stay," I told the pharmacist (far from my neighbourhood) as if I had to explain why I was purchasing a nursing bottle. I took naps and made myself all the nourishing comfort foods I'd enjoyed in childhood. I hugged and rocked myself to sweet music; I sniffed flowers and spices. I touched things, rough and smooth. I played nursery rhymes on my piano. I borrowed children's books from the library. I bought crayons and paper and drew pictures. Some were the same I drew in childhood: happy cottages with roses round the door, safe fences round the garden, trees to hide in, birds flying free in blue skies. I cut out paper people. A new family. I played! To my surprise, many pleasant scenes came back to me from my early years—happy scenes I'd blotted out with the abuse.

It was time to return to the meadow. The eleven-year-old sat by the stream quite alone. I had thought eleven was a grown-up age, yet this child was pre-pubescent, perplexed, and very scared. Her back was still toward me, but when she thought I wasn't looking she'd sneak a glance in my direction, sizing me up. Could I be trusted? I had judged her as though she were an adult. Now I recognized her tear-stained child's face. She was in acute distress and only I could heal her.

My thoughts are of suicide. Give me an opiate, forgetfulness to deaden pain. Hack out the eyes of Recall. Please God, send a fatal accident.

"Please don't kill me," the Child Within cries out. "I did nothing wrong. I don't deserve to die."

"Do something for *me*," Mary Patricia speaks clearly. "Comfort me. I need you. It scares me when you threaten to kill me."

The Child in the Meadow is calling. She is an orphan. She feels abandoned, unloved, unlovable, angry, humiliated, threatened, frightened, and damaged. When she grows up adolescence will not follow this time around, but rather old age. Where did my life go?

"You *are* okay. You *are* worthwhile. You *do* deserve," I soothe her. "I love you."

"I want to be loved so much. I expect to be hit and abandoned when I'm not bright and smiling. I'm so afraid you'll do that to me."

"No, darling child, no. Let's do something special. Just you and me." We go to the park, look at flowers and dogs and little children. How small and powerless children are. I stare at babies, toddlers, six-, seven-, eleven-, twelve-year-olds so intensely I am afraid I'll be mistaken for a child molester. I buy myself roses on the way home, borrow a book on child development from the library, and promise Mary Patricia that if she's not too tired we'll bake cookies. Suddenly I'm smiling. I'm a good woman, a nurtured child.

I had to learn to listen to my child self, to educate her, set boundaries for her, and be a positive role model. Gradually I would teach her new life skills, to risk appropriately, to talk, to trust, to feel. I would teach her about appropriate touch and about ways to play and have fun. I would be proud of her accomplishments, acknowledge her shortcomings, and forgive her mistakes. I would give her support, attention, validation, and comfort. I would help her solve her problems and answer her questions. In short, I would be my own parent and advocate. However, I couldn't do my job alone; I needed adult role models to support me to help Mary Patricia grow up through each phase of childhood and adolescence into the real me.

Fifteen months after my initial journey into the meadow I dreamed a strange, vivid dream: I find a tiny perfect child. Her eyes are closed as though she sleeps. She is tangled in socks and chains, enmeshed, in bondage. Despite the long, hard work and my exhaustion I tenderly, carefully release her. I must release her. She's thin, like a stick, a clothes-pin doll. She wears a tiny grey smocked dress with a white Peter Pan collar, spotless white underwear, short grey socks, and Start-Rite leather sandals. She is a miniature of me, aged nine. I lift her up into a grey, warm, worn blanket. She lies motionless in the palm of my hand. I look at her, then at a man and woman sitting drinking coffee in an outdoor cafe in the City of Love. I tell them how glad I am that the child is perfect and unharmed. I am so happy that she has not been molested.

The man is kind and smiles. He looks a bit like Rob, but he is not Rob. The woman, his wife, wears pearls. She looks like a young version of my mother, but she is not my mother. Startled, she says, "Why on earth would you say a thing like that?"

"Because I was very badly molested when I was a child," I reply.

The woman is quiet and seems to understand. We look closely at the little child in my hand. She is at peace, and completely safe, Mary Patricia, my Child Within. She is my very soul.

The dream was about wholeness and healing. The man was my Good Father, gentle and kind. The woman was my internalized mother, critical, judgemental, arrogant, and hiding behind clothes and make-up and "doing things right." I had yet to love her, but I had made a start. I was being a good parent to my Child Within. I started liking little children and stopped being afraid of them.

They no longer irritated or saddened me. And my imaginary audience vanished.

I dreamed about children playing, running happy. I find a small, wounded creature in the grass. I pick it up tenderly, care for it, love it unconditionally.

In the lush green meadow, eagles fly and deer graze and a child aged eleven sits by a babbling brook. She turns and runs into my waiting arms.

CHAPTER EIGHT

NO MORE SECRETS

Many survivors criticize themselves for the ways they coped. But coping is nothing to be ashamed of. You survived, and it's important to honour your resourcefulness.

Ellen Bass and Laura Davis, The Courage to Heal

I started seeing Lori twice a week as my memories and defrosting feelings swamped me. I began to trust that I could tell them to her without fear of recrimination. But the closer I let her come, the more scared I felt.

"Get right into who Lori represents. Acknowledge all your feelings, needs, and longings," said the Small Voice, during one of our conversations in the bathtub. "See what you can discover."

"I feel all split up," I replied. "I don't think I can stand this. I'm too tired."

"It's intensive, hard work," answered the Small Voice. "Keep at it. It's worth it. You're healing. I'm very proud of you. Write Lori about your feelings and your fears."

The letter came from the heart of Mary Patricia. I told Lori how much I was able to trust her with all my secrets and my feelings about those secrets. Her predictability made it safe for me. If I slipped back to drugs or booze she let me know gently, without judging, that neither was an answer. When I threatened suicide she never suggested Seven North or said, "Buck up," or "Pull up your socks," or "Don't be silly." Like Rob, she was compassionate, yet realistic. "I don't want you to kill yourself," they'd say, understanding my pain. "What plans have you made to nurture yourself instead?" she'd ask. But I was frightened by my need for Lori to think me special. It annoyed me that I always wanted permission. I worried that I was growing like Mummy.

"How do I know the things I remember really happened, Lori?" I demanded.

"Name it," Lori replied. "Name the abuse."

"Maybe I'm crazy."

"The incest happened," Lori said.

"How do you *know*, Lori?" I was practically screaming.

"Every act of child sexual abuse is done in secret," said Lori calmly. "That's why it's so hard to believe."

"If it really happened, how did I come through?"

"Many don't," she replied. "Honour the courageous little girl who made sure you're still here today."

We discussed the ways in which children endure sexual abuse, adapting basic fight-or-flight responses, which develop into adult behaviour and become inseparable from it.*

As a child I tried to stop being hurt by squeezing my legs together, lying on my tummy in my big-girl bed, futilely covering my secret places with my hands. In my marriage, sex was the threat in the night: my husband pried open my tightly crossed legs while a powerless "No" stuck in my throat. At age three my scream had been silenced by a pillow.

Leaving my body was passive resistance—even if I got turned on. A sexual abuser intends the victim get enjoyment through genital manipulation, so the child takes on the guilt. I was *meant* to be confused by sexual arousal. It was my fault—that's why masturbation was forbidden.

When the artist—with his whistling kettle, big brown teapot, and wood-burning stove—invited me in, I thought I'd found a friend. A dad. Until he touched me. He held my unhappy nine-year-old face between his hands and pulled me close between his brown corduroy-covered knees. He smelled of oil paints. He touched my temples and my hair. I kept my eyes on details—canvasses, a kettle, the stove—so I would not see the pink, fleshy thing.

No wonder I'd forgotten all this horror. It was a miracle that I'd adapted, chameleon-like, and that I could glimpse a brighter future beyond today's pain.

---

*See Appendix B.

Baby Mary Patricia, age seven months.

Mummy and Daddy helping me to walk, April 1944. I am fourteen months old.

Wearing Daddy's hat, age almost sixteen months, June 1944.

Mary Patricia, equestrian, summer 1948, age five.

Mary Patricia, ballerina, in the garden of the house I grew up in, spring 1949. I am six years old.

Mary Patricia on holiday, riding a borrowed tricycle. Summer 1949, age six, wearing toeless Start-Rite sandals.

Moments before this picture was taken, at my grandmother's house in the summer of 1952, I was crying. Clutching my handkerchief in my hand, I put on a characteristic brave smile. I am nine years old.

Mary Patricia's friend, Jean. On holiday in the Channel Islands, August 1953.

The Blonde Bimbo, hair a tiger's mane of bottled blonde, hoping to be discovered, or rescued. I am in my late teens.

Young married woman, 1967, after first coming to Canada.

Summer 1969, and happily pregnant.

Spring 1970, on a brief visit to England to show off my son, Tristram, age six months. Months later I would return for a year. Part of that time I was locked in a psychiatric ward.

Television journalist on location, 1984. Shortly after producing a program about pornography for CHCH TV, I admitted myself to Seven North, where I spent the better part of a year.

Rob and I in May 1989. Photo: Jason Harrison-Edge.

My Women's Support Circle. Our final get-together before I left for the West Coast. From left to right: (back row) Heather, me. Front row: Ruth, Karen, Penny, M. J.

My Easter party, 1990. Celebrating healing and liberation from Easter 1954, with my new friends out West. From left to right: Hélène, Janice, Tina and baby Nikolai, me, Jer, Tim, Bill. Photo: Pam Robbins

May 1990, at Jer's house. My face has softened perceptibly. My dog, Imo, lies on my knee.

Celebrating the signing of my book contract, summer 1990. Left to right: Jer, me, Jane, Tim.

My son Tristram, his friend Adrienne, and their dog
Chopper, visiting me in October 1990.

Megan and I on holiday in Mexico, Christmas 1990.

"Mary Patricia," I told the Child in the Meadow. "Thank you for all the clever ways you stayed alive. I'm proud of you."

"You're doing a wonderful job looking after Mary Patricia," Lori said. "But who's looking after you?"

I was afraid to say, I don't know. "Er . . . you are, sort of. And Rob, I suppose."

"You need to reach out more to your friends," Lori said.

I wanted impersonal small talk with near-strangers if I had to talk at all. "Lovely weather, thank you. Yes, my back's a lot better." It was far too frightening to say, "I'm recovering from incest. I feel like hell. I need support."

I had lots of acquaintances but few close friends, and I dared reach out to them only when I was in hospital. Yet, when I looked around, my room was full of cards and gifts. People cared! My telephone rang frequently but I left the machine on to take messages. I'd pick it up only when I heard Rob's voice. With a jolt I realized how I distanced and isolated myself. A week before Rob's first visit in September 1988, I held an uncharacteristic dinner party: I invited only women and I asked them to bring the food.

I also told each one beforehand that I'd been sexually abused as a child. Their reaction was consistent: I was believed and reassured that it was not my fault. Only one said, "Are you sure?"

"Yes," I replied gravely, looking her squarely in the eyes.

"I only ask," she said, "because it's a serious accusation."

"I know," I said sadly. "I wish it wasn't true, but it is."

"It sure makes sense of your life," she answered ruefully.

"It does nothing for my community standing," I replied.

That night, six women drank a toast to survival and my healing journey, and pledged whatever support they could. I explained how hard it was for me to reach out for what I needed and asked that we meet regularly, together and individually. They agreed. How afraid I'd been that I would be shunned.

At first I didn't always choose wisely whom and when to tell. One woman outright disbelieved me and two others turned away in horror; some quickly changed the subject. Gradually, however, I learned to be more selective. Several women disclosed that they too were incest survivors, or had been sexually abused as children. It was an honour to hear their stories and I felt less alone.

At home, however, it was another story. My son had reacted to my revelation of incest with "I'll kill him!" But, now he was dealing with his pain and rage in ways I couldn't handle. We had row after row until, one day, he blew up. His dark brown eyes, so like my father's but without that fanatical tortured expression,

blazed with a passionate hatred. "I hate you," he roared. "I don't
know why you had me."

They were the very words I'd wanted to say to Mummy, but
never dared. The sins of the mothers—are they visited upon the
daughters?

Pushing his chair back from the kitchen table, he threw his
dinner, plate, and cutlery into the garbage. "Well," he challenged,
"aren't you going to get the plate?"

I said nothing; I felt detached. Yet, inside I was full of sorrow.
I yearned to undo all the wrong I'd done to my son and give
back to my parents all the wrong they'd heaped on me. Incest
survivors, growing up without boundaries, don't learn how to
set them. I'd spent a year in a support group for the parents of
juvenile delinquents; most of the mothers had been sexually
abused as children. Compared to some of their offspring, my son
was an angel. It was only as I was making changes in myself that
things had started to go really haywire.

"I'll come back and kill you." My boy was brandishing a knife.
He spat at me. I tried not to flinch.

"If you're not happy," I said in my "professional counsellor"
voice, "as you don't seem to be—maybe therapy would be a good
idea."

"Waste of money," he scoffed.

"A better way to spend money," I replied, "than on hash and
grass and LSD. People use dope when they're not happy and need
to run and hide."

"Yeah! And booze," he jeered. "I've seen you blind drunk and
stoned. What d'ya know, eh?"

I tried to tell him how much I'd wanted him, although it was
for all the wrong reasons: company, unconditional love, a reason
to go on living through my depressions. When I was well I'd been
distracted by mundane chores or hiding behind my addictions.
I'd loved him as best I could, yet resented him. I'd abandoned
him, physically and emotionally, although I'd been both mother
and father when his dad had been engrossed in work or his cult.

"I've tried to do my best," I said, "but I can't do any more if
you won't pull your weight and play your part. You've had a good
life compared to mine."

He taunted me but I continued, "No, I didn't have the best
parents either." I filled in some details, but his mutterings of
"Bitch, bitch, fucking bitch" rose to a warlike crescendo.

I remembered Mummy's incantations of her rotten life and how
she never listened to *me*, heard *my* point of view, never even tried.

I hated her for that. "Tell me." I tried to keep the edge out of my voice. "Tell me about your . . . your life." I gulped. Why couldn't I talk with my own son? I was learning to talk straight-forwardly to Rob. I could be direct with Jochen. With my son either I choked up so that what I wanted to say became incoherent, or I burst out with sarcastic remarks. When I managed to be lucid and reasonable, I sounded aloof and callous. My mother's acid tongue. "Go to your room, Mary Patricia."

I looked at Tristram, the vitriolic expletives still frothing from his lips, and thought, How dare you? How dare you say you hate me? How dare you ask me why the hell I had you? Before I knew it, I became my own parent and lunged. He stopped my raised hand easily, bruising my arm, and stood up. Towering over me, he challenged, "Go on then—hit me."

"You're not worth it," I replied, still angry and resentful towards my mother.

"Not worth it, eh?" he sneered. "Not worth it."

He went to fetch a clean T-shirt and socks from the laundry room and then exploded. He shouted, screamed, cried, and threw things.

"Get out!" I yelled.

"Can I take your bike?"

"No."

"Shall I take my keys? Can I come back?"

"No."

I slammed the back door behind him.

He clattered down the side alley, swearing, beating the house with his fists, knocking over flowerpots, filled with the devas-tating fury and deep dark unhappiness I had at his age. But I had to make him leave. All told, I'd endured a lifetime of ma-nipulation and abuse. It was time to put a stop to it. I held myself accountable for all the ways I'd failed him and one day, I hoped, he and I would mend our rift. I had to take the risk, and hope that he would be safe, turn his life around, and grow into a good man. Children must separate from their parents to find person-hood; but there had to be better ways to disconnect.

The house felt very empty and quiet; although I grieved, I also felt relieved. Most of my friends supported my action and I started seeing them even more frequently.

My agitation built as Rob's planned visit, his first in four months, came closer. I was afraid I wouldn't be able to let him touch me; that I would somehow mix him up with my father, if we made love. I was as scared of rejecting him as of being rejected. I wrote to tell him how much I cared, although I wasn't sure that what I felt was love. I offered myself "just as I am without promises or guarantees" and requested that we proceed slowly and gently. To prepare him for our reunion I enclosed some articles about incest.

The night before Rob's arrival a rowdy drunken party erupted in the house next door. "Take your hands off me," a young woman screamed. Crowds of teenagers milled about in the neighbouring backyard. Frightened, I tried to ignore the incessant beat of rock 'n roll and drifted into some far-away space feeling powerless and three years old. "It's just a few teenagers having a little party," I minimized, rationalized, denying the reality of "Ow! He smashed me in the face." The same young woman was shrieking.

My father stands at the door in his brown trilby hat, shouting. I scribble in a *Punch* magazine, colouring the cartoons with the soft blue chalk Aunt Ada uses to mark her Bible.

The party next door grew increasingly ugly. Someone was going to get hurt. I should call the police. I could not move. The past had engulfed the present. I felt helpless.

When Rob walked in the front door next afternoon I hugged my dear familiar friend, but I became increasingly nervous as bedtime approached. He just held me close that night. My legs, back, buttocks, wrists, arms, right shoulder, my whole body was alive with pain. Yet when Rob made love to me the second night I was so numb I might have been paralysed. In my head, in my heart, and in my imagination I was sexually passionate. In reality I was frozen. His gentle hands caressed my body; he fondled, nuzzled, petted me. I felt nothing. I left my body and watched it happen, an impartial observer.

I clung to Rob, hoping he'd make everything all right. I wanted to love him but my feelings were as frozen as my body. I wanted to get past the incest but I would have to be brave. I knew that when I screamed and howled my way through the pain, I came out afterwards into sunshine. It might require years of intensive work. Would Rob understand?

The morning he left, Rob announced that the Californian Woman had been with him during the summer. She would probably visit twice more, for business reasons; after that he doubted he'd see her again as they'd fought repeatedly. I limped out to the garden. Maggots were devouring a sparrow's corpse in the long grass.

My gynaecologist wanted another Pap smear. When she put in the speculum flashbacks assaulted me. I became nearly hysterical. She agreed that in future I would sit up and help guide the instrument. Then I'd feel in control and better able to separate past from present. The smear came back clear.

I dreamed I told my terrible secret aloud. Around me is chaos, lots of discarded underpants. Mummy turns from me, babbling incoherently. I am angry, suffocating. Gulping hard, I try to say, "Let me speak. I have to tell you something. Why won't you ever listen?" She stops talking and turns towards me. I have her full attention. In a clear, strong, powerful voice I declare, "I'm an incest survivor."

At Thanksgiving Rob and I tried making love again. We revelled in our sensuality, massaged each other, and tried different positions. Without warning I began to come. He rolled me on my back as I plunged into orgasm, pleading hysterically, "Please, oh please."

The nursery curtains flutter in the breeze of early dawn, their pattern pale checkered blue. Is that the pear tree I can see? Or a silver birch? I'm so close I can see its bark. And spikes of coarse, stubby grass sprouting round the trunk. Box Hill!

A piercing scream rose from the pit of my stomach where it had coiled, dormant, for nearly forty years. There was no mistaking the blood-curdling scream of rape.

Rob and I stopped sexual intercourse and instead hugged each other or held hands in bed. Sex confused me and a mild depression Rob had been experiencing, worsened. We felt enveloped in pain. Once, when Rob was sound asleep, he pushed against me. I woke, startled by his erection. My dreams had been of violation; his, presumably, of love-making. Semi-conscious, I rolled to the edge of the bed. Then, mute, profoundly afraid and trembling, I moved toward Rob. He gave me protection and comfort. All I could think of was the paedophile ring and violation in the night. I fetched a bottle of warm milk and, keeping his genitals away from me, Rob cradled me in his arms, stroked my hair, and lulled me back to sleep.

I dream I am being strangled. I try to scream, "Help me!" but my mother doesn't hear. I write a message but it's unclear; no one understands. I cut the word into my skin. Help!

For the first time I experienced predictability, peace; yet, although it felt good sometimes, I itched for the old familiar bells ringing: Me . . . Me . . . Me. I wanted to create panic and crisis.

I wanted sickness, an excuse to be dependent. I wanted Rob to give me his calm caring, the way Mummy used to.

And then I spoke publicly for the first time.

Aftermath is a Toronto self-help support group for adult incest survivors and non-offending family members of sexually abused children. It is also committed to public education and the improvement of social systems dealing with abused children and their families. It holds public forums every other month.

Lori was guest speaker on a panel, November 3, 1988. During question period I was first up at the microphone. In a quiet, clear, powerful voice I said passionately, "I am an incest survivor. I was silenced as a child. Now I'm breaking that silence to expunge the shame and denial. And I'm healing." I told a little of my story.

The audience applauded; a *real* audience—appreciating the *real* me. Lori told me she was very proud of me. To be thanked for opening my mouth! Yet, afterwards, at home in bed, I cried, sucked my thumb, and rocked myself to sleep. Mary Patricia told! But I was no longer a defenceless child—even if I felt like one. I had found my adult voice, which would bring me responsibility and freedom.

CHAPTER NINE

BLACK HOLES

Own your own pain.
Why not? It's yours . . .

Give it a name.
What you possess
Cannot possess you.

Patricia Roth Schwartz, "Own Your Own Pain," The Courage
to Heal

The phlegm of memory was loosening. Innumerable painful
triggers in the present mimicked and coughed up the past. The
feelings were the same; so were the physical effects as the major
memories began to sink in. My anus bled after I remembered being
sodomized. I became afraid to empty my full bladder after the
flashbacks of being made to pee on newspapers. And with the
Box Hill memory came a vaginal infection.

"Your body doesn't lie," Lori said.

Still, I was dumbfounded that I could be multiple raped at age
eleven. Oh, Mummy, Mummy, where were you? For the first time
I let her birthday pass without acknowledgement. I felt unspeakably cruel, but I hated my parents that winter.

"This will pass," Rob said.

"You'll never have to live this again," said Lori.

They assured me that peace would return. I had to believe them
in order to go on.

A puppet; plays I put on in the nursery. I played the starring role, a princess, in "The Big Feet." My sister wanted something from the top shelf of the bookcase. I reached up, pulled on it until it toppled and I broke my doll's tea set. Mummy scolded me. "You're a witch," I shouted. Angry Mummy spanked me on the seat of my brown corduroy overalls.

Fantasy is fluid—I can change the picture, see into every corner. Reality stays immobile, things always in the same place, in the same detail. If I returned deliberately to a scene it did not change.

I'm thrown again and again against a wall. The memory is punctuated by shouts and swats. I'm sorry, Daddy, that I'm so bad. I'm sorry, Mummy, that I'm so naughty you won't stop him.

Your face is bruised, Mummy. I made him angry and he did it to you, too. Please don't let Aunt Ada punish me. She stands in the doorway of her room next to the front door, dressed in beige, her grey hair drawn into a neat bun fastened with steel-grey pins. Mummy sobs and cowers. Where's my sister?

Daddy's gone. A policeman comes—to take me to jail? The policeman leaves. The family moves on into a blur of ordinary life as though nothing happened. No one says a thing. Nothing happened.

Reality socked me squarely in the face. It really happened. Holding hands with the Child Within, I struggled against a sea of memories, not hallucinations or fantasies. Perhaps I was too broken to ever mend, but I refused to give up, although I was exhausted.

By any name, pain hurts. My childhood recollections had provoked my anger; anger frightened me. In my attempts to freeze it out, however, I froze all my feelings: love, joy, sensuality, sexuality, sadness. All I could name was depression, hurt, and manic excitement, which I mistook for love. Sooner or later I would have to thaw my pent-up sorrow and anger, and begin the healing work of grieving. I stood at the threshold, too scared to enter.

In my family anger meant dangerous violence or depression and physical ailments, according to gender. A very small part of me thought that hogwash. In general, I viewed anger as hazardous, crazy, likely to overwhelm me. If I let it out I'd lose control, cause irreparable harm, and ultimately kill someone. (At one point I'd had a recurring fantasy of my anger spilling over while I was driving my car.) Wasn't anger hatred? If I got angry wouldn't I be eaten up in self-hatred just when I was trying to learn self-love and self-acceptance. Mary Patricia piped up. She feared parental wrath and retaliation, punishment and banishment.

All my life I'd been angry. It seeped out in crying jags and temper tantrums; harsh outbursts, either at those close to me or at total strangers whom I perceived to have done me some injustice; in self-sabotaging, self-destructive acts. Mostly, however, I buried it in my spirit and in my body—depression, respiratory ailments, colds, headache, backache, neck-ache, stomach-ache— and never knew it was there.

Unconsciously, my feelings rumbled through my dreams: Rob is mesmerized by another woman. He and I maintain the warmth and familiarity of our old relationship and, although I'm currently ignored, I'm not abandoned.

The Californian Woman returned to stay with Rob at the end of September. I was quite unprepared for my jealousy: I slunk off to bed and tortured myself with thoughts of Rob and the woman. How unfair, I railed, and ruminated on the messages I'd picked up about relationships.

Be good. Be polite. Don't feel (except love). Don't ever trust a man. Look after him and make him happy. What you want doesn't matter. Don't ever get angry or he'll leave.

I adored my Daddy. He was the most wonderful glamorous daddy in the whole wide world before I was four. He was tall and elegant, in evening clothes, standing in the hall. I suppose he and Mummy were going out. Perhaps it was their anniversary. Another time, I watched in awe as my clever Daddy carved a roast. Woody, our cat, had his paws up on the sideboard, following each flick of the silver knife. Then Poordaddy was gone.

I switched off the light and burrowed underneath the blankets. Feelings tumbled inside me like clothes in a dryer. Like a fretful child—half orphan, half adult-in-exile—I waited for dawn, when the hurting would stop. My perfect Mummy and Daddy didn't exist; nor did their perfect daughter. I put the light on and wrote in my notebook, where it was safe:

> I'm hurt and sad. I've lost my appetite, I'm depressed and I can't sleep. I want to say, "Go to hell, Rob." I want to retaliate, scream, hit, and hurt. I want to run away. I'm scared he'll go away and never come back.

I'd finally found someone who cared about me and I was terrified of losing him, too. Regretfully, I perceived how I tried to fill my unmet childhood needs through Rob: that was why he said I loved him too much. The longer I held back my grief, the longer I would play out my unresolved issues in an inappropriate form.

Instead of clinging I had to take responsibility for myself. I didn't have to go on feeling sorry for myself. If I didn't like the way I was being treated, I had to say so. I could say no. I could even say goodbye. I didn't have to blame, or act out, or threaten. Rob had a right to his needs and choices, but I had choices too. I wasn't going to allow him to take advantage of me, however much he meant to me.

I fell asleep at last and had a strange, vivid dream: I'm in the hospital talking to some doctors when a woman is admitted in critical condition. An emergency team works on her; it's touch and go. The patient is my mother. I wait for her to die, but she clings to life. There is a note on her door. I expect it to announce her death—and my release. Instead, it lists tests she's to undergo the next day.

I walk around the hospital. In one room, behind glass, pretty, radiant women are having fun at the beach. In another, also behind glass, babies are being nursed by their mothers on big, soft beds. I walk past a woman who looks just like me. She limps. We smile in recognition. I pass a doctor, who leers at me.

Then I discover Rob in a dressing-room, making up his face and dressing up to look like my father. He is cold and distant. I am abandoned.

"That's a very significant dream," Lori told me. "You're still denying what happened and waiting for something big—like your mother's death—to begin grieving. Don't hold back."

If I let go, wouldn't my grief be unstoppable? I'd mourn my childhood; my adolescence; my young adulthood; my failed marriage and the baby, who neither fulfilled me nor lived up to my expectations, who was now on the streets. I'd been no better at parenting than my own mother. Yet we had both done the best job we could. Like me, my parents were the victims of victims of victims. Generations of them. My mother and I had been victimized, like all women, for being women.

I didn't deserve to be sexually abused as a child. I had a right to be angry, said the Small Voice. Did I have a right to be angrier with my mother for not protecting me? The Small Voice was silent. Unshed tears pricked my eyes.

Mummy was not responsible for *his* abuse. He was bigger, stronger, faster, and smarter than she. I needed to be very clear about who was accountable for what and act accordingly. I might even contact a lawyer and ask what proceedings, if any, I could take against my father. For the time being, I would symbolize my grief by wearing black.

At noon on October 15, 1988—my son's nineteenth birthday, the first he had not spent with me—I dug a small hole in my garden. I put a photograph of myself aged six months, a seed-pearl necklace christening gift, and the blue ribbon that tied my first hair into the minuscule potty that I was toilet trained on, and placed it in the grave. I sang some favourite childhood songs and read from favourite childhood poems and stories. In the spring I would plant a miniature Alberta spruce to commemorate Mary Patricia, the child of innocence whose soul was murdered, and to honour the child who survived. The tree would run deep into the earth of my adopted country, Canada, and grow dignified and tall. The sky clouded over and the wind whipped up the dead autumn leaves. I began to weep, with rage, not sadness; but it didn't relax the tightness in my chest.

I went to the library and Harriet Goldhor Lerner's *The Dance of Anger* almost danced off the shelf. I decided to try some of her practical suggestions for turning anger into constructive energy when Rob told me the Californian Woman was to arrive for the last time at the beginning of November.

"I'm very angry that this is happening again," I said. "Calmly, warmly, and assertively," I had written in my notebook. "Be non-judgemental, non-reactive." My heart was pounding. I took a deep breath. "I feel threatened by your impending visit, as if what I want and feel aren't important. Do what you have to do but I wish you'd set some limits and be more assertive with her. While she's with you I'm not willing to be available to you. This is neither punishment nor retaliation. Last time she was with you I felt ashamed and very depressed. This time I plan to handle things differently—separate myself from you a bit."

Rob's reaction was one of amazement and admiration. I let out a sigh of relief. "Now, *that* took courage," I laughed.

"And well done, too," he replied.

I felt jubilant. If only I could always handle my anger that way!

When the memory of the Isle of Wight came, I lashed out at all around me. I shouted at a swimmer doing a fast crawl in the slow lane. He told me to take a tranquillizer. "Jerk!" I screamed, splashing him. Later I yelled, "Get out of my way," at two pan-handlers who came too close. I blew up at Rob's daughter during a discussion of reincarnation: how could I have been bad enough in a previous life to deserve my indignities, to have chosen my parents? I stormed out of the house to rave at Lori.

"You do the mad woman very badly," she said. "Go home and punch some pillows."

I was like a pressure cooker ready to explode. Rob arrived for a pre-Christmas weekend full of cheerful stories about a party the previous night. He talked only of the men he'd met—weren't there any women there? I was distracted, my neediness and anxiety a barrier between us. I felt isolated in my shame, holding down my grief and rage. My mood became suicidal, spurred on by a nightmare:

Something I fear is around a corner. I turn it and find myself in a street market where beautiful clothes and fabrics are sold. I want to buy the white wedding dress but I know I cannot have it. I'm a prostitute and may only choose black velvet, to sew up at home.

"Each cell of your body is replaced every seven years," Rob comforted me. "No part of what is now you was touched in childhood." Then out of the blue, he said, "I know you don't want to hear this, but I'm going to tell you anyway. I understand now how you fit my pattern of women." I went numb, not understanding. I'd rather he'd struck me across my face. That, at least, would have prodded me into life.

The next day Rob thanked me for the gifts I'd given him to encourage his determination to heal. "You teach me by example," he said softly. "You're changing."

"I love you," I whispered, handing him a pot of white narcissus, the green tips bringing New Year promise.

"I know you do," he replied quietly, and left.

I felt bad and ashamed. It might have been better, after all, not to have remembered. I thought of some of Rob's early experiences. Why were innocent children so often mistreated? He and I had grown up half a world apart; yet, like me, he didn't know his emotions half the time. "My feelings for you are strong," he'd said, "but I don't know if they're love. I don't know what love is and whether I have ever loved."

"How dare anyone treat him badly," I sobbed at my startled cat. It was safer to get angry on Rob's behalf than on my own.

My melancholy increased as the days shortened. I tested Lori, calling her several times, angered that she didn't respond. Then I decided to tell her as much. She encouraged me to speak more about my feelings, and my self-confidence increased. It was perfectly okay to express my anger directly and appropriately. I was learning that if I felt my anger and acknowledged it, I could then decide what (if anything) to do about it. The difficult thing was to breathe through the feeling and think before taking action.

Three days before Christmas, miserable with pain and fatigue from nights of insomnia, and guilty about avoiding doing my exercises, I took some painkillers and stayed in bed. I began to formulate a strategy against my father. I called a lawyer I'd heard about in California who had won a number of court cases against incest perpetrators. She was sympathetic, but licensed to practice only in California and suggested I contact a lawyer in England.

My rage erupted like projectile vomit. I trashed my bedroom, hurling china ornaments, books, papers, playing cards, pens, and as a grand finale, Daddy's silver cigarette box at the closet. I swore at my father's ghost and cursed the day that he was born. Then, I smashed my old tennis racquet squarely on my bed. "Bitch, bitch," I sobbed. And stopped abruptly. I was thinking of my mother. Guilt gave way to liberation, then exhaustion.

A week later I deliberately trashed my room again and cut my foot on a shard. Hysterical and bleeding, I called the Distress Centre. The counsellor advised me to forgive my dad and forget. I yelled, "Don't you understand what incest is?" and slammed down the phone. I ran a hot bath, congratulating myself on venting my rage. It was a turning point.

The next time I was able to vent my anger by whacking my bed with the tennis racquet and yelling at the walls. In time I could just scream and wail until my throat ached and I was worn out.

Underneath the rage I found an unexpected treasure: a small, tender feeling near my heart—infinitely precious, yet fleeting—attended by a deep, pervasive sadness like mist rolling in off the sea. If I tried to hold it, it disappeared. I was afraid to let the pleasure of it flow through me and I was hard pressed to give it a name; for all I could think of was that other energy whose force I feared: Love.

The intense rage was to last for nearly a year. I tried letting it out in various ways: simulating a toddler's temper tantrum; kicking water at the swimming pool (imagining I was kicking my abusers' genitals); and remaining completely still, breathing deeply, until the rage gave way to the weeping that always followed. Then I would be very gentle with myself, as I learned about anger and how to contain or use its energy. I gave myself permission to raise my voice (asking trusted friends if I sounded as loud as I imagined). I practised assertive "I" messages, avoiding blaming or accusing others; I took "Time Out" when I felt about to lash out: a walk round the block—twice if necessary—never failed to simmer me down.

A year after my initial blow up I attended an Anger Workshop. The facilitator told us first that anger is a vital barometer of our physical, mental, and emotional well-being. We were encouraged to experience "boundaried anger," not controlled but focused and directed, striking a tennis racquet against a pile of pillows.

I was afraid to reveal my anger in front of others, but felt safe, watched over by the group leader and by the rules: "No hurting others. No hurting yourself."

I hit the pillows again and again and again. *Thwack! Thwack! Thwack!* What a satisfying noise. My anger rose in my throat as an agonized scream; tears spilled from my half-closed eyes. I returned to the Ring of Men.

"No," I screamed. "No. I won't do it. You can't make me."

The facilitator brought me back to the present. "What are you feeling?"

"Fear."

"Where?"

"Here." I pointed to the pit of my stomach.

"Do you want to move the fear?" she asked.

"Yes."

I raised the tennis racquet again. *Bash. Thunk.* "No, I won't come with you." *Smash. Whack.* "I refuse. You can't make me." The man in the flat hat drags me to the outhouse.

My wrists hurt, my screams stopped, my shouts ended. I dissolved into uncontrollable weeping, a little girl, eleven-years-old, nine-years-old, three-years-old.

"I want my Mummy," I sobbed.

"Yes," the facilitator said softly.

I raised the racquet again and saw Mummy's frightened, anxious, once-beautiful, tired face. "Where were you, Mummy?" I whimpered. "Why didn't you protect me?" I wept silently and put down the racquet.

"She could not," I said, thinking of her position of absolute powerless dependence: physically, emotionally, financially. "She couldn't." Tears of soft compassion spilled down my face. I felt adult again.

The women wrapped me in a blanket, rocked me back and forth. I was soothed. I was loved. I looked into the eyes of the women around me, trusted sisters who had suffered similar pain, horror, and abuse. I thanked them for their gift. To my surprise, they thanked me for my courage. For a while all my pain left my body.

CHAPTER TEN

DISCOVERING ME

I didn't know women could be like that . . . Resourceful, straight-forward, capable, funny, proud, independent . . .

Germaine Greer, Daddy, We Hardly Knew You

Gradually backsliding days were outnumbered by good ones; although some days I felt just plain stuck, I never slipped all the way back. "You're altering your brain chemistry," my friend Jochen said. I was enjoying my own company, discovering who I was and wondering what I wanted in life.

When a woman friend announced her impending marriage I categorically denied feeling jealous. I cynically pooh-poohed marriage as an oppressive regime. With this ring I thee own. With my body I thee ravish. No thanks. I'd done my term.

Why marry? I wondered. Romance fades; dreams and promises that "this time it'll work" melt into complacency, daily routine, and boredom. Small courtesies are forgotten, real feelings held in check. Thoughtless statements and hurtful accusations, silence and separate bedrooms; haggling, separation, and divorce. I couldn't go through that pain again. Besides, hadn't Rob and I exchanged pledges, gold-nuggeted teaspoons and a golden fish, at Green Lake? I was quite committed enough.

"Comings and goings," whispered the Small Voice. "Pleasure and pain. Round and round you go. Expectations, disillusionment, distrust, neediness, control, possessiveness. All the stuff you've been reading about." Yes, I had to admit, we had most of the characteristics typical of unhealthy relationships.

I took two steps forward. He took six steps back. We only dimly comprehended the difference between "being in love" and love; it was too scary. Sometimes I was afraid Rob expected me to marry him; sometimes I was afraid he'd never ask. By hiding our fears behind defenses, we guaranteed that sustained closeness would elude us.

Expectations. Mummy's. Family friends'. School's. My husband's. Men's. Bosses'. My son's. I always let everybody down and ended up guilty, resentful, angry, and wanting to run away— just like Rob did. My own expectations were even greater. Famous actress. Respected journalist. Ideal wife. Perfect mother. Superwoman. I never thought I'd divorce. I never expected to abandon my own child; never, I'd promised my infant son, will I do what my parents did.

I considered my present expectations: to get back to normal health and energy levels; that Rob and I would be together in some way some day; that I'd go on writing. I wanted balance in my life, yet swung from one extreme to the other. I'd be in pain from overexertion, then do no exercise until my muscles stiffened. I stopped dreaming of being a celebrity romance writer, so I wrote nothing. I envisaged Rob as my Life Partner or I was alone and forgotten.

I dreamed about the moon, silvery white, a shining, upside-down horseshoe. Bad luck. A dead ladybug. Buildings with windows. I'm living in the wrong place.

I woke to a new, mocking voice. "You can't have what you want. You don't deserve love. You're trash. Cheap incest trash. Who'd want YOU?" I breathed deeply. It was going to be a bad day. I went for a long walk, my first alone since the spinal cord surgery. My body was getting stronger. So was I. "Voice," I said, "I want you to know I don't like it when you tell me these things. I feel angry, hurt, ashamed, lonely, and afraid. About everything. Rob. My childhood. Me."

"You don't deserve Rob," the voice sneered.

"I love Rob," I struck back. I didn't have to take this. I'm adult, I reminded myself. "I do deserve him. He loves me and he deserves me. We deserve each other."

"Pshaw!" said the voice.

"I do deserve. I do deserve." I intoned over and over until I felt better. "You old hag," I said very firmly, temporarily silencing the Voice of Shame.

"Rob's your best friend, even if he's never anything else," the Small Voice piped up. I sighed. He said we'd always be friends when we first met. "Believe it," the Small Voice continued. "Stop pushing."

I wanted to learn how to relate openly and intimately without clinging or suffocating—difficult tasks. I had endless discussions with myself on love and marriage, on relationships of all kinds. I admired some aspects of the relationship between Jean-Paul Sartre and Simone de Beauvoir. They had been best friends, lovers, intellectual equals. Their relationship had room for growth; they never married. Nor would I! I'd experienced enough of white man's hypocritical, middle-class morality.

What irked me most was that the words "husband" and "wife" did not, at least in my dictionary, signify equality. A "wife" was a woman acting in a specified capacity; a "husband" was master of the house. I began to look at language in a different way and made a discovery: "I'm a Born Again Feminist," I remarked aloud and laughed with pride.

During the seventies, when I was a prenatal counsellor, the women's movement was born. It was best not to discuss the subject at home. I found it prudent to reject bra-burning, angry females, shouting for equality, as ball-breaking man-haters. Secretly, however, I admired my militant feminist sisters; and in less flamboyant ways I also fought for the rights of women: for fathers in the delivery room, for less interference by doctors touting hi-tech equipment and unnecessary Caesarian sections, for family-centred maternity care, and for the legitimacy of midwives.

By the time I was again single I was too self-absorbed to think about much more than making ends meet. I still thought in terms of finding a man to take care of me rather than finding myself and taking care of me. I overestimated men, underestimated women, and remained a victim.

I'd believed all the negative things ever said about me were me: Stupid. Crazy. Whore. Needy. Dependent. I was a people-pleasing approval seeker. My real thoughts and desires and feelings went invalidated; my ideas unexpressed. Often I derided the very things I wanted to embrace.

During the summer of 1988, I began thinking in new ways. I stopped attempting to conform to what I thought were other's expectations of me and started taking pride in being the woman I am. For a long time I felt caught between my old self and my new self; but confusion is the precursor of growth.

I had tried to sever the old deep ties to my birth country; once I even took lessons to eradicate my English accent. Now I took pride in the "English" part of me. I started enjoying music again, singing with relaxed vocal cords; playing the piano without fear of smacked fingers. It was fun holding my elbows correctly, with my fingers properly poised over the keyboard, banging out honky-tonk or attempting Beethoven's "Pathetique" and "Moonlight" sonatas. My confidence surged. It was pure joy to make music.

Intellectual failure was also part of my old self. I read little and flunked out of math, physics, chemistry, and theory of any kind. I was too busy surviving to concentrate: "Daydreaming again, Mary Patricia." No one knew then about right brain intuition and left brain logic; that some people have "felt" knowledge as opposed to academic erudition. I existed in my own world of creativity and ideas.

"Artistic," they said. Dumb, I thought. Behind my back excuses were made. "Her father, you know. A divorce." They shook their heads sadly and let me get away with things. I was the only student in the A stream who took subjects in the C stream. I played the clown; I entertained them with stories of my weekend escapades.

I was denied university because I wasn't academic; the school classified me as secretary, good-wife material. Everyone said my sister was clever (and, indeed she is, with a degree in economics and statistics). I was expected to marry, and when I did, society applauded. Good girl!

During my marriage my husband's "Who'd ever want you?" kept me in my place. As I took my first tottering steps towards independence the relationship began to crack. After spreading my wings I wanted to see how far my talents could take me. Why *not* try broadcast journalism?

A drama teacher told me that my talent at the typewriter outstripped my artistry in the footlights; but as an actress I could wear legitimate disguises and speak another's words. Writing would mean offering only my own truth. Broadcast journalism gave me an opportunity to write and perform; it also gave me an identity. My confidence grew with the encouragement of my executive producers. The creative plagiarism I'd employed in high school—writing essays based on passages from Great Aunt Ada's old encyclopaedias—translated into an ability to rewrite wire service copy, press releases, and newspaper stories. Producing current affairs programs stretched me creatively: I was not merely good on camera; I could write.

Now I was hungry to learn. Reading was a daily feast offered by local libraries and bookstores—places I'd once thought myself too stupid to enter.

My redefined goal was to balance work and home without compromising my journey toward self-realization. I wanted to make a useful contribution in the world *and* be in a committed, evolving relationship. I imagined my partner and I as intimate equals, interdependent yet growing mutually and individually, respecting each other's differences. Rob, of course, landed the leading role. I was nowhere near ready for The Big Relationship; but that didn't stop me from worrying about how to get there, rather than enjoying the steps along the way.

Gradually, bit by bit, I accepted myself as a multi-dimensional woman of many lovable, viable parts. As I mirrored those parts of myself in others I was gradually able to accept myself at a deeper level and make important, fundamental changes. At first, however, I externalized and named each part as it surfaced into my conscious awareness: Mary Patricia, the Child Within in her various ages and stages of development; Elizabeth, the nurturing and powerful Mother Within; Hope, the rebellious teenager; Amanda, my Shakti/ Wild Woman and rich, creative force; a wonderful Wise Grandmother; Helga the Hag, my very own wicked stepmother; and many more. But the one I fell in love with, in spring 1989, was Spenser, my Inner Man, named after the boy I might have been.

He walks slowly towards me across the meadow, leaning on a walking stick. Mary Patricia holds his other hand, without fear. Spenser is tall, bearded, handsome, with a lean, firm body that belies his age, and an elegance about him that attracts me strongly. I'm fascinated by him, then appalled. Dark shades cover his milky eyes.

"I will always be blind," he tells me. "Unless you can accept brown eyes. Mine. Yours. Dad's."

My Inner Man is a writer and strategic thinker, powerful and worldly. He loves nature and has a strong interest in medicine. He has visceral courage and is not afraid to be vulnerable. In some ways he reminds me of Rob, on whom I have projected the masculine part of me. "I've been very lonely," Spenser says. "Now that I've met you, I'll never be alone again." With a rush of affection, I hug myself. "Please write in my notebook, Spenser."

Dear Trysh:

I want you to know that although you're feeling sad and confused right now I love you very very much and I'm proud of you. Your courage to look inside is amazing. You *are* healing. You don't have to be "up" and perfect and peaceful all the time. You're *human*. You're becoming *real*—a Human Being instead of a Human Doing. That means being raw, feeling confused, anxious, angry, sad—as well as hopeful, loving, happy. I accept you just exactly the way you are. You're a beautiful, deserving, worthwhile woman. You're filled with goodness.

Be good to yourself. Everything is working out in the best possible way. Exactly as it should.

With my love,
Spenser

"I love you Spenser," I said aloud.

The more I got to know myself, the more I trusted and liked myself. Outward appearances mattered less. I was the same person underneath in denim or silk, with or without make-up, with or without my legs shaved. One by one my masks fell off. I had a lot of work ahead of me. I was the snake shedding layer upon layer to become my best possible self, an ordinary human.

To my eventual chagrin, however, I still waited patiently for Prince Rob to rescue me. On Christmas Day, 1988, he flew to San Francisco to say goodbye to the Californian Woman. In my dream he forgot to come back.

CHAPTER ELEVEN

DEAR MUMMY

Of course, I believe you. You're my daughter!

Sylvia Fraser, My Father's House

*After disclosure of father-daughter incest, mothers have the extraor-
dinarily difficult task of having to deal with their own feelings of
pain and rage . . . at the same time having to try to understand and
accept their daughters' rage at them for what their husbands did.*

Diana E. H. Russell, The Secret Trauma

The Child Within needed to speak, to be heard. As Mary Patricia's
advocate I had to tell Mummy.

"Mummy'll abandon me. Daddy'll come and get me. I'll be punished," she said. I reassured and soothed her.

After the back operation, I wrote to my mother that I remembered being battered. I tried to break the news gently knowing
Mummy would be devastated. I wanted to disclose the incest face
to face, but the long journey to England would have to wait until
I was physically more able. In my innocent ignorance, I anticipated
that my revelations would put our relationship on a new footing
and heal our lifelong difficulties. I told her that I was planning
to see a counsellor specializing in "special childhood trauma."

Mummy's reply stunned and disappointed me.

> I am sorry if you really believe these allegations you make against poor Daddy. Certainly nothing happened to you before he left home. The saddest thing I ever had to see was his complete rejection of you. After he left home, as far as I know, you and [your sister] never saw him separately with the exception of once when you had flu and he took her to see "Dumbo." That is, until you were much older and he had married again, after which, at one time, you went very much your own way.

I was determined to be heard. I needed desperately to know whether she'd known about the incest. If she had known, why had she done nothing? I wrote back with more explicit details. Her response contained a story about a flawed diamond: "we sometimes tend too much to dwell on the scratches."

In my rage I could no more hear Mummy's pain than she could mine. Shattered and unable to deal with my letter, she wrote that she could "only manage to cope with the present. I love you very much and always shall and despite a great deal of worry and anxiety over the years I treasure all the happy times we have had together."

I took a month to reply.

> My dear Mummy:
> Thank you for your letter. I know how hard it is for you to receive these letters of mine as it is hard for me to write them. . . . I do not expect you to be happy about what I do, nor do I expect your approval. Facing the past and . . . working through my feelings of anger and grief are part of the healing process.
> Incest tears families apart. . . . It thrives on silence and denial. . . . I refuse to perpetuate the shame and secrecy by either denying what happened to me or by keeping silent. Breaking the silence takes away the power of the past. I cannot change anything that happened but I can change now and live my life in a new and different way than ever before. . . .
> I have around me a group of friends who give me absolute honest, unconditional, emotional support. I am often very vulnerable and have created a wall of safety around myself within which to nurture myself and feel protected. I do not answer

the telephone and I see no one I do not wish to see nor go anywhere I do not choose to go.

I sympathized with Mummy's complaints of pain and insomnia and suggested she practice breathing and relaxation techniques instead of taking pills. I copied the final paragraph from a book, comforting words, I thought, that she would want to hear. I didn't know how else to say that she had been the best mother she possibly could. I wished later that I'd waited until the words came from my heart. She never referred to them in her reply, nor to anything else I'd written for that matter.

We talked briefly on the telephone at Christmas. Nothing was mentioned about our correspondence. I wrote again on Boxing Day. "Listen to me," Mary Patricia shrieked. "Listen!"

Thank you for your last letter. Frankly I am shocked that you can write to me and totally ignore the things that I tell you except to say that *you* are shattered. Yes, of course, you are. And I have said again and again that I am sorry you have to hear such news and I have tried to make you understand why I tell you. No more secrets, Mummy, no more denial. . . .

I do *not* blame you. The blame, the accountability and the responsibility is his—my father's. He is a warped and twisted, angry, powerless individual. [He] did not want sex. He wanted *power* . . . perpetrators against small children are the most pathetic because inside them there is a wounded and abused child who rages. But . . . it is not *your* fault what he did to me. It is not mine. It is his and his alone.

Still, I am at a loss to understand why you let me go to the Isle of Wight, to Bembridge, to a hotel with him at Easter when I was eleven years old. Were you afraid to say no to him? That I can understand. He was a terrifying person. I have suffered terribly all my life because of him and what he did to me. . . . Please try to understand the pain, the sorrow, the rage. . . .

You always tell me how much you love me. Show me that you do—unconditionally. Tell me you're sorry about what happened to me. Tell me you believe me. Tell me you acknowledge my suffering. Tell me it was not my fault. . . .

I felt betrayed and abandoned as a child by both of you. That does not have to happen now. . . . The past is over. The past is gone. . . .

Don't cut me off emotionally. Our relationship changes but you can support me in your letters. Otherwise I have no choice but to sever the ties. I cannot heal otherwise and I have the right to heal; to the best possible life. . . .

In terms of emotional stability and self-sufficiency I can do far more than most people. There are many things I can never do physically. I may never be comfortably able to travel to England. That is reality. I do have some physical limitations and some days I need a walking stick because my leg gives out . . . but I rest easy. Nobody has power over me or abuses me. I no longer abuse myself. I live a rather ordinary life. . . .

I urge you to talk. If you cannot share this with friends— and this subject is very very hard to discuss—ask your doctor to refer you to a counsellor. Show this letter to your doctor. . . . While incest is hardly a topic for dinner party conversation it is not the totally taboo subject it was once.

Please do not deny me the right to heal by ignoring what I tell you. Please.

Mummy's longed-for reply arrived in January 1989.

My darling Trysh:

Of course I am sorry, how could I be otherwise, very, very, sorry indeed and that you should be so unhappy just now when such a happy and open future lies ahead of you. If only you had told me then. There was no reason at the time and as far as I could see, why you and [your sister] should not have gone for an Easter weekend with Daddy but that you should have felt "abandoned" by me of all people—oh darling? My whole life was bent and spent on keeping a house for you both and it was a long, long battle, believe me, but I thought I had done so. I tried always to be there when you came in or needed me and I am very grieved to think that I failed you in any way. Financially, it was an endless struggle and very hard work to keep it all together but of love and care there was an endless supply. You and [your sister] came first in everything. It is difficult for me to go back in memory forty odd years and I can't begin to analyze all my then actions. What I did at the time was done with the best possible intentions but we all make mistakes without hindsight.

I am sorry I have been so long answering but I have been in such a turmoil and have had to do some very serious thinking to be able to assemble this reply—I do hope you will try and understand my difficulties. We have not seen each other for nearly six years and letters are not easy in matters of this sort, partly just the lapse of time or change of mood, but believe me, darling, you will always be in my loving thoughts and your welfare is as important to me as my own.

With much love,
Mummy

I replied in late February 1989, the only letter I wrote Mummy that year.

I was so deeply glad to get your letter for which I thank you. . . . I do so want to be close to you, for you to understand what I have been through. I need your acceptance as well as your love and I'd like your support. I can't talk with you yet and I am unable to visit—I will one day but I can't make commitments or promises about anything much at all right now. Knowing how my childhood was stolen has put my whole life in jeopardy; some days I fight to stay alive but by contrast I have many many peaceful days, something never before experienced. I am getting free of the horror my father perpetrated upon me . . .

You ask why I never told you. It's a very good question requiring a rather complex answer. First . . . it is [my father] who is responsible for the secrecy. He abused and manipulated his position of authority and trust. I thought you must have known what he did to me after Box Hill. Jean remembers you telling her I had a vaginal infection. She says you were distraught and she heard you crying in the night. But perhaps you were crying about something else and I must have been wrong. After all, it was you who told me (and I'm glad you did) that Daddy . . . threw me across the room sometimes when I ran to him for hugs. I know now that it's extremely common for family members not to know sexual abuse is going on; that only the perpetrator and the victim know. Children are taught to keep secrets and they do just that, come hell or high water. . . .

He started molesting me in the nursery—probably briefly during the night on his way to the bathroom. (My memories fit this.) I was little. I thought that's what daddies did. I must have tried to cry out because I remember him putting a pillow over my face. . . . After Box Hill the guilt and the shame I felt were because I thought what happened was my fault. He told me explicitly that I "must tell my mother about the worms—only about the worms." He was tall and fierce and terrifying. He had beaten me. He had battered me. He had absolute power over me.

Also I could not talk about what he did to me because I did not have the words. . . . Sex was a taboo subject. Penis and vagina were not words I knew so how could I explain? Once I made an attempt but you told me I had "such an imagination." You often said that—and it was true—but it felt like an accusation. . . .

I wanted to be close to you and I wanted to talk and be helped, but I was not able to. . . . It is only recently that I have begun to reclaim the power of those feelings, that I am deserving, that I matter.

Later on, the worst time of all:

Easter on the Isle of Wight. I realize that you could not possibly have known. . . .

I think I have to tell you about the Isle of Wight. There is no way to break the story gently. . . .

It all seemed to be my fault. . . .

When you told me the facts of life the year following the Isle of Wight you instilled in me the virtue of keeping my virginity until marriage. How could I tell you anything after that? . . .

Psychiatrists knew, I suspect, that I was an incest victim but have been afraid to confront me with the truth. Some have actually said it was dangerous to look at my childhood. There is still a chronic lack of education and training in the field of childhood sexual abuse. . . . It devastates the survivor and her (or his) non-offending family members (as you know only too well) and society by and large turns away, too horrified to get involved until it happens to someone they love.

The other part of your letter also deserves a response —about the sacrifices you made. I thank you from the bottom of my heart, for I reap now all the advantages of my privileged upbringing and education, yet I always feel guilty when you tell me about your struggles, which is sad, isn't it? I always felt, and to some extent still do, that I was a terrible burden to you for whom you gave up your entire life. You seemed always to be so unhappy and I constantly feared making you feel worse. I felt I could never please you or be good enough for you, never felt worthy of the sacrifices you made on my behalf or that I could possibly live up to your expectations of me, whatever those were. I wanted only for you to be proud and approving of me but somehow I always felt I fell short. I still do.

My father made me so terrified of him that I was afraid of all adults as a result. I was very afraid of you too. You seemed all-powerful, all-knowing and your word was law. I never knew when you were teasing me; I could not bear being helped in any way because it always felt like judgemental criticism, and the only time I felt loved was when I was ill. So I got ill a lot! . . .

I hate having this painful, sad correspondence with you but I need to try and sort everything out. In the long run it's better to be honest with you. Perhaps if we could straighten things out we can both understand how things went awry, how all the misunderstandings happened. . . .

You didn't know what a wicked man [my father] was. You did protect him but you loved him once, as I did. Now all I feel is rage and hatred; and in time perhaps those feelings will turn to indifference. I can't imagine ever forgiving him. . . .

You, Mummy, I feel entirely differently about. I forgive your mistakes with my whole heart. You did nothing wrong; nothing wrong at all. You tried to be a perfect mother, which was an impossible expectation to put on yourself. There's no such thing as a perfect mother. You lived in constant fear and pushed your anger so deeply inside you that it became a tormented mass of depression and guilt. You could never possibly ever have made up to me for all the things you lacked in your own childhood. You have every right to be angry, if you are able to experience that feeling. You have a lot to be angry about. You too were made powerless; you too were abandoned. You have every right to feel sad. . . .

I am unbelievably glad that darling "Papa" gave you his friendship, his unconditional love, and acceptance. . . . My hope for you is that you can reach beyond the pain of the past and the grief of the present and live the rest of your life in love and peace, which you deserve. And I hope the same for me.

I didn't wait for a reply. On the anniversary of the Easter trip to the Isle of Wight, I called Mummy in England. Acting as Mary Patricia's advocate, I asked her if there was anything she wanted to say to me—directly—in response to the letter. "Yes," she said immediately. "Forget all about the past."

It was not at all what I wanted to hear. "I want to hear you say you support me in all I do, whether you approve or not. I want to hear you say you're sorry you couldn't, and didn't, protect me from my father."

"All he did was push you once," she answered.

"Denial. Denial. Denial," I screamed.

"Well, I never beat you," Mummy said.

"No, but you threatened me with your beating stick and you sent me to my room for hours on end. And once you bit me on the cheek—although you claim you meant to kiss me."

Silence.

Then I disclosed what Great Aunt Ada had done.

"Now you've gone too far." Mummy's voice was cold, distant. "Aunty wouldn't have hurt a fly."

"Denial! Denial!" I shrieked. "Denial!"

"If you continue this I'll have to go," she said.

"She's going to abandon me," cried the Child Within. "Help me!"

"Daddy's right. You're not well," Mummy was saying. He'd phoned her. "Apparently you've written him some letters."

I was aghast. Was she on *his* side? Protecting *him*? Defending *him*? Sacrificing me, her own daughter?

"I have no mother," wailed the Child Within. "I'm an orphan."

"She'll never change," said the Small Voice. "Never."

"As far as I'm concerned you're dead," I screeched, slamming down the phone. I vowed never to speak to her again.

CHAPTER TWELVE

DEAR DADDY

Clinicians who treat sex offenders are frequently asked what type of person commits these crimes. The simplest answer is men . . . Many rapists and child molesters are respected members of society.

Sylvia Barrett and W. L. Marshall, "Shattering Myths," Saturday Night

Standing up to my father as an adult woman, on behalf of the child I'd once been, was a way to claim freedom. I confronted him in a series of letters, however unlikely that I'd elicit either a guilty confession or a desire to make amends. The Child Within hoped otherwise. Why should Daddy get off scot-free while she and I served a life sentence?

I began in December 1988: I had Rob mail my father a package, from a post office box number in Montreal, containing Charles Dickens' *A Christmas Carol.* On the flyleaf I wrote: "You cannot know where you are going until you know where you have been. If you want a seat in heaven, mark well what follows."

My parcel crossed with a letter from my father enclosing money for Christmas. I opened the envelope wearing surgical gloves, gave the money away, and had the post office return the envelope "undeliverable." I didn't want Daddy to know where I was. My instinct was Mary Patricia's: terror that he'd try to silence me, kill me. It took several days before I dared mail each letter to Rob, for him to forward. By then the adult part of me had taken over.

My father thanked me promptly for my gift, making it clear that he disliked its intent.

I then, later, came across your note in the book, and found myself rejecting it. I can only guess why it was written. I long ago learned that . . . I had to learn to live in [the] here and now, and to be active, forgetting, as far as I could at the time, my foolish self. I accept we are nothing as human beings, but all as God's expression—however inadequate we may be or appear to be.

The second proposal regarding "a place in heaven" is even more rejected. Heaven, which I know well!! for me is not a geographical location but a state of mind.

I pondered why you wrote as you did, what was your motive. I have the impression you must still be struggling with the past and have failed to do so; so you have tried to put the burden of it on me. That cannot be or work, for each has to work out his (her) way. Each has to grow up. One useful definition. A child looks for somebody else to love it. He (she) becomes adult when the lesson is learned that he (she) does the loving. (Ideally love is in the loving not in the object or person loved.) I have tried to learn from this quotation "Love is not sincere until every vestige of feeling that somebody owes us something is surrendered."

If I have gone too far I apologize, but the lie of distance and lack of communication have made it a little difficult to reply!

It would be nice if you considered coming over here. I have a warm bungalow and an adequate spare bedroom. Also I would have thought your mother and sister would be glad to see you again. I sent Christmas cards to almost all last month including your mother, but had no reply!

I hope I may hear from you, but only of course if you wish to write.

Much love,
DAD

Stay with him? I cringed. My second package was already en route to England, a copy of Aesop's *Fables* that had once belonged to Daddy. His childish signature graced the front page. Perhaps if he remembered how powerless he had felt as a brutalized small boy, he'd understand my plight:

Did you read the fable of "The Thief and His Mother"? You will wonder why you were instructed to read such a story. . . .

Rest assured that it is for your own good. . . . The subtleties of this tale only become evident when you think about power: how your mother took away yours by demanding your absolute obedience and thus laid the foundation for you to steal "things of greater value" when you became a man. . . .

You were only ten years old when you wrote in the front of this book, August 23, 1923. . . . Do you remember?

Your beginnings were auspicious. You were born with a silver spoon in your mouth and all the trappings of upper class privilege, yet you would come to despise your name and lineage. For what does all that mean if unconditional love is absent? Your mother. . . was not cut out to be a real Mummy. . . . Did she and your father take out their difficulties and frustrations on you? Did they snatch away the sunshine of your growing years . . . all in the name of discipline, all for your own good? . . . Your parents' job was to protect you. Instead you were betrayed. . . .

You must have been terrified when your Mummy left you on her mother's doorstep with your little brother. You must have felt that you had been convicted of crimes so heinous that you were deserving of the ultimate penalty: Abandonment. Such a wicked boy. . . .

Did anyone explain about being sent away to boarding school? Were you told simply that it was expected . . . without a single solitary thought about your feelings or your wishes. . . .

Deep inside, your spirit began to die . . . replaced by a chasm filled with increasing rage, pain, anguish and loneliness. . . .

What did school bring? An education? Books? Wisdom? Learning? Lucky for you, you were so brilliant or school might have been worse. . . . Did they poke fun at your tortured brown eyes that darted to and fro?

Did they torment you mercilessly about your nervous tic . . . ? You poor little boy. . . .

You suffered in silence year after year. The everpresent fear of the cane lashing your tender backside terrified you, didn't it? In such a vulnerable position it was so easy for the masters to take advantage. Did they touch you inappropriately? Fondle you? Masturbate you? Were you sexually abused? Violated? Raped and traumatized?

Is fear gripping your stomach in a nauseating knot as you remember?

You never told, did you? You thought it was all your fault. . . . It's hard remembering isn't it? And even harder to believe the cruelty really happened. It's easier, much easier, to deny it all, isn't it?

At home some shameful secrets. Your Mummy running off with the regimental chief—your Daddy's boss. And then you discovered at age 14(?), that you felt excited, strong and powerful dressing up in women's clothes. . . .

You would like to have made it all legitimate, wouldn't you? But your Mummy would not hear of you becoming an actor. "Nice young men of your class go into the professions. . . . "

Psychiatrists might testify that you were schizophrenic or had a personality disorder but you were simply a poor mistreated, humiliated little boy who did not receive love of any kind.

Did you enter the confusion of adolescence with . . . the awful truth that you could use that genital power against those smaller and weaker than you? Did you try to blot out that knowledge? Cover up the traces . . . ?

You would leave childhood still shackled behind its bars, always yearning to be free of its pain.

It is not yet too late. All things are possible. Goodbye for now.

On behalf of Mary Patricia.

Rob read my father's reply over the telephone, dated 15th February 1989. I had guessed correctly—where I didn't know the truth—about my father's history. He'd shared details of it with a woman he described to me once as his "spiritual wife." But my letter had obviously both angered and disconcerted him.

I received your letter (and Aesop's *Fables*) yesterday morning. Having glanced at it I thought to return it to you, but on reading it through I was at peace for the day.

What made you write it and what was your motive, why it shall be for my benefit I cannot understand. I have rejected that it was fiction—though as such very good, but rather unpleasant—but therefore written as fact. So what? To shake or surprise me by its knowledge—where did you get that, for Trysh, the facts are basically there . . . fifteen years ago I wrote eighty pages of them in red note-books. . . .

You pretend to know my feelings as a boy—nonsense! . . . It is one thing for you to go into your past, if you must. For you to do it for my past is surely an impertinence. You are a grown and mature individual able to make your own way. Nor in writing of my past do I like any criticism of my parents. I do not criticize them, nor my tutors. They all found the going tough in relation to me.

What was at the back of your letter was surely just your inability, it seems, to let the past go, and find some parable by
which to live. For me to say anything seems at the moment
to waste my time. . . .

I cannot know for you and I can only say that for me the
ever presence of God is my rock, with _____ to help and support me, and day by day I clear out the old and try to be more
loving and understanding.

Hope your writing helped you. You cannot change me. Only
I can do that.

Much love
DAD

Next, I wrote letters on behalf of Mary Patricia at age two,
nine, and eleven, detailing what I remembered. At the top of each
letter I attached a photograph of me at that age. The first letter
was dated February 28th, 1989.

You have had time to digest both *A Christmas Carol* and "The
Thief and his Mother" from Aesop's *Fables*. You've had time to
think about yourself as a small boy. I have received your letter
and the message is understood. Now I want you to take a long
look at the attached copy of a photograph taken in 1945. Do
you remember? A darling little girl with her Daddy. Me. You.
It is now time to honour what she both endured and survived. . . .

Look into Mary Patricia's eyes and what do you see? Deep
dark brown eyes like yours. Hers are filled with the innocence
and trust of babyhood. . . . She thought you were the most
handsome clever wonderful Daddy in the whole world and she
loved you without conditions, with total acceptance. Never, ever,
for the rest of her life would she love a man in such a way. . . .

She ran to you and you laughed as you picked her up and
hugged her. Danced round and round with her in your arms.
She adored you. For ever after she would remember you as
a role model for her perfect man and seek out men just like
you.

You loved to show her off to all your friends when they came
calling. You made your Tish Tosh a photo album. Remember?
With a brown cover and your neat handwriting meticulously
describes each shot. She kept it in a special place for years and
years remembering the Daddy who she'd loved so much but
had not loved enough, or so she thought, for he started battering

her, hurling, throwing, beating her. He injured her severely. And he sexually assaulted her.

Do you remember the nursery?

A doorknob turns on the door, white china. Frozen I watch, tiny child peeping wide-eyed over the edge of the sheet and well-worn, pre-war blankets. The door quietly opens in the half-light. I hear stealthy footsteps creeping closer and catch a glimpse of a blue-striped terry towelling robe. Turning my head I see the dawning sky through iron safety bars on the window. . . .

I do not know that daddies are not supposed to do this with their daughters. I only want to please and be obedient and loved. Sometimes I am beaten. To silence me? Because I am bad? Because my Daddy is a sexual deviant? I know nothing except that I feel the pain. . . .

It is over and my Daddy leaves. . . . I am bewildered by what my Daddy has done to me. The bed is wet. Ejaculate and my anxious urine soak the mattress. Stealthy footsteps creep away and the nursery door shuts softly. . . . I must have been very very bad to be so punished by him. I promise to try and be a better little girl in future.

It is all to no avail, however, because at age 3 1/2 Mary Patricia's Daddy . . . hits her Mummy and shouts at her that he wants his freedom. And when the door slams Tish Tosh knows it is all her fault. . . .

It is you who is responsible for the things you did to me when I was a tiny child. It was you who battered and sexually molested me. My own father. You have no right to be the father of the beautiful, strong, intelligent, powerful woman I have become . . .

I shall be in touch again. Meanwhile keep your dirty hands away from little children.

On behalf of Mary Patricia

P.S. No one has put me up to this.

I received no reply and sent off my next letter, dated March 15th, 1989.

At the top of this page Mary Patricia, your daughter, is nine years old. She always has such a brave smile on her face but if you look into her eyes they are sad; the eyes of one betrayed. . . .

Now, in her own way, in her own time, she is confronting the past and the things that happened to her. She is angry at the wrongs done her, sad for the child inside her who silently endured, proud that she has survived despite great odds.

Daddy: You took me to Box Hill, near Dorking, Surrey, when I was nine years old. "You *must* tell your mother," you said. "You *must* tell your mother about the worms." You made it very clear that I must keep everything else a secret. . . . I never told. Only about the worms. I did as I was told. . . .

We were in a clearing. I had needed to go to the bathroom . . .

What right did you have to do that Daddy? What right? You damaged me but you did not destroy me. You took what was not yours to take; it was mine to give but I did not ever give it to you. . . . Women do heal despite men like you who rape little children. Women are strong, intelligent, creative and powerful. You know that. That's why you did it to me, isn't it? Raping and humiliating little girls makes men like you feel "like a man". . . .

You have no power over me now. . . . It was an accident of fate that you were my father. I've used my resources, my courage, my strength and my talents and made my way in this world and found everything I ever wanted—inside myself. Because I am strong. You are weak, which is why you had to do the unspeakable things you did to me when I was a child. . . .

There is evidence—medical evidence—of the vaginal infection you gave me and the signs were all there of sexual abuse. I was asked questions. Someone stayed asking questions for hours. I didn't tell. It was assumed that little victims forgot. Wrong, Daddy, wrong. This little victim is a survivor. AN INCEST SURVIVOR. And I remember everything.

If I could I would prosecute you. I would enjoy seeing your tortured brown eyes searching wildly around for someone to take pity on you; understand your plight. You would be quite alone—as I was. I have no pity. . . .

You will hear from me again. I am not yet finished.

On behalf of Mary Patricia

I spent the Easter holiday on the West Coast grieving the first anniversary of my memories of the Isle of Wight. I still had no answer from my father. On Easter Sunday I wrote him my final letter, enclosing with it a crucifix and garlic bud to ward off evil!

Grey clouds hug the mountains and a gentle rain spatters on the window pane. A fire crackles, rebuilt moments ago, in the wood burning stove. There is a vase of freshly picked primroses on the table where I write, and a welcome pot of tea.

Earlier, I walked along the beach and watched seabirds diving in the gentle Pacific waves. . . . This is a time of remembrance and of grief: Easter 1954.

You took me to the Bridham Hotel, Steyne Road, Bembridge. I have a photograph. What happened there made me feel terribly ugly and irreparably flawed. . . . No, Daddy, I did nothing wrong. I was *never* ugly or bad . . .

I remember, Daddy, I remember that hotel room with its net curtains and blue velvet drapes to keep out prying eyes . . .

Unless I am numb I am unable to make love tenderly and passionately without the memories flashing in front of me. . . . You have deprived me of my right to sexual pleasure.

My father sucks my life blood, rapes me in Bembridge with his buddies. Four men. Or are there three and one woman? For I hear the rustle of taffeta. Red. A red dress. Lifted over me. Smothers me. . . . White bare skin of inner thigh, black hair, male genitals. *Yours*.

You wore a dress, Daddy, and a wig and make-up. You wore a woman's dress and you raped me. Then worse. You showed me off to your disgusting dirty deviant pals. . . .

How dare you let those men do those things, Daddy? How dare you? To your own daughter, eleven-years-old. . . .

You are not worth the energy required to hate you but I hate you to the marrow of my bones. . . . You could never write in enough notebooks, write enough poems, confess enough gross acts of misconduct to redeem yourself. . . .

I no longer believe in an external God. S/He would not allow such acts of criminality to be perpetrated against innocent little children. An innocent like I was. An innocent like you were once as well until the people in your childhood—*including* your parents—helped turn you into the evil wicked man that you are. My father, Dracula personified: Hitler goose-stepping through my childhood.

After that Easter 1954 (that grey-skied weekend when we walked by the shore and watched the sea—the English Channel—washing up shells and shingle and you had the unremitting gall to take photographs as if we were on some nice family outing), my life was never the same again. . . .

You stole the last vestiges of my childhood, the final tiny shreds of my innocence. And when I was taken back to the Isle of Wight at age thirteen—all I wanted was to stop the terrible pain of remembering what you did to me there. I tried to kill myself. . . .

My legs were paralysed for six weeks and scar tissue already growing inside my backbone from injuries you gave me—battering me—grew. . . .

You have not destroyed me, Daddy. Nor have you defeated me. . . . I struggle heroically to heal from the wrongs you did me. I deserve and receive the utmost respect and admiration. I deserve to have the best possible life with the best possible people surrounding me.

I AM NO LONGER A VICTIM

I AM MORE THAN A SURVIVOR

I AM A WARRIOR

"Harm the web of nature and you harm yourself." You can do *me* no more harm.

Upon receiving my letter, my father immediately telephoned my mother. They had hardly spoken to each other in thirty years, except through lawyers. Had I been hospitalized again? Had I had another nervous breakdown?

"Your Poordaddy is terribly worried about you," Mummy reported.

Reassured that I was in good health, Poordaddy penned his final, rebarbative letter on April 8, 1989. To my horror, he addressed me on the envelope as Mrs. Trysh Ashby-Rolls—as though I were his wife. The letter was uncharacteristically disjointed, peppered with spelling and grammatical errors, and crossed-out words.

I received your letter of Easter this year; a vile, hateful, very unpleasant, lying letter, full of untruth especially regarding our holiday in the Isle of Wight, and also stupid—stupid because I shall possibly keep the letter.

In no way do I accept what you write. However I have to be practical. As it seems you will write further letters, from now on I shall put them away unopened. If your attitude changes and you wish to communicate with me in an understanding non-selfish and normal humanitarian manner you will have to find another method of so doing. Otherwise it is goodbye, for at present I see no alternative.

However, although I have long since learnt to put the past behind and live here and now, it is not in God's language right to put people out of mind. Even those who have passed away, like my human parents, are nearer to me now than when here on earth. It is right to remember the warm qualities of friends and relatives—with feet on the ground about their minuses, just to remember *your* intelligence, vivacity, sense of fun and all your goodness.

"Vengeance is not legitimate." There can be no love where there is hate. To pretend otherwise is hypocritical.

I get no impression from your letters of realisation by you that others have had equal trials and tribulations as yourself, most not making them up or vilifying another.

An alternate impression is that while you ought to be grown up, you are not. Adulthood—as opposed to childish-hood—was given to me as when you love, as opposed wanting to be loved as a child. (Age does not come with this.) Therefore *grow up*.

You appear to have a far different approach to life than myself. The following paragraph is a good summary of my approach.

There followed a long religious diatribe quoted from fundamentalist Christian sources which he ended, "Yours with no recriminations, and with love." He signed his full name.

With *love*? Mary Patricia was not impressed.

Perhaps I would not have taken my next step had my father admitted his wrongdoing, had he asked me to forgive him. Perhaps I would have done nothing further had he not published several books of poetry—in which he introduced himself as being "a lover of children." Especially small children. Especially those of his spiritual wife, whom he'd doted on since they were babies. Perhaps.

"His stepchildren," said the Small Voice. "It's your duty to protect them. Just in case."

I sat down resolutely at my typewriter. Aided by the Royal Canadian Mounted Police and the Canadian liaison with Interpol, I wrote to the British police, enclosing copies of the entire correspondence, one of my father's books of poetry, and other information I thought might be useful.

The post office clerk stamped the envelope "R" for Registered, his face impassive. I struggled with Mary Patricia's tears. Daughters weren't supposed to inform against their fathers. And I was telling on my Daddy, breaking our secret childhood pact.

CHAPTER THIRTEEN

GOD?

By rediscovering our history as women . . . we can recreate ourselves in our own image. . . . Only by tapping our deep spiritual power and integrating it with action can we effect any lasting changes.

Hallie Iglehart, Womanspirit

A spasm in my leg curls my toes. I'm in the shower at the swimming pool. Excruciating pain seizes my back, which has locked into some ungodly position. I cannot move. I cried out when it happened. Everyone is staring. Why here? In public. It's embarrassing.

"Are you all right?" a woman asks.

"I'm okay." I smile bravely at her. These setbacks have been occurring ever since the surgery, apparently part of the recuperation process. I refuse to ask the question aloud, but we all ask it sooner or later: Why God? Why me?

As a little child I loved the Old Testament Bible stories and wondered whether I had a Guardian Angel in the corner. Later, the Church of England taught me that I was a miserable sinner, which I knew only too well, and drilled the Lord's Prayer into me, especially the part about forgiving the transgressions of others in order to be pardoned my own. Crime and punishment echoed through my growing-up.

I tried Roman Catholicism during my early teens. Although I liked the idea of confession, doing penance, and receiving absolution, I outright rejected a fiery hell. The theatricality of genuflecting, lighting votive candles to the saints, and splashing holy water across my breast attracted me, that and the fact that my mother had no patience with Catholics. Increasingly, however, I turned my back on organized religion and contested the existence of a divinity. Until my marriage came to its bitter conclusion I was a vehement, well-argued atheist.

Alone in 1981—hungry, cold, sick in bed, watching a damp, brown stain on the wall ooze into a rainwater trickle—I said my prayers out of bleak desperation. When the answers came I dismissed them as flukes, although I had to admit this phenomenon occurred quite often. However, I didn't articulate the coincidences out of fear that I'd be laughed at. I wondered about the Small Voice that sometimes spoke deep inside me. Was that God? And why did "Papa" often seem close by? Was he a Spirit Guide? I started going to church again, especially if I was lonely, depressed, wanted an excuse to go out, or it was Christmas or Easter and I had nothing to do. I attended a progressive congregation of the United Church from which I derived both spiritual and social comfort. At Coffee Hour, after the service, I met many prestigious members of the congregation. I enjoyed the respectable ring of, "Oh yes, he (she) goes to my church."

After Rob left, in February 1987, I was willing to try anything to soothe my aching loneliness. I tried Roman Catholicism again, investigated Buddhism, a Spiritualist Church, and the occult. But I didn't find answers to my questions. At the suggestion of a friend I said prayers to my reflection in the mirror. "Please, God, bring Rob back." When Rob returned, I wondered if there were some Divine Source.

But it was the back surgery that altered everything. That one moment, bathed in white light in the recovery room, was a spiritual eye-opener. Why had I survived? Was it an accident of fate? Was there a reason—some Grand Plan—for me to continue living? Unable to walk far, never without pain when sitting, I invented a daily Grace Space, a special time, when I was in the least discomfort, to be quietly with myself. Contemplative. I lay in a comfortable bath every morning before breakfast, eyes closed, breathing deeply, trying to clear my mind of the crowding thoughts and memories. I concentrated on breathing: In and Out, In and Out. Sparrows chirped outside the window. A streetcar rumbled by. A motorist honked his horn. Dogs barked. The sounds receded into the distance. My pain subsided. I relaxed.

"I am pain-free, whole and healed," I affirmed boldly, glad there
was nobody about to hear me. I imagined the scar tissue as white,
soft coral fronds cut back to manageable proportions. Benign. I
looked at my reflection in the mirror and told myself, "Trysh,
I love and accept you exactly the way you are." I felt very silly
doing it at first, but I persisted. I added a prayer about accepting
what I couldn't change and asking for courage to change what
I could. My tear-stained face quickly turned to smiles. What irony
saying "Please, *God*," to my obviously female reflection!

If I had any picture of God, it was pretty standard: a Caucasian,
Great-Big-Daddy-in-the-Sky stroking his long white beard, surrounded by birds and animals (especially lambs), with little children clambering over his knees. Not unlike my own father, "lover
of little children." I winced, disgusted. Only a misogynist God
would allow misogyny. A male authority figure ruling over me
neither made sense, nor did anything for my peace of mind.

On Christmas Eve I went back to church. I didn't know of any
other way to give thanks for survival. The minister preached a
sermon about love—real love far beyond romance, making sacrifices. At midnight we sang "O Come All Ye Faithful" amid spark-
lers, passed from one person to the next. "God bless. Merry
Christmas." We prayed for Lockerbie and Armenia, political prisoners everywhere, welfare recipients, and a solution to world pov-
erty. I thanked the Great Spirit, The Goddess, Whomever, that
I could be there celebrating communion. Wonder Bread and Con-
cord wine.

Christmas Day was sad, simple, gentle. I opened my presents,
estimating that Rob was halfway to California. "Happy Christmas,
Rob," I whispered, missing him. The previous night I'd filled a
stocking for the Child Within, which I opened with my cat and
teddy bear. Guatemalan worry dolls. An old-fashioned puzzle. A
decorative box. Fruit. A dollar coin. Cookies. Chocolates. Beads.
Bath goodies. A gorgeous coloured shawl, a gift from Mummy—
how carefully she'd chosen it. I pulled it close around my shoulders. Somehow it protected me in ways she never could.

Daddy and Mummy had opened their stockings sitting up in
their beds. My stocking, crunchy and full against my legs in the
night, seemed huge as I carried it into their room in my little
arms. Between early morning and mid-afternoon is a long black
space I can't remember. At tea-time, in the drawing-room by the
tree, we ate iced cake decorated with a Father Christmas. Daddy

carved a capon at dinner and we pulled crackers, wore paper hats, blew whistles.

The memories had no power. They passed across my mind's eye, as on a distant screen. The black space would open in its own time.

I took my scrapbook, made for me in 1944, to Nellie's, a safe house for battered women, and shared it with a three-year-old boy. I thought of Bobby Bitsy, the boy Rob had once been, and Mary Patricia, of the children my father and my mother had been, of my sister, of my son. The little boy snuggled close and we talked about the pictures in my book. I showed him my worry dolls, hidden in my pocket with a tangerine. Out of the blue he hit me. "I don't like being hit," I told him quietly. He stopped and held my hand instead, staring intently. Several women eyed me curiously. Some smiled. One, an elegant older lady, like Mummy, offered me tea and cookies. I wanted to reach out to others this Christmas, not as a do-gooder but as a fellow traveller, learning about survival, about other women, about my mother, about the human spirit. When I left, alone but not lonely, I felt accepted, connected, spiritually nourished. "I surrender myself to the healing process," I whispered on the way home, snowflakes flying in my tear-filled eyes.

I opened myself a little to the beauty of the world around me. I was a part of it; it was part of me. My contribution, no matter how small, could make a difference. And all our small "differences" would help toward the healing of the planet.

"Do you think it's possible that if we have a dark side, we also have a golden side?" I asked Rob. I hesitated. "I mean, a god part? Is that crap?"

"Not at all," he answered seriously.

"Well, in you, a god part. In me, a goddess part. Is that a crazy notion?"

"No," said Rob. "I think it's entirely possible."

We talked a lot about the Jungian concept of animus and anima: feminine and masculine energies in men and women. "Maybe there's a golden, 'higher,' spiritual part in every living entity. God . . . or The Goddess . . . is in every leaf, every rock, every cell. . . . " I stopped—hardly an original theory but I was flushed with excitement. My personal discovery marked a turning point. It was like being handed a spiritual sextant to navigate my journey through life.

I learned to sit with my pain, breathe through it, knowing it wouldn't last. The setbacks, however difficult, were temporary, there to make room for new growth. Whenever I felt unable to get beyond a barrier, whenever I felt tense, anxious, depressed, emotionally overburdened, I shut my eyes and held an inner conversation. "Help me," I asked the Highest Part of me, "to get past being stuck." Visualizing my impasse as a great sheet of paper, I imagined how easy it would be to break through it. Answers came in curious ways, books, the radio or television, a friend— ideas, feedback, or support in unexpected moments. Seemingly random events dovetailed in synchronistic patterns. Everything was working out.

As I slowly uncovered the raw bleeding wound of my childhood, I realized how much I tried to hide my fears behind angry, hostile walls of defenses. When a friend told me she found me arrogant and controlling, I turned inward for guidance from my Higher Self. What sword do I need to fight my shadow? I asked. This answer came in a dream: Vulnerability. Calm. A cottage on the West Coast.

Acknowledging my difficulties, admitting my mistakes honestly, and getting in touch with other parts of me helped me release the tension. Rituals helped, too, to move me forward.

We cut the wedding photograph in two, my women friends and I. Silhouettes of a man and a woman once very much in love. Or so we'd thought. Who knows what he had projected onto me. I'd wanted him to keep me warm, safe, dry; be a father to my wounded inner child. This was a bittersweet occasion, my divorce, a time to let him go. I put a match to one corner of his photograph. The flames burned briefly, brightly, and died down. I released the remains into the evening breeze, setting my ex-husband free; setting me free.

Yet, without my marriage I might not have come to Canada, escaped the clutches of my past, and found my present measure of serenity. I didn't understand why my beginnings had been so devastating or why I had survived. I trusted that there was some purpose in everything. One day, when I had completed more of my basic healing work, I would dare explore more deeply into the spiritual realm.

CHAPTER FOURTEEN

LETTING GO

Letting go of anger toward parents, an important step toward emotional well-being, often requires three separate processes: 1) expressing your anger; 2) understanding your parents; and 3) forgiveness. True forgiveness usually occurs through understanding.

Jordan Paul and Margaret Paul, Do I Have to Give Up Me to Be Loved by You?

"*Never*! I'll *never* forgive Daddy," I vowed.

"That's understandable," said Rob.

"You don't *have* to," said Lori.

"Why should you?" said the women in my support group and most everyone else.

During my more composed moments I could see the brutalized small boy he once was, and my compassion ran over for his Inner Child. He'd identified with his tormentors in his attempt to master his torment.

"There's no excuse," the Small Voice said. "*You* haven't sexually abused children."

"I've done a lot of other rotten things." I reeled off a list.

"Stop blaming yourself. Take responsibility instead. Forgive yourself. Forgive the Child Within."

"Forgive Mary Patricia," Lori concurred, "for being there."

"I do forgive Mummy," I told Rob.

"I think you have to," he said.

Forgiveness is not wholly a conscious decision. My task was to see my parents as they really were, acknowledge my pain in the context of theirs, grieve for it, accept it, let it go, and move on. It's a process that cannot be forced, but when it happens it's like sunshine melting a chilly morning fog.

I dream I go far to the other side of Vancouver Island. Safe in a little house, I burn sweet-scented wood in the fireplace. Daddy tries to follow but withers away. He no longer has power over me.

Something shifted in me. The only way to resolve the past was to face the reality that my parents were wounded adult children like me. It was painful, but I had to give up the dream of a perfect happy family and an all-loving Mummy and Daddy taking care of me forever. Being adult seemed a desperately lonely, difficult business. Remaining a child—having others take care of me—appealed far more.

Shattering news snapped me out of my inertia. Rob told me, mid-January 1989, that he'd found someone else.

"Why?" I wailed. "What did I do wrong?"

"Nothing," he replied. "You did nothing at all." I felt fragile and alone. Numb with shock, I hoped Rob's announcement was just a bad dream. I tried to maintain my dignity, do what was right for me; but I went to pieces. "Bastard," I screamed. How could he? On New Year's morning I'd woken to his kiss, his loving gaze. He really *does* love me, I'd thought then. "Realistically," he'd whispered, "we're more than friends." What had he meant?

Well, I had wanted the truth. I had wanted predictability. Now I had them, and they hurt. He'd kept to our agreement, telling me when another lover came along.

"Is it because I'm an incest survivor?" Used dirty goods, disgusting, a reject.

"No," he said.

"Is it because I'm a cripple?" I was deeply flawed. That was why he was doing this.

"No, Trysh. No."

"Then why?" I shouted hysterically. "Why?"

"Oh, Trysh," he sighed.

Once I had acquiesced to everyone's wishes, apologizing for being a nuisance and a burden because I had needs. I had lashed out at the innocent bystanders in my life; I had persecuted my son.

"Please help me with this, Rob. I can't handle it by myself. Not with everything else."

"I will," he consoled me. "I have some ideas about how to continue our relationship."

"You have?" I was amazed. It wasn't over? The Sartre/Beauvoir relationship that I admired so much wasn't looking quite so good any more.

"We have a very deep close friendship," Rob said. "We support and help each other's healing."

We talked again next night. I was more dignified. (How had Simone been under similar circumstances?) Rob met the Montreal Woman at a party. Hearts pounded. Pulses raced. Adrenaline flowed. After the mire of pain that Rob and I were bogged down in, this woman was a breath of fresh spring air. It was easy and light.

"I seem to be paying a very high price for my healing," I said. My sadness was almost intolerable, yet the pressure to hurry my sexual healing was lifted.

"I think that'll take a long long time," Rob said. "Now you won't have to worry about me. I'm your brother."

My brother? It was the last thing I wanted Rob to be. Yet I knew it was exactly right. We talked about sexuality and closeness, about our fears. "You know me so well," he said. "Better than anyone."

"I love you," I said simply. "What's your idea about being friends?"

"All our elements can remain intact except expectations of marriage or living together," Rob said.

"What if we want to be sexual?" I asked.

"Sex is out. I'm too vulnerable," he answered. "I assumed you weren't interested."

I wasn't. But I heard myself say, "I can't have a friendship without sex." I was willing to do anything to keep him. "I could consider a sexual friendship without commitment," I bargained.

"Let's talk again tomorrow," Rob said wearily.

The following night I pestered him again. "Why, Rob? What did I do?"

"I wanted to give you all my support but you always seemed to expect more," he said. "Every time I did something helpful, I paid a price. I was being pulled toward commitment, a future exclusive partnership."

It was more than I could handle, more than I could comprehend. I'd been so ill. I didn't really know what I'd done or why everything had gone wrong. Our lack of communication hadn't helped. "What if I just say 'Get out, stay out?'" I threatened. "It would be for good. I'd never see or speak to you again."

"I'd feel deep regret and loss," Rob replied. "I'd lose my friend and confidante, my soul mate."

Soul mate?

"And sad you would be giving up someone who could be of lasting comfort and value."

I felt overwhelmed. "Lori," said the Small Voice. "What would Lori counsel?"

"How would you feel about seeing a counsellor together?" I asked. "I'd like to resolve our parting with minimal harm, with a measure of grace. Certainly kindly."

Rob agreed. "I'd like to come down for your birthday," he said. "I'd like to take you to dinner." I was amazed. Leave his new woman and come five hundred miles to take *me* to dinner!

Snow was in the air. My birthday was two weeks off. I sat at the piano wanting him. Who? Rob? My father? I tried to nurture myself: long baths, good food, sleep, rest, seeing friends. Time heals, they said. It won't last. He'll come back. Rob always does. Be friends. Forget him. There's other fish in the sea.

Once, when a relationship broke up, I slashed my wrists, overdosed. Self-hatred, suicide? Not this time. I bought myself red roses. "I love you, Mary Patricia," I said. "I love me." I trudged home through the snow, tears spilling down my face.

I dream I travel in a train to meet Rob at a certain place, a certain time. I change seats so I cannot easily be found. I'm taken off the train. I'm sick. Rob calls to reconfirm our arrangement. The doctor says my sex organs are not ready. I must be hidden from Rob, who arrives and cannot find me.

I thought of Mummy's involvement with "Papa." Like Rob, he'd been a gentle man. Although sometimes I'd resented him, I'd yearned for his closeness. How I'd loved it when he called me "my beautiful!" But he was Mummy's and I thought I didn't deserve his love. He did so much for us in quiet, discreet ways. Always compassionate, always kind, he was my role model for a "good" man.

Nevertheless, a question gnawed at me. Why didn't he do something when I was raped at age nine? He knew; he received reports from the hospital after the gynaecological examination. When I revealed to him, in 1976, that Daddy was a transvestite, he'd replied, "I didn't know *that*." What else *did* he know? My heart sank. "Papa" hadn't been perfect, after all. Mary Patricia howled her betrayal and frustration. "Why didn't he protect me?"

"Maybe he didn't know who to point the finger at. You didn't tell," the Small Voice said months later. "People think that kids who appear reasonably normal after a trauma, are okay. It was the 1950s. Things were different then."

I dream I forgive "Papa" with my whole heart.

There are many non-offending, decent men who, knowing what's going on, cough and shuffle their feet and stand impotently by. Tacit. Afraid.

On bad days I wished I hadn't remembered. I longed to wake up some morning without "incest" my first thought. Incest. I saw the word everywhere. I misread—and occasionally mispronounced—interest, insect, incense. I, former news junkie, stopped reading newspapers, stopped listening to the radio. Too many ghastly stories piqued my rage and grief. Life was beyond my control. Why had Rob left me?

"What Rob does is about Rob," Lori said. "His new relationship is not about you."

At my prompting, Rob told me more about the Montreal Woman. I'd imagined her an archetypal mother. She'd been married and had three young children.

Flashbacks of my marriage. Housewife. Mother. Prenatal teacher. Sad, lonely, anxious lady. In such pain. Ours was a traditional, patriarchal, inflexible relationship. We kept our emotional distance. How I despised my weakness for allowing my husband to dominate me. I'd nurtured myself by looking after the mothers-to-be. Counselling them made me feel needed. Being needed made me feel loved.

Yet I was sensitive, capable, perceptive, intelligent—much like Rob, very much like Mummy. I felt a rush of loving compassion and empathy for Rob. So why couldn't I feel the same for Mummy? For me?

Giving up what Rob represented was like tearing out roots. I blamed him for not loving me, not being here for me; abandoning me by being with someone else.

Daddy. Daddy. Mummy. Mummy. "Papa." What am I repeating?

I refused to let go. I was determined to be right. Daddy was wrong. Mummy was wrong. "Papa" was wrong. Rob was wrong. Round and round spun all my unresolved conflicts—blame, self-blame, anger—until I choked on my resentment.

I had a nightmare in which Mummy disapproved of my healing work. I woke up sobbing. "I want my Mummy."

"Only you can take care of you and approve of you and love you," the Small Voice said. "The rest will follow."

I had to find some middle ground, some compromise, especially in thinking of my mother. In judging Mummy I judged myself, my mothering. What I didn't like in her reflected back at me, and I couldn't accept the mirror image. If I let go of my hard anger I had to let go of the Mummy who lived in my imagination. I accused her of being authoritarian; of judging, criticizing and punishing me; of not protecting me. I'd been permissive. Yet I'd judged, criticized, punished, and barely protected my son. He might have been sexually abused without my knowledge. Mothers aren't secret police, keeping their own children under round the clock surveillance in their own home, alert against their *own partner*. It's an absurd expectation.

I dream Rob lies ill in my father's bed. Everyone is wounded. Crying. Hurting. Grieving.

Where are you Rob? The Child in the Meadow is lost, distraught, helpless. Would I ever grow up, stop crying? Would I ever be whole with equally whole Rob? I didn't hold out much hope.

"I want him to come back," Mary Patricia sobbed.

"Everything is as it should be," whispered the Small Voice. "Breathe. Keep breathing."

"When does this pain end?" I asked, exhausted. "When? All I see is pain and wounded people in wounding situations."

I began giving up the dreams of Rob, the illusion of a perfect Daddy and Mummy. Too sad to notice where I cried, I sniffed and wiped my nose on my sleeve. My eyes were swollen and red. My pain was profound and endless. The world was in pain.

Eleven-year-old Mary Patricia has invited three-year-old Mary Patricia into the meadow, promising to take care of her. She made her a baby bottle and rocked her to sleep; fetched her juice after her afternoon nap and hugged her; took her to the bathroom and stayed to protect her. Then she tidied up the bedroom and made tea for Big Trysh. Later we'll find the nine-year-old who is feeling neglected and unheard. Rice pudding is on the menu tonight.

"Don't forget the teenage part of you," said the Small Voice quietly.

I ignored her. Why would I want to know that hostile, rebellious girl? She was nothing but a trouble-maker. Despite my pain I laugh. Here I am carrying all these people inside me, conducting internal conversations with them all! On the outside I look completely normal, softly sad, beautiful in a fragile way.

I hug myself, take Mary Patricia in my arms. Lately I've noticed specific traits in each inner child. My three-year-old is mischievous, playful, affectionate, and terrified of abandonment. It's she who misses Rob most. My nine-year-old is shy, serious, and thoughtful. She's also excruciatingly lonely. My eleven-year-old is responsible, fun, intelligent, very sad. Her budding sexuality scares her. All three children are angry. As I slowly integrate these aspects into me I feel an overwhelming love and compassion. Warmth floods my body that has risen from a deep bright place in my soul. For how could any one of them have been *bad*? Soft tears fill my eyes. I forgive you, Mary Patricia. For being there.

I dream a long dream about climbing stairs, gritting my teeth, respected and supported and realizing I cannot compete. I dance to my own rhythm. I'm less attached. Daddy is not a threat although he's present.

I woke up to medieval music on the radio. My father had lost more of his power. My anger had diminished. I felt love for Rob. Suddenly I realized that I'd been so self-absorbed that I'd paid virtually no attention to Rob's obvious pain and depression during the last six months. He'd been seeing a counsellor and going to a therapy group, yet I was demanding his full attention. How could one think about "forever" with so emotionally frail a partner? But that's what I thought—like a magically-thinking child. Melting snow dripped from the roof; the optimism of spring was in the air. A year ago I'd had the hysterectomy.

I dream another strange dream. I run away on a train. Rob chases me. I tell him I'm going to marry my ex-husband. Aghast, Rob says, "I still refuse to marry you." "I can't stay where I am," I reply. "I'm going to Vancouver."

It was the third consecutive dream I'd had of leaving on a westbound train, the third dream from which I awoke refreshed and feeling powerful. Lori told me that I was doing very well indeed, healing and moving forward. The sadness, the loneliness meant real health was approaching. By mid-March my depression lifted.

I dreamed about Daddy getting weaker, about my parents dying. While my childhood fades into the past, I keep my humour and power. I move forward.

In May I dreamed another powerful dream: I visit a hospital where all parents are dying of terrible wounds. Mummy is nowhere to be found and it is too late to say goodbye to Daddy. He's dead.

In mid-June my frustration and anger at Rob resurfaced. He'd called regularly, as we'd agreed, but I felt shoved aside, kept around "just in case." I wanted to pick a fight. My timing was appalling. Rob's brother was dying, he was going home to Vancouver to say goodbye. When he returned a few days later I blew my stack. The Montreal Woman was becoming increasingly significant; I was filled with anxiety and self-loathing. Jealous, accusatory, wanting to hurt and spite him, I screamed, "I hate you," and slammed down the phone. "I hate you. I hate you," I sobbed. I fetched my tennis racquet. "I hate you, Daddy," I yelled. "Go to hell—all of you. *I hate you!*"

The following evening I went to a birthday party for one of Jochen's daughters. A charming man told me how much he enjoyed my company. So many men said that. Yet I always ended up alone, while the men went on to someone else. I watched Jochen and the man mock fly-casting on the lawn, aiming at imaginary fish under the red currant bushes. "Teach me," I asked Jochen.

"Sure."

It was harder than it looked. "I can't do this," I said, defeated.

"Yes, you can," Jochen encouraged me.

"My wrists hurt."

"Let go."

"What d'you mean?"

"Let go."

I sighed. Hopeless. Helpless. "I'm trying to get it perfect," I confessed.

"Yes," Jochen smiled. "Do it again. Give up the control." I took a deep breath, consciously relaxed, and flicked the rod. Jochen roared and we both laughed. I'd done it!

I'd wanted so much to "get it perfect" with Rob. However, just because he'd found someone else didn't mean I was a failure. I could learn from the experience. I could ask him to share with me his reasons why he preferred we be "just good friends." The difficult trick was to ask the question with real curiosity and warmth.

Rob wasn't interested in pursuing any conversation. He'd spent the weekend alone in the country. Clearly, I'd hurt and angered him. "Do you have some goal in mind for this conversation?" he asked coldly, when I phoned.

Someone was clattering dishes in the background. The Montreal Woman? I had nothing to lose. Taking a deep breath (as usual) I proceeded with my question. "Did my expectations make you feel controlled?" My genuine curiosity made my defenses fall away. So did his.

"When I left you in 1987, after your birthday," Rob began, "I was daunted by your expectations—we've been through this. They were way beyond my willingness or ability to fulfil. When you were so ill I got scared. Your neediness was excessive. I never felt capable of responding to it. Neither was I willing to."

"Is my neediness the reason men end up only friends with me?" I asked.

"I can only speak for me," Rob replied.

"Tell me," I said gently.

"You're interesting, resourceful, sympathetic, empathetic, and a pleasure to be with," he said. "Rewarding in friendship. Steadfast, loyal, brave, and true." We laughed. "All the elements which should be part of a healthy, normal relationship. But you cling. I back off. We come back together. You supplicate . . . "

"Oh," I whispered almost inaudibly.

If I'd driven Rob away with my overwhelming neediness and expectations, what kept bringing him back? Daddy *never* came back. Jochen said, "Let go. Take all your projections off Rob. Be your own father." But I didn't know how.

I closed the bathroom windows and turned on the taps. I didn't fear that the neighbours thought me crazy—they probably did already—but I was afraid someone would think me in trouble and call the police. I *was* in trouble. The tremendous rage against my father made me understand why people kill. Stuffing a towel into my mouth, I screamed and screamed and screamed.

"If only I could simply have hated you, Daddy. But I loved you once. I loved you. And you loved me and left me." The resentment I'd held on to—since I'd watched my father yell and slam his way out of the house, out of our lives—released. Suddenly I understood why he'd gone. I imagined myself as an adult observer at the scene.

He stands there enraged, bursting with frustration: my father, aged thirty-three; an adult child, emotionally unstable, damaged; responsible for a young family in a postwar situation. He is married to a needy, wounded woman who is totally dependent upon him, coping with two small children, expecting him to provide for her emotionally, financially. He is her whole life, the key to her existence, her sustenance, the centre of her world.

I put myself in their shoes. He was no god; nor was he the devil. He was just another of the walking wounded, a weak human man, an abundant sinner but too powerless to be evil. Yet, for his acts of molestation there is no excuse and no forgiveness. I don't know why he did what he did. Universal karmic law says we get back what we give out. So be it. He was my flesh and blood. He played a part in my creation. Without him, I would not be here.

To my amazement, a great well-spring of forgiveness and a profound, raw, vulnerable sadness surged from deep inside for my father's abandonment of me. I stood alone in the kitchen yet sensed the presence of a force behind me, protective, comforting. "Spenser?" I whispered.

Tears trickled down my face like a delicate spring rain. Spenser was no longer blind.

PART THREE

WARRIOR

The warrior is a lover of life, whose movements are in balance.

Diane Mariechild, The Inner Dance

I have no armour: I make benevolence and righteousness my armour.

Anonymous Samurai, Fourteenth Century, "A Warrior's Creed," Ralph Blum, The Book of Runes

CHAPTER FIFTEEN

BIRTHDAYS

Fear not the transformations you must face,
changes of state.
The cocoon of love arrests you
for a time, in its silken embrace.
You will endure it. You will emerge,
Your smile threadbare but intact.

Gary Geddes, "To the Women of the Fo Shan Silk Commune,"
Changes of State

If Rob had unconditionally comforted and supported me through all my physical and emotional pain, I told myself, then surely he was the Man of My Dreams. So I lapsed into long-term grief and occasional bitterness. But nothing is accidental: death, birth, rebirth, and transition—each piece of the puzzle fits. The Montreal Woman came at the perfect moment.

After the shock wore off, I saw her as a challenge: relationship roulette had long been a favourite pastime. All I needed was a strategy to win him back. Hot on the heels of this idea, however, came a completely unexpected turn of events that shaped my future as irrevocably as had my meeting with Rob in 1986.

Penny left an article in my mailbox about the survivor of incestuous abuse who'd committed suicide in prison. I was devastated by the story; I howled and cried and beat my fists on the table. No more of these stories, please, I begged the piece of newsprint in my trembling hand. Why couldn't someone tell about the healing instead of the horror? Couldn't someone bring a message of hope instead?

"Breathe, Trysh. Breathe," the Small Voice said. I put the kettle on for tea while my hysteria turned to a colder, more focused anger. If I wanted to protest, why not go directly to the author of the piece, June Callwood.

I have a recurring dream about white wedding dresses, of being a virgin.

In the cool light of dawn, after another sleepless night, a thunderbolt of realization hit me. If I let Rob look after my life I sacrificed all my dreams, relinquished part of me. I thanked Rob for having been honest with me, for creating the predictability that leads to trust. It had forced me to be honest with myself and, by extension, with the world.

June Callwood interviewed me on Friday, January 20th, 1989. So great was my reluctance to tell every detail of my past to a complete stranger that I carefully planned what I would say in advance, and the order in which I would say it. Yet I knew that without telling my story it would be impossible to understand my healing. My qualms vanished in the safety of Ms. Callwood's respectful, caring grace. I spontaneously told her about the abusive incidents I'd remembered, and she was profoundly moved, but I wanted her to know that I was a survivor, not a victim. I wanted to honour the child I'd been. She understood.

"Of course, you'll do a book," she said.

A heart-pounding challenge thrilled inside me, with a sense of urgency. I was in transition, hatching, a small wet chick knocking against a hard shell with its tiny beak. Hard work. Exciting. Scary. Moving forward. The reason I'd come back to life in the recovery room was abundantly clear. A book. But what if I became a success? Would I lose Rob? What if I failed? What about my lack of technical know-how; I wasn't academic; I hadn't been to university. If I asked for Rob's help would he think me too dependent? Too bad. I had a serious job to do—not to betray my essential self.

"I feel very strange," I told Lori. I felt real, part of the human race. I'd become an adult woman, no longer isolated, although still in pain. "This must be what it's like to be well!"

"Yes," she smiled.

"Lori, I think you and I, among many others, have been put on this earth to help heal the planet. You do it as a therapist. I believe my way is as a writer and speaker. Our medicine is communication." Lori nodded. I told her what June had said and that

I was thinking about devoting my life to helping other survivors of child sexual abuse. "When the book is published," I said, "I'd like to go to school and train to be a counsellor. Perhaps on the West Coast—follow in my grandfather's footsteps and live where I've always wanted to, in Vancouver."

I'd decided to go out there for Easter to look around. The decision seemed symbolic of the new emerging me. I was more assertive, tougher, yet tender and vulnerable. My face had softened; I held my head high. I felt a burgeoning sense of authentic power—and a humility. "From survivor to warrior," said Lori. Then she posed the question I didn't want to hear: if I was strong and changing, could Rob meet me as an equal when I didn't need him desperately?

My story appeared the following Wednesday. I opened the newspaper excited and wary, not knowing what to expect. The headline—THE COMPLICATED, TORTURED PATH TO SELF-HEALING FOR AN INCEST SURVIVOR—made me sob with sadness and humility; the way the story was written thrilled me. It felt like a day that never should have been, yet was worth waiting for. A true birthday. A warrior birthday that I could share with friends from British Columbia to Newfoundland, Rob in Quebec, unknown people across Canada ("Across *Canada!!*" shouted Mary Patricia, very impressed); people who'd touched my life, whose lives I'd touched.

The telephone calls started just after 8:00 a.m. I was getting out of the bath when the first came in. I stood, towelling myself dry, listening to the answering machine. "Wanna gimme a call sometime," growled an old familiar male voice. "I'd like to hear from you." I stood rooted to the spot, frozen. It was John, and with him some primeval force calling me back to Daddy. I fought a deep compulsion to call him. And won!

I dream about my father being weak, pathetic; about my birth; being pushed into the world all slippery and damp; someone touching my head. Going home to England. Looking out of my old bedroom window. An adult.

It was just before dawn on February 2nd, 1989, my forty-sixth birthday. I went downstairs and decorated a wreath on the front door with dried flowers and a large white bow. For Mary Patricia.

"Is this a truce?" asked Rob, letting himself in later that morning. I laughed. "I need a hug," he said, extending his arms. I melted into his embrace as though nothing untoward had happened in the month since his last visit.

"You look terrific," he said.

"Vancouver CBC is interested in doing an interview," I said excitedly. I'd just been talking to a producer who'd seen the newspaper story. "So is Newfoundland." I'd also been approached by a radio phone-in show and a national TV interview show.

"Your story is sensational, inspirational. You could help a lot of people," he said. "That's why I've kept on at you to write your journals."

"It is?" I was amazed. "For my book?"

Rob nodded. "You'll need a good editor," he cautioned.

I swallowed hard. "I'd like to ask you," I said, a little shyly.

"I'd be honoured," he replied.

I wished that everything could go back to the way it was before, but that wasn't reality. I'd started taking charge of my own life, making decisions about what I wanted instead of trying to control Rob all the time. (Although, I must confess to frequent slips in the form of declamatory speeches. "You don't like women very much, yourself even less. You're a good man, not a bad little boy." Blah-blah-blah.)

We went to see Lori. I stroked the brassy scales of the Golden Fish, which Rob had returned to me, and thought of "Papa." I'm sure I heard him say, "Don't do anything rash, dear."

Lori said she was impressed by Rob's and my determination to cut through our misunderstandings. They may have fuelled my expectations, fanned the fires of my dreams, but I was willing to douse them with reality and Rob was willing to listen. Facing each other, toes touching toes on Lori's peach-coloured sofa, we dedicated the cornerstone of our non-defensive friendship based on dignity and respect.

One of my friends had suggested that saying goodbye to Rob would be a gift. Once the blush of his new liaison wore off, she theorized, his loneliness, emptiness, and pain would be so great it would precipitate his healing. "His healing isn't my responsibility," I'd retorted. But I knew I wasn't yet complete with him. "Papa" had been Mummy's friend for thirty years. Their strong, mutual bond was rare and special. So was ours.

Friendship: Being real. Being there for one another; a commitment without romantic illusion. Stating and negotiating boundaries. Communicating. Checking things out. Sharing. Checking again. Being angry. Loving. Crying on each other's shoulder. Being awkward, boring, predictable, irritating, scared, vulnerable. Learning to trust; becoming trustworthy.

We'd have to be patient; it wouldn't be easy. It'd demand work and time and persistence. It'd be fun and stimulating; supportive, nurturing, caring and loving, non-controlling—truly free. I could be me, do whatever I wanted with my life and be loved. So could he. I wished I could love him with my body too, but sex isn't as intimate as opening one's soul, surrendering judgement.

"It's honesty, clarity, generosity, humour, reliability, respect," Rob summed up, splendidly succinct. "Absence of manipulation, hidden agendas, or bean counting. No creating a ledger; no holding points against the other or creating one's own record of gold stars."

He and I had once written a contract in the snow in which we promised "to eschew abandonment both mutual and singular for as long as we shall both be together in a significant way." I had no idea what would happen with the "we" in "he" and "me" but it occurred to me that a relationship of equilibrium—rather than striving towards some kind of goal—in which we could take off our skin and be in our bones together, lovingly accepted, was supremely special. No more assumptions. No more second guessing.

Late that night, after we'd celebrated the birthday of bombs and almond blossom when baby Love-Child Mary Patricia slipped into the world, I said, "Rob, I'd like you to sleep in my bed. The guest room is made up. Where would you like to sleep?" His choice to take the guest bed made the little girl me feel rejected, although the adult me very much respected Rob's boundary. Sadly, I got into my own bed, took Mary Patricia in my arms with my teddy bear, and fell asleep.

My body ached horribly next morning—and would for several weeks. (In defiance of grim predictions that I would never dance again, and out of sheer delight in being alive, I had danced with Rob until the wee hours.) I invited Rob to join me for tea in my bedroom. We chatted and laughed just like old times—except he sat on the edge of my bed instead of in it.

While Rob cooked breakfast I took stock in the hot soothing water of my bath and Grace Space. In the crowded club the night before we'd danced without intensity, but our ordinary conversation this morning had turned me on. Words had caressed me; the intimacy of sharing had brought us very close. That Rob should have found another woman after we stopped making love—with whom he'd chosen monogamy—was ironic, hurtful. Quickly putting on a housecoat and wrapping a towel around my wet hair, I went downstairs to confront him. "Can I be angry with you?" I said.

"You can do anything you like." He paused. "But please don't hit me."

"I'm terribly, terribly angry with you," I burst out. "And afraid."

Rob said something about not deserving but whether he referred to me or himself wasn't clear. We sat down to eat. Anger is compatible with love, I thought. There was so much in my heart that I could not speak. I tumbled inside a black hole, churned through a roar of chaos and pain. Abandoned yet not. Rejected yet not. Loved yet not. Unlovable. No. I had the Golden Fish. Rob had his freedom. Perhaps we both had what we wanted.

Spiritual warrior. Born in love and sadness January 25th, 1989. Celebrating a mortal birthday in love and sadness, February 2nd, with my good friend. I was not with you in my body, Rob, when I was born a warrior. Your spirit and mine communed, two small flames of love burning deep and fierce; indestructible old souls, unable to consummate passions we fear.

Was it not possible for one human being, one man that I choose, to want me—every inch and scrap of me; every vital throbbing cell; skin peeled back to soul, dancing together with throbbing life-force in a partnership of love? Equally. Forever?

"I love you," I said, pushing back my plate. (I'd hardly touched the food.) Rob stood up, put his arms around me, held me close.

"I love you," he said.

"I know you do," I whispered.

Later, grieving, my body racked with pain and sobs, rocking with my teddy bear, wanting Rob to hold and comfort me, I had the feeling he was close.

I looked at my roses, knowing everything was all right. Little girl, I told my Child Within, nothing is forever, except you and me embracing. We are tender young shoots of springtime. Alone together, free and independent. For one year I'll be celibate, for two years walk alone. I'll rechannel my passions into the book which Rob will help me write; anger to action, sexuality to creativity. And, as I let Rob go, my love will change, in time, to the affectionate tenderness of ordinary friendship.

CHAPTER SIXTEEN

BODY BEAUTIFUL

By finding, knowing, monitoring and loving our bodies, we can greatly enhance our recovery.

John Lee, I Don't Want to Be Alone

Summer 1989. There's a work-to-rule on the transit system. A woman who is late for work lashes out at the streetcar driver. He takes advantage of the situation to goof off for coffee, leaving us trapped until he comes back twenty minutes later. I'm on the way to Lori's.

The return journey is worse. In a park adjacent to a cathedral, a wino is stabbed during an argument over a bottle. A woman, stupefied with shock, sits hunched on the ground, alone. Onlookers goggle. Ambulance drivers pack the taped-up body onto a stretcher. Police take notes, question bystanders. A man, half-naked, his fleshy stomach bulging over beltless, dirty trousers, is bundled, handcuffed, into a cruiser. The arresting officer looks grim.

Is this enlightenment, seeing all this, hearing all this, feeling the pain of life around me?

Since my return from the West Coast at Easter I'd viewed Toronto in a different light. Restaurants and bars, galas and opening nights held no glamour when bums panhandled, homeless youngsters hustled, strangers harassed me. Increasingly, I experienced insensitive rudeness and indifference to us, the differently-abled. And the roar of traffic kept me awake at night.

My bones ached, my muscles hurt, anxiety nipped at my heart. 3:00 a.m. Tossing and turning achieved nothing more than to induce further anxiety. I'd stopped taking pills, habitual since adolescence, to battle my insomnia.

Get comfortable. Close eyes. Breathe. Pull the covers closer. Try counting sheep. Woolly ungulates contemplate a hedge. 1 . . . 2 . . . 3 . . . Bo-Peep eggs them on. 4 . . . 5 . . . 6 . . . Bo-Peep pokes a sheep with her crook, adjusts her bonnet. 7 . . . 8 . . . 9 . . . I bet Bo-Peep wasn't an incest survivor.

Distracted suddenly, the speculation started, the worries, the memories. I craved a sleeping pill, a Valium, something to stop the babble in my head.

"A bath!" suggested the Small Voice.

"At this time of night?" said a shocked Helga the Hag, my internal "wicked stepmother." I procrastinated until dawn.

Two more similar nights. On the third the Small Voice said, "It's perfectly okay to bathe at 3:00 a.m." Permission was all I needed. The bath relaxed me. I got back to sleep quickly. After sleeping right through the fourth night, I congratulated myself. The fifth, sixth, and seventh sleeps varied in length—three, five, and three hours respectively. I was worn out. The baths helped, but I succumbed to afternoon naps. My insomnia increased.

I read that the trick was to acclimatize the body; train the brain. I made myself a timetable. Bedtime: 10:00 p.m. Get up: 8:00 a.m. No more afternoon naps. No more working in the bedroom—it's for rest, relaxation, quiet play. No working after dinner—too stimulating. Prior to retiring, star-gazing and deep breathing looked like promising ideas, but Toronto air was conducive to neither. I made more rules: no more wandering the house during wakeful periods. Make sure the temperature is right. I played with the thermostat setting, bought a humidifier and an electric blanket. I turned on the fan, opened the window, shut the window. Soft music helped—until it turned itself off with a *click* and startled me awake.

Sometimes, waking from a dream or seeing shadows in the room that reminded me of long ago, action was required. One night I yelled, "Get out, Daddy. Go away. Leave me alone." (I'd stopped worrying about the neighbours by this time.) I shut the closet door, opened the bedroom door, kept a light burning by the stairs, kept a light on in the bathroom. I burned votive candles, then decided it was safer to comfort the Child Within with a plug-in nursery night-light than risk an accident.

Tuning into feelings sometimes helped. Holding back the pain never did. It was better to face it, let it out, howl into my pillow. I wrote in my notebook, soothed myself with a warm drink. An immersion heater in a mug of milk beside the bed was less disruptive than an excursion to the kitchen. I was determined to teach myself to stay in bed. Cuddle my teddy. Get some extra pillows—one underneath my knees, one in the small of my back. Comfort was everything. I breathed: "Everything is working out in the best possible way. I'm safe. I'm sleeping through the night. I wake refreshed."

On the inevitable nights when the cat padded into the room, and the fear clutched at my gut so tightly that I couldn't cry out, when I couldn't stand the exhaustion another minute and I guiltily swallowed a couple of pills, the rule was: no beating-up on myself. So I slipped. Two innocuous aspirins were better than Percodan, Valium, or sleeping pills. Breaking a twenty-five year nightly ritual ain't easy, I told myself. Tomorrow I'll do better. Patience. Perseverance. Gentleness. Next week I would be a lot better. Next year's improvements I could not imagine.

By the fall of 1990, it was unusual *not* to sleep right through. Even getting up to pee was a minor interruption. If I woke in the night and couldn't get back to sleep I used a tape urging me to "enjoy a full, completely restful night's sleep" and other subliminal messages. Occasionally, I used a mixture of skullcap, hops, and valerian; but, as anything can be habit-forming, I took it only in extreme cases. By spring 1991, I stopped worrying about not sleeping—it was so rare. One night of insomnia can easily be made up for. Daily exercise and fresh air play an integral role in combatting insomnia. So does a proper diet—part of another problem I've had to lick.

Anorexia and bulimia. Eating disorders. Secrets from my past:

A Dickensian asylum for the insane, 1971. Refusing to eat. Throwing my breakfast tray at the Charge Nurse. He threatens to tube-feed me.

Standing by a fireplace at a friend's house, aged twelve. Someone remarks on my breasts, swelling underneath the itchy wool of my red sweater. Developing into a woman is embarrassing, threatening. Rising hormones curve my hips, round my breasts, bring menstrual blood and male invasion. In the semester following the Isle of Wight our home-room teacher taught us the shocking truth about how babies are made. Devastated, I wondered how many babies grew in my tummy? Like a hawk, I watched for signs of pregnancy thereafter—only half aware of what I was doing.

Not eating meant death, oblivion, an end to pain. No more loneliness and fear and abandonment. No more pricks stuffed in my mouth. By refusing food I had the power to control what went in my body. No one could force me to eat except the Charge Nurse with his hosepipe; still, the gnawing hunger and the need to eat had to be acknowledged, the empty spaces filled. Food became my obsession.

I ate the other children's leftovers at school, wolfed down the remaining mashed potatoes, beef stew, comforting custard and rice pudding. The girls hooted and catcalled when I told dirty jokes— mine always the scummiest, the filthiest, as I stuffed myself some more.

Sometimes at home, when it felt safe, I tucked in. I even stole from the pantry, especially leftover meat from Sunday's roast. Preserved eggs, good sherry put by for guests, ingredients for Monday's baking. Fruit pies, Eccles cakes, rock buns, and my favourite: butter pie. Next to the meat safe sat a big tin of powdered egg. I'd scoop up the yellow powder. Great gobs of it stuck to my wet-licked fingers and the roof of my well-fucked mouth.

In adolescence I was a stick doll in a school uniform. Improper eating caused frequent constipation. Pig-outs and premenstrual tension distended my abdomen. I was afraid I looked pregnant. In the mirror I saw a big fat ugly blob. I gobbled down enough laxatives to induce volcanic eruptions of cramps and diarrhoea. As an adult I used enemas, although they frightened me —subconscious reminders of humiliating times gone by.

Dancing. Stretching. Cycling. Swimming. Yoga. A woman can never be too thin. I weighed in every morning; every evening. If the scales indicated more than 115 pounds, I'd go on a diet. My height, until the operations, was over five feet, seven inches.

It was Rob's daughter, Megan, who told me that on Fat Days I looked no different than on other days. My mind's eye distorted the mirror image. Awareness is halfway to cure. Once able to identify which days were which, I dressed more carefully on Fat Days, careful to wear exactly the same clothes as on Thin Days. I talked to my reflection; affirmed my self-esteem. "You're beautiful, Trysh, just the way you are. It's okay to eat a normal diet. Your body is perfect just the way it is."

Until Rob came along I didn't think I deserved good food. The restaurant where I met him served mediocre food to its misfit patrons. I went there often, feeling I belonged. Watching Rob rev-

erently chop, slice, dice, cook, and serve subtly flavoured, aes-
thetically presented dishes was like observing religious ritual. Rob
gave me permission to nourish my body appropriately and well.
At the elegant, gourmet restaurant chosen for the celebration of
my forty-sixth birthday, I knew I deserved every morsel, every
mouthful, every sip.

In the early months of healing I hung a menu on the refrigerator
with a suggested list to choose from for each meal.

The menu helped me plan ahead, shop for ingredients, and
remember to eat. I bought a larger variety of fresh foods in small
quantities and cooked smaller portions. Little by little the feelings
of fear, shame, and unworthiness abated: I stopped obsessing
about food, elimination, exercise, and weight. I reminded my Child
Within that it was okay to eat, that proper nourishment would
not make her fat or appear pregnant. As my taste-buds perked
up and my desire to eat grew, I wanted to buy everything. I curbed
the urge for instant gratification by gently reassuring the Child
Within that her newfound delight in food would continue. The
aim was balance.

Impromptu invitations to eat with friends provided the healing
ingredient, fun! One holiday weekend began with hamburgers
with Jochen on Friday. Then Ruth came to dinner on Saturday.
I roasted cornish hens, she brought a raspberry pie. On Sunday,
Karen and I tried out a new cheap Chinese restaurant that had
opened round the corner. Another friend took me for Indian fare
on Monday.

Proudly, I watched my scrawny, weak body grow stronger. I
began to like what I saw in the mirror. The weight I was gaining
made me chuckle gleefully—up ten pounds since leaving hospital.
One hundred and thirty pounds. I didn't look fat at all. My body
was ripening from girl into woman. To mark the milestone I indulged myself with pretty lingerie, including a brassiere. I hadn't
worn one since I'd been a nursing mother. I purchased it one
rainy day. "To give myself a lift," I wisecracked.

The better I felt about myself, the better I nourished myself
and paid attention to my bodily needs. I gradually lost interest
in the compulsive behaviours and substances that I'd used to cover
up my shame, my fears, my awkwardness. In 1987 I'd kicked a
twenty-eight-year cigarette habit. The craving continues sometimes, but I can't risk even a puff. Chewing sugarless gum helps.

A fellow patient in Seven North diagnosed me alcoholic in 1985
and suggested Alcoholics Anonymous. Shocked, I stopped drinking for several months. I abstained again after I became ill in 1988,

and I'm now able to take it or leave it. But I have one strict rule: no drinking on blue days. Just in case.

My longing was for tranquillizers, sleeping pills, and narcotic painkillers, closely followed by sexual addiction. As the first step in my sexual healing I stopped myself masturbating, which had been a comfort since early childhood. It's been one long battle saying no to myself, nurturing the Child Within, being patient and kind to myself. After many trying months the compulsion would fade, and with it, my associated need for drugs.

By summer, 1989, all self-destructive behaviour had stopped. I paid attention to each bodily need and protected myself in ways I'd never considered before. I took cabs after dark; once I was able to use public transportation I sat close to the driver. If I visited neighbours during the evening I walked home on the outside of the sidewalk underneath the street lights. I used a walking stick wherever I went, regardless of my physical need. Banging my cane down on the sidewalk made up for my lack of brawn, particularly on my right side. Had anyone tried to attack me, I had more weapons than house keys and a rape whistle. During the 1970s I'd taken a course in self-defence, which was empowering as well as practical. The sad truth is that the world is not a safe place for women: read the newspapers, the statistics, the tip of the iceberg.

Being good to myself had almost become ingrained, so it came as something of a surprise to discover that I was having difficulty accepting pleasurable sensation. It scared me; I wanted to fight it. I decided to teach my body's largest erogenous zone, my skin, to enjoy.

I sat in the bath stroking the skin on my left arm. It felt good. Tingly. Sensual. I breathed deeply, wanting to remember the pleasurable sensation. Next night I stroked the skin on my right arm. The night after I touched my face. Stroked my forehead. Eyelids. Cheekbones. Nose. Mouth.

I stopped, uncomfortable with the rest of my body, yet. I did want to like it, all of it. I treated myself to special soaps, lotions, and massage oils.

I had stopped seeing Carolin, my massage therapist, because the memories, coming thick and fast through late 1988 and early 1989, made all forms of touch unsafe. In May I returned to regular sessions. This time the massage felt good; there were no flashbacks. "Your body is opening," Carolin said. "Stand tall. Think wide. Open yourself more and more."

Standing in the bathroom in front of the brightly lit mirror, waiting for the bathtub to fill, I stared at my body. The stiffness in my body had eased; my shoulders had dropped. I felt more limber; I looked more toned and svelte. I examined every part of my body and discovered I could love all of me. *Viva!* I ran my hands all over myself, laughing and crying at the same time.

Dr. Perrin, at my one-year check-up, told me he was delighted with my progress. "You've worked very very hard," he said.

"I still do," I replied. "Each day."

"I know," he nodded sagely. "You always will."

Then I broke my news. "I'm going to live in British Columbia," I said. "I'm going to write a book."

"My God," he beamed. "You'll be a millionaire." We laughed. He asked me to keep in touch. I took his hand and thanked him from my heart, for helping me to stand on my feet—not only physically but as a whole human being. We moved slightly, hesitantly toward each other. But we were Anglo-Saxons, after all, and he a true professional. "Thank you, Richard," I said quietly.

I devoted my summer working hours to my book—sometimes making notes or reading at an outdoor swimming pool. Sunbathing had become more comfortable, a sensuous diversion. In the water I was mermaid, porpoise, dolphin—unafraid; a year ago the underwater had terrified me. I admired other bodies without embarrassment; my own body felt like an acceptable part of me, not split off. I walked the half mile to the pool easily, including a hike up a small hill. I love you, legs. Thank you for supporting me. I love you, feet. Thank you for walking me. I love you, back. I love you, body. You're beautiful.

CHAPTER SEVENTEEN

LEARNING LOVE

the need you
grew
still remains.

but less and less
you seem the way
to fill that need.

I am.

Peter McWilliams, "Changes,"
How to Survive the Loss of a Love

Rob and I made an agreement to call each other on Tuesdays. Sometimes, when it was his turn, I was so afraid he'd forget that I deliberately left the house to avoid disappointment—only to find his message on my machine when I returned. His sudden predictability made me feel ambivalent, pursued. He had invited me to share a friendship free of possessiveness. Why would he stick around being "my friend" when he had the Montreal Woman? Maybe he was just being nice to me, telling me what he thought I wanted to hear. Why did he want a friendship with me and a sexual relationship with someone else? To force me to look elsewhere? Was he trying to say, "I'm afraid of being hurt too. So I'll hurt you first. If you leave, it's your fault."

When he added a second "phone date" later in the week—ostensibly to discuss the book project—I felt unworthy, undeserving.

I overreacted to everything he said and perceived the slightest criticism as imminent dismissal. Then, afraid he'd hang up, I babbled, gave unsolicited advice—anything to keep him on the line. I was like a broken record trying to control him, feeling sorry for myself, and getting nowhere fast.

Hoping I could stop being a love junkie, I continued a guided imagery exercise which I'd begun after my birthday and spread over several weeks:

February 4, 1989: I release a pink balloon from my front door into the sky containing my dreams of Rob and me being together. "I let you go. I let go my dreams."

February 6: The pink balloon floats in the atmosphere. Inside a bride and groom become Rob and me, ordinary mortals. I send them on their way. Friends. Someone once told me that friendship is the Kiss of Death. The balloon bursts. I start the exercise again next day, but I can't let go.

March 7: Rob and I are inside the balloon. At last I've managed to move it from outside the front door to a spot halfway between my front steps and the middle of the road. I cannot shift it further.

March 9: The balloon, covered in confetti, is in the middle of the road, preparing for lift-off. "Rob is a good man. I let him go."

March 11: The balloon still refuses to lift off. A small foot holds down the string. Three-year-old Mary Patricia won't let go.

March 13: Mary Patricia still has her foot on the balloon string. I give her all the time she needs to let go. No conditions. With my love.

March 15: No change. I tell Rob about the child and the balloon and giving up Daddy. "I know all about that three-year-old of yours," he says. We talk about how I use and want him in that role.

March 27: En route to Vancouver for my Easter holiday I offer a list of miracles to the universe—lasting friendship with Rob one of them—and let them go so the universe may send them back to me when the time is right. The balloon flies high over the Rocky Mountains. Life is filled with possibilities, much better than the fantasy I lived in.

Later: At last! The balloon that I've dragged across Canada finally floats free over the Okanagan Valley, high up into the clear blue sky, over snowcapped mountain peaks into the crisp cold air towards the coast.

Giving up Rob and my dreams of a future with him was far harder than sending an imaginary balloon into the atmosphere, it precipitated a new stage of grieving. I thought I'd never stop crying. "The deeper the grieving, the deeper the healing," Lori said, when I got back to Toronto. Mary Patricia was furious that Rob refused to look after her as he once had. The adult me welcomed the opportunity to explore an equality in which I could let down my guard and explore being truly known. Rob remained steadfast despite my relentless testing. Gradually, our friendship freed me to decide my future and to heal sexually. For that I needed lots of time.

The last time Rob and I made love. Screams. Flashbacks. Shadows on the wall that stirred something deeply revolting, consciously unknown. Sex terrified me. I didn't know how I was going to become a healthy sexual woman, but my commitment to a year of celibacy gave me time. I'd made a start with the affirmations, the slow touching exercises in the bathtub, and taking care of my body.

If I had confused my partners with Daddy, it was logical that I was able only to freeze and fake. I needed to learn to trust and delight in my natural responses; accept sexual pleasure as something I deserved; get to know my body and stop being afraid of it. I wanted to be playful like a child without being a child. I wanted to give pleasure and to enjoy touching my partner's body. I'd bathed with Rob, massaged him, trying to be comfortable with his masculinity. He'd responded with cuddles and tenderness but I had work to do with myself. I needed to understand that sexuality is far more than penile/vaginal contact.

My biggest sexual handicap was thinking ill of my genitals, fearing their power. They'd got me into trouble enough. I affirmed *viva la vulva* over and over again with my legs spread in front of the mirror. I looked at pictures of female genitalia—what a variety! I insisted to the admonishing voices inside my head that my vulva was beautiful, that sexuality was normal—not disgusting or dirty. Feeling that I had the right to be my own woman was vital to reclaiming my right to be a sexual person and have sexual pleasure. It was an issue of power and control. In teaching myself healthy sexual response I held both.

My second problem was stamping out the sado-masochistic fantasies that I had used obsessively for so long. Deliberately calling up the negative images, I overlaid new, positive images of lying in a warm sea on a beach in a magical, fantastical place I called Rain Island until the new fantasy became the turn-on. After a while, the old fantasies usually sickened and disgusted me.

Not allowing myself to masturbate was terribly difficult, but I did become less compulsive. When the longings snatched at my genitals—with urges to use the old fantasies—I breathed slowly and deeply, went for a walk, took a bath, or diverted my attention into constructive channels. "I deserve to be sexually fulfilled," I affirmed. "I deserve sexual pleasure." Not certain, sometimes, whether I was feeling genital anxiety or a true need for sexual satisfaction, I asked myself some basic questions: Am I feeling good about myself or down on myself, bored or lonely? Am I feeling open and spontaneous? Or anxious and empty?

I quickly discovered that if I lied to myself I had very different sexual experiences. Sometimes I made genuine love to myself, tenderly, feeling sexual and sensual all over. Mere clitoral masturbation was a way of lessening anxiety. It required sado-masochistic fantasies and orgasm; it was neither loving nor self-caring. I stopped forcing myself to orgasm allowing instead the warm sensuality to float through me, tingle down my arms and legs, experimenting with positive sensual images. My favourite was of a big tree with a mossy patch beneath, a picnic basket, and my lover, on Rain Island. It was this fantasy that I chose to use with a trigger word, "Moss." Then, if the old images popped up uninvited (and to my chagrin they did—exciting me), I said, "Moss" and immediately superimposed the picnic scene, which I elaborated upon gently, sensually. Bit by bit, the orgasms became more connected to my entire body. My sexuality was unfolding.

At the beginning of April I told Rob, straightforwardly, that I felt sexual again. It was part of our deal to be open and not to have hidden agendas. "But," I warned, "I can't include sexuality in our friendship while you're with someone else. My body is too precious to have sex casually. And you're too special to have casual sex with. Are you interested?"

"No," he replied, directly. "My love for you is brotherly."

I wanted to make a speech about the high risk of sexualizing friendship: there's so much more to lose. It's easy to confuse sexual attraction and love; to underestimate the intensity of love by calling it "brotherly." But I was so choked up with jealousy that he had someone to cuddle, make love to, share his life with, that I couldn't speak. "The blush of romance wears off," Rob was saying. "Friendship lasts a long long time." Was it all off with the

Montreal Woman? "When I'm free," he continued, "you'll be the first to know."

I missed him, the adrenaline rush of being in love; its drama and excitement. I wanted so much to create what we'd had elsewhere I had to resist calling John or maintaining the correspondence with my father. Instead, I allowed my emptiness to be. It hurt that Rob described his new relationship as "easy and supportive," that they were "better suited than you and I." Regret overwhelmed me. "It's okay to make mistakes, especially with trusted people," said the Small Voice.

I dream about Rob and me, familiar friends, walking together in Montreal. I leave him in the care of a grey-haired healer. For my own good I must leave. I kiss Rob goodbye, telling him I'll see him when his therapy is over. I go away, supported by my walking stick, to be taken care of by women. Years pass. Rob arrives whole and healed. We're glad to see each other, good old friends.

I decided to stop taking his relationship with the Montreal Woman personally and get on with my life. I tried dating but realized how much I was drawn to wounded men. Dating could wait until I was healthier. Then I'd attract healthier men.

I'd told everyone but Rob about my plan to move. I experimented with letters explaining that it was time to make major changes; that I'd always intended following in my grandfather's footsteps. But it wasn't the whole story and I never sent them. "May I come to Montreal for a couple of days?" I asked. "There's something I want to tell you in person."

"Yes," he replied without hesitation.

I took out the Golden Fish, symbol of loving friendship. I wanted to give it back. Unconditionally. It was time to get off the fence and commit to a genuine friendship—knowing Rob was there for me, and I for him. All-weather friends. I had to stop my steps in our dance: Cling, smother, overwhelm. Retreat, pause, supplicate.

I intended to let him know, warmly and calmly, that while I needed some separateness with him for now, I remained open to a future Life Partnership. But, as usual, it didn't come out that way.

"I once said if it got too painful I'd say goodbye," I blurted out as soon as we arrived at Rob's cottage outside Montreal. "My house is up for sale. I'm going to live in British Columbia." It was as if I'd struck him. "I'm *not* abandoning you," I continued softly. "I'm doing this for *me*. I've been waiting for you to come back. I'm wasting my life."

"Let's have tea," Rob said. I followed him silently across the garden, sensing his pain.

It wasn't until the next day that I asked him how he felt about my plans. We were weeding his vegetable patch.

"I'm shocked that you're going," Rob said. "And that it has so much to do with me."

"I'd like to share more with you," I replied, "my feelings about you getting involved with someone else. Why I'm angry. Sad. And glad."

They were days of honesty, self-disclosure, affection, and support. "Our friendship is quite wonderful," Rob said on the second afternoon. "Better than it was. Although I miss the magic sweetness and innocence we once had."

"Me too."

On the last morning we walked by the river. "I have something for you," I said, handing Rob the pouch containing the Golden Fish and a card. He laughed at the picture of a white-haired, elegant man in his fifties, alone with his dog on a beach. I'd agonized over the wording. "If you ever want to explore the challenge of a Life Partnership . . . " I began. Rob stared at the river, withdrawn and quiet. It wasn't until I reached the paragraph reiterating our promise in the snow that he turned toward me again and gazed lovingly into my eyes. Taking my hand tenderly he thanked me.

"Do you love me enough to let me go?" I asked him. He closed his eyes and nodded. "You must love me very much," I said.

"Uh-huh, yes, I do," he whispered.

We went up to the house for breakfast. Raising our glasses of champagne and orange juice, I proposed a toast. "I acknowledge that the form of our relationship has changed. Bless what has been and let it go."

I dream Rob and I have to overcome enormous obstacles. We must leave a very high, steep mountain and go down a narrow, twisting path in a bus. We are terrified and must be courageous. Rob sits calmly fishing in a little boat, surrounded by ice floes and water lilies. The boat is attached by a long line to someone safe. I'm told that I must not forget him. I walk alone. I pass a couple who take no notice of me. I meet a wise woman with long greying hair. I follow a labyrinth to reach a special room with women in it. I must join the women.

With only four months left in my self-imposed year of celibacy I realized it was time to deal with some present-day realities. A television commercial about safe sex prompted my next step toward sexual healing.

I'd had innumerable sexual partners whose partners were unknown to me. A trip to the Hassle Free clinic quickly proved me lucky—and HIV negative. I asked Heather, from my women's circle, about condoms.

First, she taught me how to open the package, how to handle the condom, how to check for tears. It looked so *big*. It'd be much easier just to avoid sex altogether, I thought. "Then you won't completely triumph," said the Small Voice. "You don't yet know what good sex is."

Suddenly, I remembered a recent dream about corn on the cob. Beautiful. Smooth. Perfect. Hesitant and scared I slowly peeled back part of the green husk to gently bite the succulent corn.

"How d'you have oral sex with condoms?" I questioned Heather, putting it in my mouth. It tasted awful.

"Carefully," she answered. We laughed. "Buy the non-lubricated kind and always use a water soluble lubricant—never petroleum jelly or cortisone cream. Using a spermicide may kill the HIV virus."

A week later, as though to demonstrate to the world that I was my own woman, I cut my hair short like a boy's. The odds were that Rob would hate it but I'd lost interest in being a fairy princess. On the way to the hair salon I stopped by Lovecraft. Maybe—just maybe—I'd buy a vibrator.

The store mesmerized me. I saw books and rubber ducks (rubber ducks?), cards and lacy lingerie, but no vibrators. Reluctant to ask, and about to scurry back to the safety of the street, a young saleswoman greeted me. "Can I help you?" she asked cheerfully.

"Er, I'm looking for er . . . a . . . um . . . vibrator," I stammered.

"What size?" she asked.

What size? "I'll tell you what I need it for . . . " I tried to explain. "I mean, well, apart from the obvious . . . "

I told her that I was a recovering incest survivor. She didn't bat an eyelid. She lead me to a table covered in pink plastic penises, picked one up, and held it out to me. "This is a good starter size," she said. I gaped. It looked friendly enough, familiar almost. Without thinking, I started stroking it. It had been a long time . . .

"This is the next size up . . . " The young woman startled me from my reverie. "Oh no!" I said, scared. "I'd need to . . . to graduate to that. I'll take this one." She took a box from a drawer over to the desk and opened it. "Batteries aren't included," she smiled, clicking the vibrator on. Zzzzzzzz.

"You can't return it," she said. I laughed. How easily we exchange lovers if they don't measure up. I thought sadly of my neediness, how it scared away men who might have loved me but always left for less intense, more self-sufficient women.

When I got home I lay on my bed with the vibrator. Looked, touched, then tucked my strange little friend away in a drawer with my new lingerie. After all, it was our first date!

Saturday night. Preparing for a long, slow sensuous, sensual rendezvous with my special lover. Mr. Ziz Ziz. Resplendent in silk, pretty earrings, and expensive perfume I set the table with silver candlesticks, fragrant pink rosebuds, and lace mats. Soft music, complete with birdsong. The answering machine is on. I have no intention of being interrupted tonight. The air is filled with the tantalizing aroma of gourmet food. I nibble on an olive and toss the salad with balsamic vinegar, fresh herbs, and extra extra virgin olive oil. I'm an extra extra virgin too. There may have been many sex partners but I've never made love alive, present, and aware. Tonight I will. My mouth waters, my entire body tingles in anticipation of the erotic evening ahead. I sway to the rhythm of the music, exulting in my body's flexibility. No wine— tonight I want to be absolutely focused.

Every mouthful of dinner savoured, I light candles and run the bath. I add mint and lavender bubbles, stretch luxuriously. Undressing seductively in front of the mirror I touch and stroke my body reverently, admiring and affirming its beauty but avoiding my breasts and vulva. A long, slow bath is followed with an equally long, slow self-massage in my candlelit bedroom. Teddy bear sits ignored on a chair in the corner. The bed is made with fresh sheets, invitingly turned down. Mr. Ziz Ziz is waiting. Condoms and lubricant are ready under the pillows.

I leave no part of my body untouched. My nipples stiffen. I kiss my flesh wherever possible, wishing I could suck my own breasts. My vulva moistens. Time to fit Ziz Ziz with his safe. I get it out of the package but roll it incorrectly, forgetting to check for tears. Then discover that it's lubricated. A mistake. Like using vanilla scented massage oil—I smell like a pudding. Good enough to eat! Giggle. Giggle.

Ziz is close to my vulva. I'm scared, wonder if I've gone dry. Relax: I deserve sexual pleasure. I hug myself and open my legs wide. With a little help from the lubricant Ziz Ziz inserts easily. I'm not scared at all. My body is moving. I'm slow-dancing. Turn on Mr. Ziz. Oh, he's turned on all right. Sounds like a lawn mower. Hope the neighbours can't hear.

Exploring what I like, what I don't like. Mustn't touch anus then vagina, otherwise there are no rules. Try a long, slow fuck. Everything's long and slow tonight. Try a quick fast fuck. Nice Anglo-Saxon word, fuck. I will stop using it in other contexts. In, out. Ziz Ziz, you're terrific. I like you. In, all the way out. In again, moving. My body's moving. I rock back and forth, delighted. The cool sheets feel so good against my skin. I'm alive. Responding. Loving it.

I move the vibrator around, rubbing it in circles. No! Gang rapist moves inside me. I stop at once, hug myself. The present is not the past. Must keep my eyes open. Get a mirror. Look at my lovely vulva. I'm fine. I'm safe. I deserve sexual pleasure, passionate, sexual, sensual Aphrodite.

Ripple. Thrust. Starting to come. I've been playing for hours. Who cares. I'm having fun. No hurry. Ripple, ripple. Thrust. Thrust. Next time I do this I'm going to watch my genitalia in the mirror. The time after I'm going to watch my face—see if I agree with the comparison between orgasm and marathon running. My breathing certainly sounds like I'm approaching the finishing line. Building. Building. My throat opens. I get a sudden rush. "I love you," I shout spontaneously. "I love you" again. In an orgasmic joyful spray of moans and cries, I come. I did it! I did, I did it. Not once. Not twice. Multi-orgasms I am too amazed to count. My pulsating yoni pushes Mr. Ziz Ziz out. I take off the condom, tie it properly, get up to dispose of it and pee. I fall into a marvellous sleep, and dream of being a powerful woman whole unto myself.

CHAPTER EIGHTEEN

BOUND FOR GLORY

What we must do to protect our own recovery doesn't always appear to others as the "nice" thing. We may be judged as selfish, thoughtless, ungenerous. But we owe it to ourselves and to those we love to go to any lengths to recover.

Robin Norwood, Women Who Love Too Much

It was my son, Tristram, who gave me the opportunity to practice making boundaries when he asked to live at home again. To my surprise he never once trespassed on them or accused me of being stupid, as he had before. In fact, our relationship thrived: he shared some of his story with me and I was able to really listen, hear his pain, respond.

For a while he'd lived on the street before being taken in by friends. From there he got a job and moved into a low rental tumble-down house, which was about to be demolished. "No," he said, when asked if he'd like to come out west with me. Toronto was his home, his life. He'd get another place. He'd formed a rock band with friends; they played gigs for money or beer or both. He made extra cash painting leather jackets and T-shirts and weaving bracelets. I was filled with admiration. My son was another survivor of a dysfunctional family, creative, resourceful, intelligent, sensitive, street-smart. He talked openly about his childhood, about his grade one teacher who had dragged him across the classroom by his hair. (I remembered her preferring little girls.)

"How dare she!" I burst out indignantly. "You were just a little boy. How dare she do that." I said how sorry I was that I didn't stand up for him. I was so spaced out, depressed, absent. "That's what it's like being sexually abused as a kid—you just don't know how to be a good parent, how to shout on behalf of your own child. So I'm shouting now." Tristram laughed, genuinely pleased. I laughed, too. It was better to stand up for him late than never.

No means no. No, I'm not willing. No, I don't want to. No, that's *not* okay. No, not now. NO! NO! NO! No means being good to myself. No takes practice. No is a way to negotiate or stand firm, depending on the situation. Trusting my intuition, shouting a loud unladylike "NO" aggressively and rudely gradually felt as acceptable as a quieter, more gracious *no*.

"Are you having fun yet?" asked Jochen.

"Yes," I said. "Saying no and meaning no."

Saying "I don't know" was more difficult. I still feared being thought stupid.

Layers of old defenses dropped away. I often jumped over my fears and anxieties to say and do what intuitively felt right. I listened a lot to my Small Voice. When I followed her I stayed on track; when I ignored her, I made—and forgave myself—mistakes.

My new straightforward manner had an affect on people: I was taken seriously, treated with respect. I stopped flirting and seeing every man I met as a potential bedfellow. I no longer saw myself as a sex object but as a person with rights and self-respect. Friends commented on my dramatic changes.

"You've lost that drugged look," said one friend. "You look me in the eye."

"You're alive now," said Heather.

"You look radiant," added her daughter. "Grounded."

"You're not moody any more," Ruth said. "You're always nice to be with."

Even strangers made comments. "You take good care of yourself, don't you?" said a woman at the swimming pool. "You're so peaceful." I nodded. I was surprised and delighted. "I never used to be," I thought.

New friends came into my life; close friends came closer. But not everyone took to the new me. One woman slammed down the phone after I told her I didn't like her use of expletives. "God," she snorted irritably, "you've changed so much. Go fuck yourself." It was the last I heard from her.

Mid-August. I could make choices and set events in motion but I learned it took patience and detachment to await and accept the outcome. Instead of worrying that my house hadn't sold, I visualized the cottage out west. I continued sorting, packing, planning my move. I came across some old letters from my parents. My father's filled me with loathing, my mother's with regret. I missed her. A lump caught in my throat. "I want my Mummy," I sobbed. It was a blue, rice pudding day.

Two weeks later my house sold. Ahead was an action packed two months. I was about to leave for New York to talk to my favourite lodger, Jean, about her memories of my childhood. In mid-September I'd speak at a conference in Prince Edward Island and on a television show in Newfoundland about healing from incest. I planned a visit with Megan, who had started at university in Nova Scotia. And I'd booked a flight to London mid-October. Before I could settle in the west, I had unfinished business in England. I wanted to roam the neighbourhood where I grew up, talk to childhood friends, search the archives where certificates of births, marriages, deaths, and divorces are stored, follow up on the letter I'd sent to the British police.

My visit with Jean was marvellous. To her astonishment I thanked her for being my ally as a child. What an important role model she had been: capable, strong, independent, intelligent, fun, straightforward.

I was curious to know about myself from age nine to twelve, when, as a young grade-school teacher, Jean rented rooms in our house.

"You were fun, interesting, creative, very bright . . . "

"Mummy always said my sister was the clever one," I interrupted.

"Yes," Jean replied. "She was convinced of that. But you were much, much brighter."

"Mummy always seemed so disapproving of me . . . " I faltered.

"Your mother was so bloody proper," Jean exploded, recounting how honoured she felt to be invited to tea in the "inner sanctum." It was a rarely granted privilege. "Suddenly, your mother sent you to your room. I thought it terribly unfair. You went without protest, instantly obedient."

"Was I always so docile?"

"No. You laughed sometimes when your mother lectured you."

"Laughed?" I was incredulous.

"You were afraid of her, really. It was nervous laughter. It made things worse. She couldn't bear being laughed at. One summer we all went on holiday together. Your mother found a fly in her food. Everyone cracked up. It upset her dreadfully. She flounced off to her room."

"Go to your room" rang in my ears. Dismissed. Abandoned. Mummy always seemed so angry with me. "Perhaps she had trouble with you," Jean speculated, "because you were so like your father."

"She seemed to accept my sister more than me," I said sadly.

"Perhaps because your sister was more like her," Jean explained. Was my sister the favourite child?

"Did you ever guess I was being sexually abused?"

"If I had, I would have made a stink," Jean said indignantly. "We never thought about incest in those days."

"No clues?"

"There was a lot of upset over the vaginal infection," Jean answered. "Your mother was dreadfully distressed. And you were sexually very precocious for a nine-year-old. I always thought it odd. Now it makes sense."

On the return journey to Toronto I pondered the misunderstood, mistreated child whose spirit flickered for those who could see it. Jean had corroborated innumerable facts for me, but telling me I was bright made my heart leap with joy.

They gave me a standing ovation on Prince Edward Island without knowing I'd had a terrifying fantasy of my father bursting in, disrupting my presentation. I was asked, "Do you have any fears?"

"I go beyond my fear," I answered. "Because I have to."

"You're on a mission."

"Yes."

They called me "Warrior" in Newfoundland where I spoke amidst the scandal of child sexual abuse at the Mount Cashel orphanage. The public was rightly outraged. I knew church fathers were the tip of the iceberg: most perpetrators are fathers and stepfathers within the sanctity of the family.

Less than a month later, I sat opposite Detective Sergeant Peter White of the Sussex Criminal Investigation Department in Southern England talking about my father.

The interview lasted nearly four hours. The detective was not only experienced in paedophilia and child sexual abuse cases, he had been trained by international experts. My story didn't surprise him in the least. The incident in the Isle of Wight was typical of kiddie porn rings. "Have you heard of PIE?" he asked.

PIE stands for Paedophile Information Exchange, the British link to a network of men of all ages and classes. Members exchange pictures of children, lists of children's names, child pornography, and even children.

"You believe my father is a member," I stated flatly. Sickened, I went to stand at the window to gulp down some fresh air. I had come to protect two young children as well as to advocate on behalf of Mary Patricia. It was as though, all of a sudden, I belonged to—and was advocate for—a massive family of sisters and brothers.

"Do you hate your father?" White asked. I shook my head. "No," I said from my heart. "I think he's despicable." Why waste my energy hating such a pathetic creature?

I recounted a recent visit with one of my father's former friends. "Oh, he's quite dotty," the man said.

"He had an incestuous relationship with me," I said.

"Yes," he said, matter-of-factly. "I'm not at all surprised. He was a bit inclined that way." The conversation was hearsay, inadmissible evidence.

"Are you willing to testify at trial?" White asked. My answers were faithfully copied onto sheet after sheet of official police stationery.

"Yes."

"I shall arrest your father."

I stared at him, stunned, disbelieving. Mary Patricia cheered. I took a deep breath, trying to look dignified. I'd been believed by the authorities, not only in Canada but in the country where the crimes had occurred.

The case might never come to court, White warned me. There was not much concrete evidence and the only other witness available, my sister, barely remembered Easter 1954. (Box Hill didn't count. I couldn't remember seeing my father's *face*.) My father would probably state that I was crazy, that he'd visited me in the mental hospital. If my father was sent to trial, it would be a brave jury who'd dare convict a man in his seventies.

Elderly convicted offenders usually get probation, even though age doesn't stop them from molesting children. Two paedophiles, aged 79 and 81, had recently been arrested. They lived a stone's throw from my dad.

"They're incurable," White said. "All we can do is quarantine them for a while."

When it was all over I walked the length of the town's quaint High Street in a daze. Perpetrators are put on probation; victims get life.

It was a relief to say goodbye to my birth country. My trip down memory lane had filled me with sadness, a deep sense of betrayal. I felt like a foreigner in England, far from home. I flew back to Montreal for a last few days with Rob.

A bomb scare delayed my plane for twelve hours in London, and it was long past midnight by the time Rob got me out to the cottage. He bundled me into bed, where I stayed for three days nurturing the heartbroken, orphaned Child Within who'd turned in her own father and brought grief to her mother. "You did the right thing and you know it," said the Small Voice. "The shame's not yours." Nevertheless, I felt suicidal.

"Tell me," Rob urged.

I described the bottomless pits of neediness and loneliness inside me. "It's why I'm so overdependent—trying to get those needs met. I've opened a door to my childhood, to hell. And with it an emotional door. I feel . . . " I blew my nose, took a breath. "I feel all the terrible longings to be loved and special and wanted and held and touched."

Snippets of my previous visit popped into my head. I'd wanted to meet Rob's lady, for as long as I denied her existence, I wouldn't be able to let him go. Generously, she'd invited me to dinner and to stay at her place in town.

I could have been compliant, eager-to-please Mary Patricia, bottled up my feelings and left with a thank-you-for-having-me handshake. But I'd learned to say no. As soon as I spotted the thick, gold wedding band and matching diamond engagement ring on the third finger of her left hand I realized Rob and she were . . . ? I hurried from the apartment, weeping, defeated.

"It's not what you think." Rob tried to explain later, but I was too busy shouting to hear his answer. All I knew was that he didn't love me. "I do love you," Rob said, impatiently. "It's different."

"How can it be?" I yelled.

"I'm *in love* with her," he shouted.

"You don't have to *say* it," I screamed back.

A light went on. I'd been replaying the old drama: Daddy's Gone and I'm Going to Get Him Back and Damn Well Keep Him This

Time. I'd never win. I wanted to climb inside Rob to fill my unmet needs. He'd be too fragile to resist. Little by little, if he let me, I would wear him down, destroy him like the beautiful parasitoid that lives in victim-killer relationship with its host.

"I understand why you can't manage my neediness," I sighed.

"I'm not strong enough," he admitted sadly, taking me in his arms. I loved him. The last thing I wanted to do was hurt him.

"The relationship is young," he said, "but I'd leave it tomorrow if it ceased to be satisfying. I think it'll last a long time." It was in his best interests for me to leave him alone.

As if reading my mind Rob said tenderly, "You will see me again. You know that, don't you?"

"Yes," said the Small Voice firmly.

"Yes," I whispered.

"Were you ever 'in love' with me?" I asked. Rob thought for a moment. "I guess I skipped that part," he said. "I went straight to loving you."

"And you still do," I said quietly. He nodded. Relief flooded through me. It wasn't over.

"I've been testing you," he said, "though not always consciously. Are you testing me?"

"No. Not any more."

"Now come on," Rob grinned. "If you're going to learn to fish out west, we've got to buy you a magic fishing wand."

CHAPTER NINETEEN

FINDING MY FEET

It is in this refuge that dignity is restored, more of our preciousness is discovered, and we are mended in the broken places.

Rusty Berkus, In Celebration of Friendship

Simone de Beauvoir hiked the French Alps to develop her self-sufficiency. I moved west. The cottage I rented from the only friend I had in British Columbia was a far cry from my townhouse in Toronto. Its only heat source was a wood-burning stove, the shower was on the porch, and I cooked with propane gas, which ran out every ten days or so. Things I'd taken for granted in the city demanded my full attention and energy. I had to learn to light a fire. Until I bought a car, I would flag down the once-a-day rural bus to go shopping. A day in the city meant catching a ferry. I congratulated myself on my resourcefulness and determination, which had brought contentment, inner peace, and a sense of safety.

But the month before Christmas has always been a difficult time for me and November 1989 was no exception. I thought of Rob, of all the reasons why we weren't together. Like lightning zig-zagging across the sky I shot back to the time when Daddy left and Mummy, numb yet relieved at his departure, turned in on herself. Unable to attend to my emotional needs, my grief perhaps an unbearable reminder of her own, she soldiered on with a stiff upper lip and breaking heart.

I had a series of nightmares. Of Rob. Not being able to ask his help. Being alone, needy, anxious. Hiding in a friendless terrain with a predatory animal out to get me. A wolf. I dreamed increasingly of wolves.

My friend Penny had moved to Vancouver Island. She invited me to stay for a much needed break. I loved Victoria's jolly British funkiness, its elegant Empress Hotel. It reminded me of my paternal grandmother. For the first time I felt a compassion linking me to all the women in my family. (A few days earlier my mother's birth certificate had arrived from England, along with other research material I'd requested while in London. My maternal grandmother's first name had been Mary, like mine. She'd gone to London from her home by the sea to have her baby out of wedlock. She was a survivor. Like Mummy, like me.)

My confidence and energy surged after three days in the comfortable warmth of friendship. On the way home I whispered hopefully, "Good friends are coming to me easily and effortlessly." A fat iridescent rainbow plunged into a gorge to the right of the road. An omen, surely. Within a few days I found an Adult Children of Alcoholics group. At the end of the evening a woman gave me her phone number and invited me to call. "I'd love to introduce you to people," she said. Later that week I found the woman who would become my counsellor.

Lori had given me six possible therapy referrals. I spoke to three counsellors on the telephone and interviewed two personally. In the end, I relied on my instinct and chose Pamela. She is a feminist, knowledgeable and experienced in incest and child sexual abuse counselling and education; compassionate, warm, caring—yet tough and direct. She'd also just completed a book about women's experience of childhood sexual abuse. As a bonus, she fit a dream I'd had of a wise woman with long greying hair who would be my teacher and role model.

Other avenues I explored to ease me into the community were the local writers' group and Transition House, a safe home for battered women, where I hoped to work as a volunteer. There was no such program but I was invited to meet and share experience with the staff. Feeling supported and nurtured, I headed home. Before I got there, I heard on the car radio that fourteen female engineering students had been murdered at École Polytechnique in Montreal. A misogynist gunman had made innocent young women the scapegoats for his rage and powerlessness. From that moment I would align myself with women.

I tried writing to the Montreal Woman for Christmas but I couldn't get past the pain of her being with Rob. I wrote him a couple of letters; he didn't reply. I didn't call him, or he me. I replaced his photograph with a mirror. "I love and accept you, adult woman Trysh," I told my weeping reflection.

Christmas was one of the best I've ever had. I felt surrounded by the unconditional loving acceptance of my new friends: like-minded men and women committed to living honest, uncomplicated, mindful lives. It was like being part of a huge family. Sharing. Listening. Checking. Sharing. Our interactions were clear, open, direct, respectful.

My dreams and thoughts revolved increasingly around my relationship with Mummy. I recognized so many parts of myself that mirrored parts of her.

Mummy always made a big deal about dressing well. She always looked nice. Part of me thanked her for being a fine example to emulate; another part recoiled in anger and humiliation, remembering: "Let's see what kind of a clown you've made of yourself this time, Mary Patricia. You can't wear *that*." (Paradoxically, she stood up for me when some nosy local woman griped about my tight yellow cutoffs, sloppy sweater, no shoes and underwear. "Mind your own business," Mummy told her in no uncertain terms.) I see her standing by her dressing table, dabbing cream on her face from a white porcelain pot. She always looked neat, perfectly groomed, and clean. Perfumed. Brushed. An English rose.

Suddenly, I turned on my son, who had come to visit for the holidays. As we walked along the street, I recalled the shame and unworthiness I felt whenever I was in public with my Mum; I never lived up to her standards and expectations. I scathingly attacked the way he dressed; criticized the way he shuffled his feet. He grew darkly angry. Guilty and confused, I pulled myself up short, attempted to make amends. "Let's have coffee," I suggested desperately. In the restaurant I admitted my mistake. "I've made many mistakes," I said. "I'm sorry." We talked, trying to understand the other's viewpoint, and resolved the matter in an atmosphere of calm respect.

Rob called on New Year's Day 1990. I was painfully aware of the distance between us, that I'd been rejected as his Life Partner. "My feelings are the same for you," I faltered, "though somehow different." More real, perhaps. Less needy and obsessive. "It's over," I heard myself say. The romance, the denial, the anger. I felt only soft, silent sadness. Two weeks later I called him, to share a letter that arrived from Detective Inspector A. Snelling, Sussex Police, England.

I write to inform you that the matter which you reported to us and subsequently made a Statement to my Detective Sergeant White on 25th October 1989 has been fully investigated and resulted in your father being arrested on 14th November 1989.

It has been decided that no further action can be taken against your father having regard to all the available evidence. I can assure you that a full and thorough investigation has taken place.

My Detective Sergeant White worked closely with the local Social Services and I am satisfied at this time that [the children about whose protection I'd been concerned] are being well cared for, are safe and in no danger.

I would like to thank you for taking the time to call at this Police Station and to relive what I know was a most painful experience for you. Sergeant White has asked me to wish you well for the future, and I do hope that this letter will go some way to explain the current situation.

At half-past midnight I called Detective White. It was his day off. White's assistant arresting officer told me that my father's house had been searched under warrant, but nothing turned up: no porn, no lists, nothing suspicious. "Did my father threaten you?" I asked.

"He did get a bit stroppy," she admitted. He'd ordered them out of his house, angry and raving.

"What happened?" I asked. "Did you put cuffs on him?"

"I thought we might have to," she answered. "We got him calmed down."

"How?"

"I told him we had no intention of leaving," she said. "We had a job to do." I was incredulous. A *woman* standing up to *my Dad*? No meant nothing to my Daddy. I wondered how tall she was. He was like a great dark shadow over *me*. I still thought of my father as an adult; myself as a little child.

"He simmered down and went with us quietly to the station," she said.

My father denied he'd done anything to harm me. He told the police he couldn't understand my motivation for making the statement against him, insisted that I was crazy. They questioned him for hours in the presence of his lawyer. He spent six hours locked in a jail cell for his lawyer to come from London. I wonder what he felt in that cell? Did he experience the anger, isolation, stigma, humiliation, loneliness, and emotional hunger that I endured for all those years?

No other witnesses came forward. The children who were interviewed denied that they'd been hurt. Their mother "has been made fully aware of the situation," the constable told me. My half-sisters were neither found nor interviewed. (I believe they live in Holland, their mother's homeland.) I *do* know that one, or both, has children whom my father visits. His grandchildren. My half-brother was located in an institution—too ill to be of any use. I asked after my father's health. The police officer said she doubted he'd last much longer. "He's on his last legs," she said.

My Daddy taught me how to dance. I stood on his shoes, on my tippy toes, my little arms clasped around his long, lean legs. And I laughed up . . . up . . . up into his smiling face. Round and round he twirled me to the music of the 1940s. In the days of my innocence, long, long ago. My first love. My first lover. My Daddy.

News of my father's arrest and its aftermath left my soul bleeding. "I'm concerned you're doing too much," Pamela said. "Why not invite one of your friends to stay from back east?" I tried to think which friend I wanted but Mummy's face flashed in front of me. My forty-seventh birthday was around the corner; I'd do something really special to celebrate. I called Heather in Toronto. "How about spending our birthdays in San Francisco?"

It was a brilliant gift to myself. I'd been holding it against Rob that he hadn't taken me there, but in the airport, I let go my resentment. Rob wasn't a god or a hero. Just a good, kind, caring, vulnerable, wounded man. I sent him my love, holding him in my mind's eye healed and whole. "Thank you for being part of my journey," I wrote him. "Everything is working out in the best possible way. Everything always has." I also wrote my mother. Before I mailed the card I read it aloud to Heather:

Dear Mummy:

Today is my 47th birthday and I am thinking of you sadly and lovingly, thanking you for your part in creating me, nurturing me and bringing me through childhood.

Hold me in your mind's eye a maturing, beautiful, healing woman—that would be a gift for me. We may be estranged,

in retreat behind protective walls, but we are sometimes pre-
ciously close.

"You have changed," said Heather. "You're much more grown
up."

A card from Rob awaited me on my return home. He and Megan
had also jointly called me on my birthday. "It's quite safe," the
Small Voice whispered, "to let him go."

Life was looking up. I felt more loving, self-accepting, closer
to my new friends, less needy, more assertive, less uptight. I was
beginning to surrender control, stepping back to observe myself,
listening to feedback, sifting the possibilities before choosing a
response. I was changing. Being true to myself gave me great
satisfaction, increased my self-esteem and power.

"You're finding the mother in yourself," said Pamela.

On February 19th, walking up the mountain, I slipped on
melting snow, tearing the newly healed tissues around the spinal
cord surgery. Within days I lost bladder function. In extreme pain,
my leg purple and lifeless, I was transferred by ambulance from
the local hospital to a neuro-surgical unit in Vancouver. It's all
over, I thought. Excruciating surgery or the wheelchair. "Promise
me, Rob," I asked him on the phone, "to finish my book if I don't
pull through. I'm at peace this time, surrendering to what is, but
I feel no sense of future in the optimistic way I did then. I know
I can manage alone now. I can fill those empty spaces without
a man but I need my physical strength. I need wholeness in body
that I don't have and wonder if ever I will now."

My month-long stay in the hospital taught me some very important lessons: I was assertive, no longer a victim, I had choices.
"You're present in the here and now," Pamela said in one of our
daily telephone conversations. "Acting and speaking from a strong
centre." For the first time, I allowed the older nurses to mother
me. Instead of being ferociously defensive, as I had been in the
past, I lapped up their kind attention. My friends came visiting
regularly, even in the city, particularly Tim and Jer.

The moment I met him, Jer reminded me of my father: brown
eyes, glasses, hawk-like nose. But you only had to look *into* his
eyes to see the difference: he had gentleness and wisdom. In the
past I would have flirted outrageously and made a play for him.
I would have fallen in love with him, overwhelmed him with my
neediness and demands, guaranteed that he would abandon me.

Jer would be the man with whom I'd free myself from confusing all men with my father.

Tim was thirteen years my junior, divorced with two small daughters, with many of Rob's tastes and interests. The resemblance drew me to him. I recognized my task with both Tim and Jer: to separate the present from the past. I genuinely wanted to get to know both men, and let them get to know me. Be friends.

I went home in mid-March, still in great pain, but I refused a wheelchair. I limped slowly on a walker.

"Flawed! See, you're flawed," Helga the Hag taunted. "I knew it. Flawed. Flawed. Flawed."

"No, I'm not," I yelled, throwing my walker across the room. "I refuse to be disabled."

Very slowly, very very slowly, I could walk again. I put back the weight I'd lost, sat in the sun until my skin glowed, started writing again and, as my energy picked up, built up my strength walking and swimming. Friends continued dropping in, surrounding me with love. I felt safe, secure.

I don't know whether the memory came first or the dreams. Hands. Big hands. Grasping, calloused, workman's hands around my naked, budding body. I squirm and wriggle, terrified. The man in the hat with ice-blue eyes leers. I've re-entered this memory. I'm struck in the face. How could he do that with his hands around my writhing naked body? The smack is sharp, stinging across my face, humiliating me. I can't stop the man. I can't stop the memory in the middle of a chill March night.

In the morning I called Pamela. She talked about "felt" memory, at cellular level. It was safe now for me to feel, smell, taste, touch, see, hear. With one notable exception: my dog's red tongue licking me and the smell of his breath repulsed me.

A few days later another flashback enveloped me.

The man holding me has a hard-on sticking through his unbuttoned trousers. He rubs up against my skinny thighs. His eyes glaze over crazily. He throbs against me. Sticky, messy stuff like egg whites squirts against my vagina and partway inside.

In the wake of each memory came intense grief, followed by peace. I began to feel more spontaneous, playful. Yet, at other times, more serious than before. "That's adult," Pamela said. "The good, ordinary enthusiasm is integration."

Heather came to visit at the end of March. Tim helped me get my garden started, turning over the sod while I sprinkled seeds.

Our friendship was comfortable, comforting, easy. We laughed a lot together, had fun. I told him I was worried about Rob. I had the feeling he was headed toward, if not actually in, a depression. I wanted to offer him solace, invite him out west. "Rob's a very very lucky man," said Tim. At last I wrote the Montreal Woman thanking her for her part in my healing. She replied saying she was glad her presence hadn't been all negative.

At the beginning of April a small, closed group formed out of our larger group to work intensively through the Twelve Steps for Adult Children of Alcoholics. Over the next year, it proved to be a powerful tool for change, a chance to connect with others without losing my self, in a supportive atmosphere.

By Easter I felt much stronger. To celebrate my healing and liberation from Easter 1954 I gave a party. While I was getting things ready I listened to a choral concert on the radio. "I hate that stuff," said Mary Patricia.

"It reminds me of Mummy," I said. I felt close to her that morning. On impulse I dialled her number.

She was cold, distant. I guessed she was protecting herself, fearing I might hurl more accusations. I spoke quietly, from my heart, melting her defenses. She asked where I was. I described the scene, my dog, myself. We talked of Daddy's arrest and how the British police had asked Interpol to track me down. The local police had finally found me but I'd already been to England and made my statement. I wanted to impress on her that the authorities believed me, even if she didn't.

"Nothing like that ever happened to me," she said. "Forget the past now. Don't bury it—I don't mean that . . . "

"Let it go?" I suggested. She sounded relieved. "Yes, that's right," she said.

At last I felt heard, believed, understood. It wasn't a perfect conversation. She got in some digs about my poor parenting. "Yes," I admitted. "I am accountable for my mistakes but Tristram and I are mending fences now." I wanted her approval but it was not forthcoming. I said I was helping other survivors of incest and child sexual abuse. "Oh," she replied sadly, as if she wished I did something else. "Are you happy?"

"Yes," I said emphatically. Being happy had always been her highest priority for me. For the first time I felt I hadn't let her down.

My increasing self-confidence and inner strength was reflected in my writing but I wanted Rob's input. I'd sent him several chapters with letters of encouragement but heard nothing. At the end of April I called. "I've made some notes," he said listlessly. "I'm very fragile, but I've yet to hit bottom."

"Don't worry about the book," I insisted. "Rest, get strong and well again. Then we must talk."

"Thanks for your letter," he said. "I like it that you love me as a fuck-up." We laughed.

"I'm really worried about him," I said to Jer.

"Don't worry," he replied. "Pray."

"I need support with the writing," I said. "I'm ashamed of my grammar."

"I'll help you," Jer offered.

"You will?"

"I'm not a professional editor like Rob," he said. "But I can spell, I'm good at grammar, I give good hugs."

"You're right there," I grinned.

I thought about all the times I'd been weak, needy, depressed; feeling I was letting people down. Those who loved me rallied to my side, did what was in my best interests. Perhaps it was time to let Rob make his journey without my help or interference.

"Yes," agreed the Small Voice firmly.

"I love Rob," I shouted. I was walking up the mountain in the pouring rain. A deer ran across the path ahead of me. "Pam's right. It'd be more loving to let him be."

"You never know what's going to happen," said the Small Voice.

"Huh?"

I dream that Rob, looking very glamorous, is not able to escort me to the dance. If I ask, he'll reject me. Instead, I invite Bob, a more ordinary version of Rob with whom I feel extremely comfortable. He won't reject me.

"Congratulations," Pamela said at my next session. "Rob's fallen off his pedestal flat on his ass. You're not in love with him any longer."

"I love him for the real person he is," I said. When the right moment came I would talk to him. I'd be clear, open, confident that what I said would be more than adequate.

"Know that the right words will come," Pam assured me. "When in doubt, describe."

Bits and pieces of memory filtered my waking hours, my dreams and nightmares. I was open to whatever was coming. I continued writing four or five hours daily, and visited friends. Hélène massaged me once a week. She and I were becoming good friends.

A black shoe. A man tying his laces. Diamond rings. Fear. Disgust. A fat white belly hanging out.

"What happened?" I ask the Child in the Meadow. "What else happened in the basement?"

"I'm scared to tell you," she replied. "I need you to protect and take care of me."

"I will," I promised.

Hélène massages my toes. She wiggles each one individually. I used to wiggle my toes as a child whenever I felt acutely anxious. Last night I had insomnia and genital anxiety again. I covered my vulva with a pillow as if to forbid access. Flash. Flash. Flash. Black jeans. Rob's with two buttons at the waistband. Pamela's. I hate it when she wears them. For the last week I've worn my black jeans. I feel invincible in them. The man tying his shoelaces wears cheap black trousers with a shiny seat. He gets up and tucks in his rumpled white shirt. He has Y-front underpants. White. I saw his penis sticking out.

He ties his laces. Waiting. While I . . . The memory rips through my whole body. Urine splash on newsprint and I am enveloped in humiliating shame, fear, anxiety. My eyes are focused low on black shoes. Black laces. Black moment. Two other men are coming into my awareness. The man with flashy rings is like a fat white slug. His stomach hangs over his boxer shorts that button at the waist. The button is yellow with age, what they called a utility button during the war. He leaves slime down my legs. The other man has a tattoo on his right biceps. A bulging snake or a dragon, something wriggling and blue.

Images of men crowding round me while I struggle to escape. One man stamps on my right foot, holds me tight. I feel nothing. See only a picture in the far distance. In the far corner of the basement where men molested me at age eleven. I have this odd, uneasy, flickering recollection of a matronly figure in black evening dress. Soft tears trickle down my face for the little girl I was.

There were eight of them. Brothers, sons, and fathers all chaotic, excited, writhing flesh. I'm stripped naked. A small defenceless sacrifice. First served, first come. Paedophiles on a long Easter weekend. Stinking bodies. (I thought it was me who was dirty, who smelled.) Ejaculating on me, in me. In my mouth, my hair, my face, on my body. Everywhere sticky snail slime traces. Burning, choking hotness in my throat. Pain pierces. Sharp firebrand poker. Poke her. Pain shooting blinding interplanetary penetrating HOWL of a little girl. Me.

A great big slobbering German shepherd with a toothy grin, long pink tongue, wagging tail, bounds in. Like a great wolf, it stands up with its paws on my shoulders. I smell its breath. It slobbers on my face, licks me. Its furry tummy feels familiar; we have a dog at home. It's almost comforting, a relief after . . . The men close in on me, pushing, shoving, squeezing, jeering, knocking me to the ground. They're above me, rolling me around. I'm stomped on. Stepped on. Hoopla. Party-time. "Doggy's wanking off in pretty baby." The photographs were the easiest part.

I go to sleep crying. I wake up crying. How can I ever let anyone know? Pamela's voice breaks the rage, the wanting to kill my dog. "It's the most difficult, accepting an animal . . . "

"You mean, this has happened to others?"

"Yes," she replies. "Moreover, what you've described is quite consistent with the things you've already remembered happening in the Isle of Wight." I'm flabbergasted.

My inclination was to isolate myself. Hide. Instead I confided in my group, in my friends. "I've scrubbed and scrubbed," I said helplessly. "I still feel dirty. Even though I know every cell in my body has changed five times over in the last thirty-six years I feel soiled, sullied."

"Use a smudge," suggested a friend versed in native Indian customs. "Waft the smoke from cedar or sage over your whole body. Use a cedar-scented soap."

When Jer and Tim offered hugs, I recoiled. "No," I said. "I'm unclean, unworthy."

"No, you're not." They shook their heads sadly, enraged that grown men should have done such things to a child, to me their friend, to anyone. At last I allowed their embraces, both at once. I sobbed, mostly with relief: I'd remembered the very worst that had happened to me.

CHAPTER TWENTY

DANCING IN MY BONES

Through the power of mindfulness, of not clinging, condemning, or identifying with what arises, we break that chain of conditioning and open to the possibility of genuine freedom.

Joseph Goldstein, Seeking the Heart of Wisdom

When the seals returned to inlet waters at the beginning of June, I moved from my cottage on the mountainside to the large rambling white house Jer rented by the ocean. He needed a roommate; I needed temporary accommodation during the four-month visit of my landlady's relatives.

The first week was disorienting. Jer was the first man I'd lived with apart from my father and husband. Not surprisingly, a barrage of memories and projections assaulted me. I fought another skirmish with the past.

Headlights sweep across the wall; he's coming home late at night. I stir, terrified. Frozen I listen to his footsteps coming towards my room on his way to the . . .

The spell breaks. It is Jer, on his way to the kitchen for a cup of coffee. My doorknob does not turn; the bathroom is the other way. The present is not the past.

"There's something I'd like to share with you," I told Jer after a few days. "I want to tell you about mixing you up with my father and my husband."

He was stunned.

I laughed. "I'm rushing around tidying, cleaning the counters, doing dishes—getting everything ship-shape for six o'clock."

"Why six o'clock?"

"That's when my husband came home. I always got antsy—terrified actually—that he'd be angry, that something would be wrong. I'd always need a drink to calm down."

"You don't need to do any of that with me," Jer said.

"I know," I replied. "I just wanted to tell you. Saying it aloud takes away the power of the memories."

"Would you like a hug?" he asked. Ever respectful of boundaries, he always asked before touching me.

I laughed suddenly as he embraced me. "Anyway, I'd make a terrible wife," I said, testing him.

"I don't think so," he said. "You'd be wonderful."

"Oh, I mean in the traditional sense," I said, earnestly.

"I wasn't talking traditional," Jer replied.

"Really?" I was delighted. I'd worked out what I wanted in relationship—to be accepted for who I am in a passionate best friendship—but I'd never considered what my partner might want. "What qualities would you want in a partner, Jer?"

Jer thought carefully. "I want to be accepted for who I am. I want to matter. I want her to have her own purpose in life. I want her to be an independent, free-thinking person." He stopped to sip his coffee and light a cigarette. I waited, wondering what was coming. "I want her to have strong boundaries like you do. I don't want to be a father to a needy little girl."

That evening, I walked on the deserted beach with my dog and gazed up at the first twilight star. Before I made a commitment to anyone I would make a commitment to myself, "marry" myself. I slipped a silver ring from my right hand to my wedding finger and vowed never again to lose my separate, unique, individual self in a relationship. Lights twinkled on the far shore. Leaves and grasses quivered in the evening breeze. It would be dark in a few moments. I was ready to let Rob go, and to get on with my life without him. "Call him," said the Small Voice unequivocally. It was easier said than done.

For the next few days I felt mildly depressed, irritable, bored, and indecisive.

"Being flaky doesn't suit you," Pamela said. I was infuriated. How dare she?

"Told you to get off the pity-pot, eh?" said Jer. I stuck my tongue out at him and went outside to roar my anger into the wind. Energy burst through my block. Next morning I called Rob.

"Working together isn't working," I began.

"You don't need me," he said. "You're a strong writer."

"It's not only the writing . . . " I faltered. "I need to let you go. I've made a fool of myself over you. I've woken up and realized I've been playing a game with myself that, really, you love me more than her and that any minute you're coming back. I need time to heal the shame, to let go of all the hopes and dreams. I don't want any contact until after your birthday."

"You've given me a most loving gift," Rob replied. "It feels clean. I no longer need feel obligated to you, although you know it's not finished."

"It's not over." I fed his statement back.

"Oh no," he replied, "but I'm freed to do my healing—it's my top priority. And there are things I have to finish up here in the east. A year ago I'd have been devastated. Now I'm relieved."

"I hope you'll come home, out west, one day," I said. "I hope you'll find me . . . that we'll find the magic innocence we had before all the pain came. I hope I'll see you again."

"You're going to be seeing a lot of me," Rob answered.

"At Megan's graduation," I smiled. "At her first wedding . . . second wedding . . . Ph.D graduation." We both laughed.

"I'll see you at the launch party," he said.

"You're a good man, Rob."

"You're a fine person—a loyal and loving friend."

"I'm not abandoning you."

"Oh no, I don't feel that."

"I want you to know I'm wearing a wedding band. I don't want to get involved with anyone. My healing is top priority too. It's to remind me."

We tied up some business ends before bringing the conversation to a close. "Have a good summer," Rob said.

"You too," I replied. "I love you very much, Rob."

"I love you, Trysh."

I lit a red candle (for transformation) and burned in its flame a piece of white paper on which I'd written:

> I release all past shame and guilt and cleanse myself of the karma connected to mistakes with Rob: overwhelming neediness and expectations; pain, drama, chaos and creating unhealthy excitement; attempts to recreate parents in him; attempts to recreate unhealed childhood with him.

May they stay part of the past to do no further harm, freeing
us/me for a new relationship to come.

I scattered the ashes on the sea. Then I pushed into the waves
a doll-house Hope Chest with a rose attached to its lid containing
my wishes for a deeper love in future. "Au revoir. Goodbye, Rob.
I let you go," I whispered into the salty air. I ended my ceremony
by throwing blue irises into the sea and reading some poetry.

A little over a month later a police officer was shot and killed
in the small Quebec village where Rob was living. The ensuing
armed stand-off at Oka would dominate the news until after Rob's
birthday. The nightly TV news was of familiar territory, including
Rob's front gate. "You may be letting Rob go," Jer said. "But, obviously, you're not meant to forget him."

I spent the summer cementing my relationships with Jer and
Tim, making and developing new female friendships, writing, attending workshops, healing. I met innumerable survivors. Every
time I bore witness to a courageous story, I knew that countless
women, and men too, have risen again from the ashes of trauma
to lead normal lives.

My face was changing rapidly. The blank, drugged expression
in my eyes, the hallmark of a murdered soul, had disappeared.
There was a fullness about my features, a wholesomeness.

"You look like the girl next door," Tim said. I was thrilled. No
one had ever said that to me before.

"You mean you could take me home to Mum?" I joked.

The Mary Patricias were growing up, no longer external images
but incorporated into myself. The teenage part of me, which I
called Hope, was maturing as I gradually accepted her idiosyncrasies. I understood how hard it must have been for my mother
to cope with me when I entered puberty; yet I also sympathized
with Hope's instability. I worried that I was becoming too aggressive and sharp-edged, too overbearing, stubborn, arrogant,
controlling. I knew I still needed to swing into middle ground;
but strong men and women respected me, liked my assertiveness,
accepted and loved me the way I was. Yet something held me
back—a fear that blocked my path to being a complete, whole
woman.

When I was with women my own age, whom I admired, part
of me still felt like a child. And in some deeper place, I felt a
sense of not quite deserving to be a woman. I feared Aphrodite's
sexuality, her passion, her capacity to love, her creativity.

The part of me I disliked wore a tight leopard-skin mini-dress, black fishnet pantyhose, and high-heeled boots that showed off her long, skinny legs. Hair cascaded over her face and down her back, a tiger's mane of bottled blonde, green where she'd left the dye on too long, and black at the roots. She was a Barbie doll hooker waiting to be rescued and transformed. She hurled herself at me from the far corner of the darkness.

"What do you need or want from me?" I asked softly.

"To be held," she said instantly.

"How have you served me as a Blonde Bimbo?" I asked, my arms around myself.

"By being an object I helped you to survive," she answered.

"Now you needn't do that any more," I reassured her. Within weeks I felt more womanly, more graceful, more sentient, more relaxed. I felt grounded, integrated, whole. My legs felt strong, my back tender but pain-free. By fall I weighed 150 pounds and felt magnificent.

In a ritual ceremony at a women's workshop I placed before me an iron bar, a piece of green prickly seaweed, and a sea-shell. "I leave behind my fetters and take back my strength," I stated to the assembled group. "I leave behind my prickles and take back the green of unconditional love. I leave behind my shell and take back my femininity, which I've seen reflected in each of you."

The next night, I sat laughing and chatting in the hot tub under a harvest moon. I was comfortably nude, in a circle of eight naked people. Six were men. It was a rite of passage.

I wanted to let go all the anger and blame against my parents, against all my childhood perpetrators. Although I sometimes felt anger and sadness that my father was never a real "Daddy," my grief was fleeting. In order to concentrate on a new future, I de-vised two letting-go rituals. The first, a Fight Back against the men in the hotel, Easter 1954.

From eight pieces of paper I fashioned eight erections and wrote on each the word RAPIST with whatever I could remember of each man. Then I penned an appropriate punishment underneath. The owner of the dog, for instance, received "violent murder." Lighting a red candle I burned each "penis" in its flame, chanting my hopes that each man be brought to justice somewhere, some-how, caught by his own stupidity in an ego-tripping slip. "Guilty," says the judge. "Guilty as charged." I threw the ashes on the sea and turned toward home without looking back.

Two weeks later, I held the second ritual. The table is set with an old lace cloth. There are flowers, candles, a photograph of my father in a heart-shaped frame, and a copy of his birth certificate. A single chair is at the table. My father's. I have cleaned and polished it with reverence as if it had belonged to some beloved person. It is the only possession of his that I have. I hadn't intended bringing it out west—I was going to burn it in Rob's fireplace—but the movers packed it. Now it's been retrieved from its dusty corner in Jer's garage. Today is my father's seventy-seventh birthday. I shall consider it his last.

I headed the procession down to the beach holding two giant rainbow-striped candles. Jer carried my father's chair high in the air. On its seat lay a large fungus, *Fomitopsis pinicola*, which native medicine people believe restores a part of the soul that is diseased or dead. Tim came next, toting a box of firewood. Five women friends followed. Tim collected a ring of stones to contain the fire that Jer built underneath the chair. As it caught I threw the birth certificate and the photograph, knotted together with a white ribbon, into the flames. "I waited all my life for you, Daddy," I stated. "Now I release you to the fire. I release you to the air. I release you to the earth. I release you to the sea. May you go in peace. Leave me in peace." The women contributed readings, songs, a Buddhist prayer. One drummed. Another threw a fat pinecone on the fire. After the feast I knew the ashes were gone, taken out on the afternoon tide. Jer said I'd never find the "gravesite," but I did once. A bird had graced it with a white feather. *Pax vobiscum*. By late September a storm had moved the rocks around. Where once there were sandy patches was seaweed.

I hadn't bargained for my father's ritual to open a doorway and propel me into working through my mother, but it did. For six weeks I dreamed about Mummy while I grew from child to adult grieving her. The final dream was about a spotted powerful snake rising up from my dog's basket. I'm not certain whether to be afraid so I run to Mummy for help, comfort, and advice. I stand beside her single bed. Her white hair is spread out upon her pillow. She gives me all that I need. I look at her again with love. She is me. I'm looking at myself.

On a golden afternoon in early October I walked once again along a beach. I felt free. The sun warmed my face and bare arms. I watched glinting ripples of light dance upon the sea, then I watched the waves lap at the pebbly beach. Jer had taught me to read tide tables but I'd neglected to look at today's details. I'd loved living with him. Although we often got together since my return to the small cottage, I missed him.

He'd taught me so much about relating, about trust and acceptance; the specialness of being ordinary. Not only had we worked out all those irritating small details about who likes what, but he'd also given me the confidence to know that I was capable of a completely normal adult man/woman partnership without losing my self, without being needy, dependant, or possessive. Living with him had softened my hard edges. I loved him.

I sensed a presence and turned, wondering who'd crept up beside me. It was Spenser and Elizabeth, my inner parents. They'd been with me, faithful and loving, since January 1988. It was time to say goodbye, to integrate them into me, for I was my own good father and mother.

A week later I was waiting in the cinema line-up and saw a man who, from the rear, looked so like Rob that my heart leapt. Unexpected tears forced me to turn away.

This man was Rob's height, with the same shoulders, hands thrust deep in pockets, slim hips, long legs. Even the shape of his head was the same although this man's hair was grey. (Maybe Rob's was, too, by now.) As he turned his head slightly I turned so I could see him full face. The lump in my throat felt like a rock. I wanted to cry out. The man was not Rob, of course. Yet in that moment I knew I no longer felt possessive. Rob was with someone else now. It felt okay, acceptable. I felt no jealousy, only a profound affection and a feeling that the past was long ago, a misty memory for a rainy day. One day I'd see him again. I'd learned to let him go and knew he'd always be my friend.

Another surprise awaited me on my son's twenty-first birthday in mid-October. Tristram and his girlfriend arrived at my door with all their belongings and large dog. They stayed a month. For most of the time I felt like a good mother—loving, accepting, comfortable—but I worried they'd never leave.

I talked with Tristram. I handled it a lot better than the conversation about his appearance the previous Christmas. Then I'd been unable to suspend critical judgement; this tiff was about my difficulties in setting boundaries easily, speaking my truth clearly, without defenses. Even so, my words came out wrong. His anger erupted in a burst of tears. "You like Megan more than me."

I reassured him that I loved him. "But it's hard," I said, "when I don't hear from you for months on end. Both of you know you can call collect. You're my son. She's not my daughter." But I felt torn.

"Megan is a feminist, shares many interests with me. We exchange ideas and information. We laugh at the same jokes. We both love her father. With you—well, you're my flesh and blood, who I nurtured and nourished and nursed and did the best job parenting that I was able to at the time, given the circumstances . . . But I do love you."

"Why d'you always think you were such a bad mother?" Tristram asked.

"Because I didn't fill your needs when you were a little boy," I answered. We cried in each other's arms.

Next morning I said, "I'm sorry about the way I handled things last night. I did it better than I would have a year ago. In another year I'd do it even better."

"I'm sorry too," he said.

"Can I have a hug?" I asked. We embraced.

"I love you, Tristram," I whispered.

"I love you, Mum," he replied.

"Oh, thank you," I wept. "Thank you for that."

In a few days he'd be on the road with his girlfriend, carving out his life and destiny. I hadn't done so badly, after all. I was willing to listen, to learn, to talk. Filled with relief and love I knew this visit had been a new start. He was his own man now, and he'd be back.

Two nights before they left, the three of us lay sprawled on my bed watching television, the dogs snoring beside us. When the telephone rang I didn't want to answer. "It's urgent," whispered the Small Voice.

Jer had collapsed in his garage and had not regained consciousness. He was on life-support systems in the hospital. He was to be flown to the city. A suspected aneurism.

I watched the helicopter take him above the tall trees, among the bright stars that he loved. One fell, leaving a silvery trail across the sky. I knew my dear friend would not come back.

Jer died the next evening, at peace. For the first time in my life, I didn't feel abandoned.

CHAPTER TWENTY-ONE

INTO THE LIGHT

There is . . . an arrow of time through which we are forever becoming, changing, and enfolding all that has ever been and still is. The most and the least we can do is try to keep up with this becoming.

Roy Laurens, Fully Alive

It's more than three years since I began my healing journey. During the first year, as my pain got worse, I often questioned whether to go on, for my chances of getting through seemed slim. Like millions of others abused as children, I blocked out almost all my early memories until I was mature enough, and it was safe enough, to deal with them. Love, often from unexpected quarters, has sustained me. Now that I know what happened, I'm rid of all the addictions and compulsions. The craziness is gone. Life is cleaner, clearer, saner. The future holds endless possibilities, and I know that everything works out in the best possible way.

My one regret is that I have not reconciled with my mother. During the preparation of this book I agonized about its impact on her. For most of my life I tried hard to love her, placating her in guilty duty, behaving in the way I thought a daughter should towards a mother. Once my story tumbled out, I was able to see more clearly.

For years I railed against her, latterly that she did not protect me. How could she? My father held us hostage. Constantly on the alert, never knowing what's coming next, a battered woman's only friend is exhaustion. We have hotlines in the 1990s. Family problems are publicly discussed, yet battery and rape and incest still flourish. In the 1940s and '50s, silence reigned over the domestic brutality behind the dream of upstanding breadwinning husband, content wife, and happily obedient children.

I've stopped hating or blaming my mother. In coming to terms with my own story, I found deep compassion for her. She is a wounded, damaged woman who, to protect herself, has had to deny. Sometimes I feel as if I'm healing for her, too, by breaking a generational cycle of shame and abuse. A family friend told me that my mother "didn't know *how* to love." When a woman has never felt loved, how can she unconditionally accept another? My father stole her from me, turning us against each other by his manipulation and deceit. A child made to carry the secret shame of sexual abuse does act out, becoming difficult to manage and less than endearing.

My mother did what she could to protect me after the divorce. She appointed legal guardians who, in the event of her death, would provide for me and my sister, safe from my father's overt and dangerous violence.

When I slammed down the telephone on her and yelled, "As far as I'm concerned you're dead," she mourned my rejection for months. She could not understand that I was protecting myself against her inability to hear my pain; but it's not something I'd do now. Now that I am who I really am, I can let others be who they really are as well.

My sister has tried to tell her about the book but she doesn't want to talk about me or my life. She "wishes me no harm and hopes I find peace" and "can't bear any more hurt" from me.

I doubt I'll see my mother again. She is quite frail and the news of my father's arrest "shattered her." I'm glad now there was no trial, for she'd have been called to testify on behalf of my father. Clearly she couldn't have withstood the pressure. I wrote her for her seventy-sixth birthday, enclosing photographs, news of her grandson, and telling her, truthfully at last, "I love you." Months later she sent a message through my sister that she prefers "silence and memories." She was pleased that I look "well and happy" but "wasn't keen" on keeping the pictures.

I sit on the stairs outside the drawing-room listening. Mummy plays the piano. Debussy, Chopin, Beethoven, Bach. I'm supposed to be in bed, but I've been coming every night since Daddy left. I want so much to climb up on her knee, to be held; but I dare not interrupt. She's inside a private bubble of solace, unreachable. Night after night I sit here, avoiding my lonely bedroom and the dark. I haven't reached her yet.

It's been an uphill battle to see my mother through the eyes of an adult rather than through those of the Child Within. Mary Patricia is grown up now and able to give up the longing for a perfect Mummy. She did the best she could, of that I am convinced. I've come home to her in my heart. I can forgive her because I can forgive myself.

Collecting tadpoles. Riding my bike in the park. Shuffling through rust-coloured leaves in autumn. Planting a flower garden. Nasturtiums, hollyhocks, poppies, delphiniums. Building a cabin in the old vegetable garden from bean poles and leaves. Watching raindrops dance on shiny streets. Mummy said they were fairies. Learning to watercolour. Winning a drama competition. Lines from Shakespeare. Swimming in the river by moonlight.

I close my eyes, and visualize a box. It's made of cedar, inlaid with mother of pearl, coral, amber, lapis lazuli, obsidian. Into this box I've poured every memory of childhood, each washed clean. I take the box to the cemetery beside the old white house where I grew up. I walk up the path and take the second gateway on the left. It's closed and locked, but it wasn't always. On the right-hand side, halfway down, underneath a holly tree, is a grave decorated with a large white marble cat. The grave honours a child who died, aged seven. I used to wonder why she'd died, not me. I place the precious box in this special place; my perpetrators have not won.

There are a million and one things I am grateful for, and know that I deserve: the beauty of the shining sea, the snowcapped mountains, the lush forest, the trust of children, my dog wagging his tail in friendly greeting, my friends. For those of us who choose to heal and go beyond survival, my prayer is that we find serenity and dignity. Healing is a way of life, a spiritual path.

I feel liberated, adult, whole; connected to other women, worthy of a Life Partner. I belong in the world, responsible for my part in its growth and healing. The past is not forgotten, but it is over. I'm not attached to it. I've opened up to unconditional love and anger. I've come into my womanhood, my sexuality, my power. I'm proud to be in the circle of women protecting the children. I've found my self and I love her.

I still have flashbacks now and then, but the "bad" days are the exception, and within the normal range of ups and downs.

They are the tests and challenges of recovery. During them I realize how far I've come on my journey.

I'm decreasingly introspective, keep my own counsel more, ask for help when necessary. I am more serious and a lot calmer, but I have more fun. I allow my feelings to flow one into the next while I remain centred and focused. I aim to speak my truth from my heart and make my choices wisely. It's imperative to see things from many directions and take responsibility for what I see.

In December 1990, I lodged a formal complaint with the Ontario College of Physicians and Surgeons against the psychiatrist I saw between 1971 and 1978 in Toronto. A hearing is "highly probable." I'll be going to bat for the young married woman that I was and, in a way, for the child I was too. For to be scrutinized by male medical professionals won't be that much different from being surrounded by men in a hotel basement. They'll be looking at my private self, holding the power. The big difference is that I'm doing the challenging this time. Mary Patricia learned to protect herself from adult authority. I have emerged from those armaments to correct, as much as is possible, the past.

I had a dream the other night in which my mother and Megan helped me prepare for a meeting with my father. I thought he would apologize, but I was wrong. Knowing that he'd forever hide behind denial, I faced him, adult, strong, compassionate. Accepting reality.

And the future? I want to go to university. I want to give workshops and lectures; to write about and educate people about healing from incest. Beyond that I want a very private life. Be married. Live in a house by the sea. Be a grandmother. Tend my garden. Make jam. Knit.

The end is the beginning; life is a circle. Mary Patricia, the self-possessed toddler, has come home to herself.

Spring came early this year.

POSSIBLE INDICATORS OF CHILD SEXUAL ABUSE

Sexual abuse cannot be identified by racial, cultural, or socio-economic background. It is also rare to observe overt physical symptoms. Sexually abused children, however, *do* share some common characteristics which, although not conclusive, are suggestive of sexual abuse when observed over time and in particular combinations.

Behavioural Indicators

- Unusual sexual knowledge.
- Persistent and inappropriate sexual play for the child's age and development level (including sexual play with toys).
- Sexualized expressions of affection.
- Excessive masturbation.
- Simulated sexual acts with siblings or friends or sexual attention to pets or animals.
- Precocious or flirtatious behaviour.
- Sexualized kissing in relationships with parents and friends.

Courtesy of The Metropolitan Toronto Special Committee on Child Abuse, revised July 1990.

- Sexual preoccupations.
- Compulsive sexual behaviour (i.e., grabbing breasts or genitals or compulsively removing clothes).
- Confusion about sexual norms.
- *Sudden change* in feelings about a particular person or place (e.g., "I hate Uncle So-and-So").
- Unusual fear of a particular person or people (e.g., men); fear of going home; fear of going to daycare or being left alone; fear of real or imagined objects or persons; fear of monsters, masks, uniforms, persisting beyond the normal time period, immobilizing the child, causing extreme patterns of flight and fright.
- Evidence of an unusually secretive "special" relationship with an older person, particularly one involving elements of bribery, trickery, or coercion.
- Nightmares, night terrors, and sleep disturbances (nightmares are uncommon for children under age three).
- Self-destructive behaviour such as drug/alcohol abuse, prostitution or indiscriminate sexual activity, self-mutilation, suicide threats/attempts, being "accident-prone," running away.
- Dramatic behavioural changes (e.g., acting out or disruptive behaviour causing difficulties with other children and affecting school adjustment and play).
- Overly compliant or, conversely, overly aggressive and destructive or anti-social behaviour.
- Compulsive lying and/or confusion regarding personal reality (e.g., dissociation, multiple personalities).
- Global distrust of adults or specific distrust of adults of the same sex or resembling the perpetrator.
- Regressive toilet training problems resulting in child being toilet trained again.
- Possible learning disabilities that may not be evident for some time and might show up at later developmental stages.
- Regressive infantile behaviour (such as bedwetting, thumb-sucking, dramatic and persistent crying unrelated to any other event); tantrums or conversely, pseudo-mature behaviour.
- Clinging or compulsive seeking of affection or attention by both boys as well as girls.
- Chronic depression, anxiety, withdrawal, phobic behaviour.
- Poor peer relationships, self-image, overall physical care.
- Attempts at disclosure either verbally or through artwork, essays, or journals.

Physical Indicators

- Pregnancy.
- Sexually transmitted disease.
- Vaginal infections.
- Torn, stained, or bloody underwear.
- Trauma to breasts, buttocks, lower abdomen, thighs, genital, or rectal areas.
- Foreign bodies in the genital, rectal, or urethral openings.
- Pain, itching in the genitals or throat; difficulty going to the bathroom or swallowing.
- Enlarged vaginal opening or redness in the genital area.
- Recurring physical ailments with no apparent somatic base (e.g., frequent stomach-aches, persistent sore throats, vomiting).
- Eating disorders (e.g., refusing to eat or eating constantly).

APPENDIX B

COPING SKILLS

These are some of the coping skills used by child sexual abuse survivors that develop into adult behaviour and become inseparable from it. This is by no means an exhaustive list.

- Numbing.
- Dissociation: "forgetting" traumatic incident while it's happening.
- Spacing out.
- Mental and physical illness.
- Minimizing: "It really wasn't that bad."
- Rationalizing.
- Denying.
- Wearing masks: acting one way while feeling another, wearing too much make-up, bizarre dress, hiding face behind hair or sunglasses, etc.
- Performing to get attention and/or to conform with expectations.
- Need to be controlling: bossiness, talking too much, manipulation.
- Acting out: destructive behaviour, being "accident-prone," aggressive, tough, cynical, feigned indifference, lying, stealing, cheating.
- Objectifying self: wearing revealing or tight clothes.
- Self-mutilation.
- Suicide attempts.
- Multiplexity (multiple personalities).
- Depression, hyper-vigilance: always checking that you are safe.

- Running away: moving frequently, changing jobs.
- Living in a fantasy world or in the intellect, watching TV excessively.
- Sleeping difficulties: insomnia, over-sleeping.
- Workaholism.
- Creating drama and excitement.
- Addictions to substances or sex, to gambling or shopping.
- Being so busy there's no time for memory or painful feelings to steal into the empty spaces deep inside.
- Eating difficulties: anorexia, bulimia, over-eating.
- Compulsive behaviour: caretaking, co-dependency, belonging to cults or sects, over-exercising, gambling, shopping.

BIBLIOGRAPHY

Books

Abrams, Jeremiah (ed). *Reclaiming the Inner Child*. Los Angeles: Jeremy P. Tarcher, 1990.

Anand, Margo. *The Art of Sexual Ecstasy: The Tantric Path of Sacred Sexuality for Western Lovers*. Los Angeles: Jeremy P. Tarcher, 1989.

Bass, Ellen, and Laura Davis. *The Courage to Heal: A Guide for Women Survivors of Child Sexual Abuse*. New York: Harper & Row, 1988.

Beatty, Melody. *Beyond Codependency*. New York: Harper & Row, 1989.

————. *Codependent No More*. New York: Harper & Row, 1987.

Berkus, Rusty. *In Celebration of Friendship*. Santa Monica: Red Rose Press, 1990.

Black, Claudia. *It Will Never Happen to Me*. New York: MAC Publications, 1981.

Block, Joel. *Friendship: How to Give It, How to Get It*. New York: Collier Books, 1981.

Blum, Ralph. *The Book of Runes*. London: Eddison/Sadd Editions, 1982.

Blume, E. Sue. *Secret Survivors*. Rexdale, Ontario: John Wiley & Sons, Inc., 1990.

Bolen, Jean Shinoda. *Gods in Every Man*. New York: HarperCollins, 1990.

————. *Gods in Every Woman*. New York: Harper & Row, 1985.

Boston Women's Health Collective. *The New Our Bodies, Our Selves*. New York: Simon & Schuster, 1984.

Bradshaw, John. *Homecoming: Reclaiming and Championing Your Inner Child*. New York: Bantam Books, 1990.

————. *Healing the Shame that Binds You*. Deerfield Beach, Florida: Health Communications, Inc., 1988.

Budapest, Zsuzsanna. *The Holy Book of Women's Mysteries*. Berkeley, California: Wingbow Press, 1989. Originally published by Susan B. Anthony Coven No.1, 1980.

Butler, Sandra. *Conspiracy of Silence: The Trauma of Incest*. New York: Bantam Books, 1978.

Campbell, Susan M. *The Couple's Journey*. San Luis Obispo, Ca.: Impact Publishers, 1980.

Caplan, Paula J. *Don't Blame Mother: Mending the Mother-Daughter Relationship*. New York: Harper & Row, 1989.

Carnes, Patrick. *Out of the Shadows: Understanding Sexual Addiction*. Minneapolis, Minnesota: CompCare Publishers, 1985.

Carson, David, and Jamie Sams. *Medicine Cards: The Discovery of Power Through the Ways of Animals*. Santa Fe, New Mexico: Bear & Co., 1988.

Chesler, Phyllis. *Women and Madness*. Garden City, New York: Doubleday, 1972.

Colgrove, Melba, Harold H. Bloomfield, and Peter McWilliams. *How to Survive the Loss of a Love*. New York: Bantam Books, 1981.

Danica, Elly. *Don't: A Woman's Word*. Charlottetown, P.E.I.: gynergy books, 1989.

Dass, Baba Ram. *Remember: Be Here Now*. San Cristobal, New Mexico: Lama Foundation, 1975.

Dodson, Betty. *Sex for One*. New York: Harmony Books, 1987.

Dowling, Colette. *Perfect Women*. New York: Summit Books, 1988.

————. *The Cinderella Complex*. New York: Summit Books, 1981.

Downing George. *The Massage Book*. Co-published New York: Random House, Inc., and Berkeley, California: The Book Works, 1975.

Duerk, Judith. *Circle of Stones: Woman's Journey to Herself*. San Diego, California: Lura Media, 1989.

Eisler, Riane. *The Chalice & the Blade*. New York: Harper & Row, 1988.

Engel, Beverly. *The Right to Innocence: Healing the Trauma of Childhood Sexual Abuse*. Los Angeles, California: Jeremy Tarcher, 1990.

Farrell, Warren. *Why Men Are the Way They Are*. New York: McGraw-Hill Book Company, 1986.

Forward, Susan, and Craig Buck. *Betrayal of Innocence: Incest and Its Devastation*. New York: Penguin Books, 1978.

————. *Toxic Parents: Overcoming Their Hurtful Legacy and Reclaiming Your Life*. New York: Bantam Books, 1989.

Forward, Susan, and Joan Torres. *Men Who Hate Women and the Women Who Love Them*. New York: Bantam Books, 1986.

Fraser, Sylvia. *My Father's House: A Memoir of Incest and of Healing*. Toronto: Doubleday, 1988.

Friends in Recovery. *The 12 Steps—A Way Out: A Working Guide for Adult Children of Alcoholics and Other Dysfunctional Families.* San Diego, California: Recovery Publications, Inc., 1989.

Gawain, Shakti. *Creative Visualization.* Mill Valley, California: Whatever Publishing Inc., 1978.

Gil, Eliana M. *Outgrowing the Pain.* San Francisco: Launch Press, 1983.

Gleick, James. *Chaos: Making a New Science.* New York: Penguin Books, 1988.

Goldstein, Joseph, and Jack Kornfield. *Seeking the Heart of Wisdom: The Path of Insight Meditation.* Boston, Massachusetts: Shambhala Publications, Inc., 1987.

Gravitz, Herbert L., and Julie D. Bowden. *Recovery: A Guide for Adult Children of Alcoholics.* New York: Simon & Schuster, Inc., 1987.

Greenspan, Miriam. *A New Approach to Women & Therapy.* New York: McGraw-Hill Book Company, 1985.

Greer, Germaine. *Daddy, We Hardly Knew You.* New York: Random House, Inc., 1989.

H. Julie. *Letting Go With Love: Finding Peace of Mind and Heart for Those Who Live With a Practicing or Recovering Alcoholic/Addict.* Los Angeles: Jeremy P. Tarcher, 1987.

Harner, Michael. *A Way of the Shaman: A Guide to Power and Healing.* New York: Bantam Books, 1982.

Hounam, Peter, and Andrew Hogg. *Secret Cult.* Hertfordshire, England: Lion Publishing, 1985.

Iglehart, Hallie. *Womanspirit: A Guide to Woman's Wisdom.* New York: HarperCollins Publishers, 1983.

Johnston, Robert A. *She: Understanding Feminine Psychology.* New York: Perrenial Library, 1989.

_____. *He: Understanding Masculine Psychology.* New York: Perrenial Library, 1989.

_____. *We: Understanding the Psychology of Romantic Love.* San Francisco: Harper & Row, 1983.

Kelly, Liz. *Surviving Sexual Violence.* Cambridge, England: Polity Press, 1989.

Kopp, Sheldon B. *Rock, Paper, Scissors: Understanding the Paradoxes of Personal Power and Taking Charge of Our Lives.* Minneapolis, Minnesota: CompCare Publishers, 1989.

_____. *If You Meet the Buddha on the Road, Kill Him!: The Pilgrimage of Psychotherapy Patients.* New York: Bantam Books, 1988.

Kreps, Bonnie. *Subversive Thoughts, Authentic Passions: Loving Without Losing Your Self.* San Francisco: Harper & Row, 1990.

Laing, R. D. *Knots*. London: Penguin Books, 1972.

Larson, Ernie. *Stage II Relationships*. New York: Harper & Row, 1987.

Lasatar, Lane. *Recovery from Compulsive Behaviour*. Deerfield, Florida: Health Communications, 1988.

Laurens, Roy. *Fully Alive*. Dallas, Texas: Saybrook Publishing Company, 1985.

Lee, John H. *I Don't Want to be Alone: For Men and Women Who Want to Heal Addictive Relationships*. Deerfield, Florida: Health Communications, Inc., 1990.

_____. *The Flying Boy: Healing the Wounded Man*. Deerfield, Florida: Health Communications, Inc., 1989.

Leonard, Linda Schierse. *On the Way to the Wedding: Transforming the Love Relationship*. Boston: Shambhala Press, 1986.

_____. *The Wounded Woman*. Athens, Ohio: Swallow Press, 1982.

Lerner, Harriet Goldhor. *The Dance of Intimacy: A Woman's Guide to Courageous Acts of Change in Key Relationships*. New York: Harper & Row, 1990.

_____. *The Dance of Anger: A Woman's Guide to Changing the Patterns of Intimate Relationships*. New York: Harper & Row, 1989.

Lew, Mike. *Victims No Longer: Men Recovering from Incest and Other Sexual Child Abuse*. New York: Harper & Row, 1990.

Madaras, Lynda, and Jane Patterson, with Schick, Peter. *Womancare: A Gynecological Guide to Your Body*. New York: Avon Books, 1981.

Mariechild, Diane. *The Inner Dance*. Freedom, Ca.: The Crossing Press, 1987.

Marshall, W. L., and Sylvia Barrett. *Criminal Neglect: Why Sex Offenders Go Free*. Toronto: Doubleday, 1990.

Miller, Alice. *The Untouched Key: Tracing Childhood Trauma in Creativity and Destructiveness*. New York: Bantam Doubleday Dell Publishing Group, Inc., 1990.

_____. *Thou Shall Not Be Aware: Society's Betrayal of the Child*. New York: New American Library, 1984.

_____. *For Your Own Good: Hidden Cruelty in Child-rearing and the Roots of Violence*. New York: Doubleday, 1984.

_____. *The Drama of the Gifted Child*. New York: Basic Books, 1983. Originally published as *Prisoners of Childhood*.

Newman, Mildred, and Bernard Berkowitz. *How to Be Your Own Best Friend*. New York: Random House, 1971.

Nicarthy, Ginny. *Getting Free: You Can End Abuse and Take Back Your Life*. Seattle, Washington: Seal Press, 1986.

Noble, Vicki. *Motherpeace: A Way to the Goddess Through Myth, Art and Tarot*. New York: Harper & Row, 1988.

Norwood, Robin. *Letters from Women Who Love too Much.* New York: Simon & Schuster, 1988.

————. *Women Who Love too Much: When You Keep Wishing and Hoping He'll Change.* New York: Pocket Books, 1985.

Osherson, Samuel. *Finding Our Fathers: How a Man's Life is Shaped By His Relationship With His Father.* New York: Ballantine Books, 1987.

Paul, Jordan, and Margaret Paul. *Do I Have To Give Up Me to Be Loved By You?* Minneapolis, Minnesota: CompCare Publications, 1983.

Paulus, Trina. *Hope for the Flowers.* New York: A Newman Book, Paulist Press, 1972.

Peat, David F. *Synchronicity.* New York: Bantam Books, 1987.

Peck, M. Scott. *The Road Less Travelled: A New Psychology of Love, Traditional Values and Spiritual Growth.* New York: Simon & Schuster, 1978.

Perls, Fritz. *Gestalt Therapy Verbatim.* Moab, Ut: Real People Press, 1969.

Plaskow, Judith, and Carol P. Christ. (ed). *Weaving the Visions: New Patterns in Feminist Spirituality.* New York: Harper & Row, 1989.

Rabin, Barry J. *The Sensuous Wheeler: Sexual Adjustment for the Spinal Cord Injured.* San Francisco: Multi Media Resource Center, 1980.

Rush, Anne Kent. *Getting Clear: Body Work for Women.* Co-published New York: Random House, and Berkeley, California: The Bookworks, 1973.

Russell, Diana E. H. *The Secret Trauma: Incest in the Lives of Girls and Women.* New York: Basic Books, Inc., 1986.

Sams, Jamie. *Sacred Path Cards: The Discovery of Self Through Native Teachings.* New York: HarperCollins, 1990.

Sanford, John P. *The Invisible Partners.* New York: Paulist Press, 1980.

————. *Dreams and Healing.* New York: Paulist Press, 1978.

Sanford, Linda Tschirhart, and Mary Ellen Donovan. *Women & Self-esteem: Understanding and Improving the Way We Think and Feel About Ourselves.* New York: Penguin Books, 1988.

Sargent, E. N. *Love Poems of Elizabeth Sargent.* Toronto: New American Library of Canada Limited, 1966.

Shain, Merle. *Courage My Love.* Toronto: McClelland-Bantam, 1988.

Siegel, Bernie S. *Love, Medicine & Miracles.* New York: Harper & Row, 1988.

Sills, Judith. *A Fine Romance: The Passage of Courtship from Meeting to Marriage.* Los Angeles: Jeremy P. Tarcher; New York: distributed by St. Martin's Press, 1987.

Silverstein, Shel. *The Missing Piece Meets the Big O.* New York: Harper & Row, 1981.

Singer, June. *Love's Energies.* Garden City, N.Y.: Anchor Press/Doubleday, 1983. Originally called *Energies of Love: Sexuality Re-visioned.*

Staude, John-Raphael. *The Adult Development of C. G. Jung.* Boston, Massachusetts: Routledge & Kegan Paul Ltd., 1981.

Thomas, T. *Surviving With Serenity: Daily Meditations for Incest Survivors.* Deerfield, Florida: Health Communications, Inc., 1990.

Tenov, Dorothy. *Love and Limerance.* New York: Stein & Day, 1979.

Trungpa, Chogyam. *Shambhala: The Sacred Path of the Warrior.* Boston, Massechusetts: Shambhala Publications, Inc., 1984.

Walker, Barbara. *The Woman's Encyclopedia of Myths and Secrets.* New York: Harper & Row, 1990.

————. *The Crone: Woman of Age, Wisdom and Power.* New York: Harper & Row, 1988.

Wegscheider-Cruse, Sharon. *Coupleship: How to Build a Relationship.* Deerfield, Florida: Health Communications, Inc., 1988.

Whitfield, Charles L. *Healing the Child Within.* Deerfield, Florida: Health Communications, Inc., 1987.

Williams, Strephon Kaplan. *The Jungian-Senoi Dreamwork Manual.* Berkeley, California: Journey Press 1, 1986.

Wholey, Dennis. *Becoming Your Own Parent.* New York: Doubleday, 1988.

Wolkstein, Diane, and Samuel Noah Kramer. *Inanna: Queen of Heaven and Earth.* New York: Harper & Row, 1983.

Women's Resource Centre. *Recollecting Our Lives: Women's Experiences of Childhood Sexual Abuse.* Vancouver, British Columbia: Press Gang Publishers, 1989.

Zweig, Connie (ed). *To Be a Woman: The Birth of the Conscious Feminine.* Los Angeles: Jeremy P. Tarcher; New York: distributed by St. Martin's Press, 1990.

Publications

Armstrong, Louise. "Daddy Dearest." *Connecticut Magazine*, January 1984.

Browne, Angela. "The Traumatic Impact of Child Sexual Abuse: A Conceptualization." *Journal of the American Orthopsychiatric Association*, October 1985.

Butler, Sandra. "Incest: Whose Reality, Whose Theory." *Paper Aegis*, Summer/Autumn 1990.

Feminist Review (Special Issue). "Family Secrets, Child Sexual Abuse," no. 28, Spring 1988. Published three times a year by a collective with help from women and groups from all over the United Kingdom. London, England: Methuen & Co. Ltd.

Feinblatt, John. "Blood Relations: Violent Couples, Battered Children—Can Americans Survive the Nuclear Family?" *Vogue*, March 1988. Book review of *Heroes of Their Own Lives: The Politics and History of Family Violence* by Linda Gordon.